MW00388683

NEPTUNE'S NOR'E.

A STORM AT SEA

THE TRUE STORY OF A BOMBOGENESIS STORM

THE UNEXPECTED NOR'EASTER STORM OF
NOVEMBER 14 thru 16, 1962

The saga of men at sea, and the six ships and thirty-six men who were lost,
when an Extratropical Cyclone visited the Western North Atlantic.

These losses included the fishing vessel *Midnight Sun*,
a New Bedford scalloper, and her eleven-man crew.

Paul J. Doucette

HOVE DOWN ON GEORGES BANK

THE ESCAPE FROM NEPTUNE'S TRIDENT

ANCIENT MYTHOLOGY

The Romans knew him as Neptune!

The ancient Greeks knew him as Poseidon!

He was their God of the Sea!

He carried a "Magical Trident," and it was believed
that if he was angry, he could slam his Trident into the ocean
floor, and it would create earthquakes and violent storms at sea.

The Romans knew her as Venus!

The ancient Greeks knew her as Aphrodite!

She was the Goddess of Love and Beauty!

It was believed that she could grant prosperity and victory.
She was considered the mother of the Roman people.
It was said that she was born from the foam of the sea.

Venus and Neptune linked by the Sea!

Forever!

"There was very little that your father didn't know about fishing."

Captain Ole Andersen

Spoken to me on November 27, 2016 at the
New Bedford Fishing Heritage Center,
38 Bethel Street,
New Bedford, Massachusetts,

"His father saved my father's life."

Mrs. Kirsten Edvardsen Bendiksen

Spoken to author and filmmaker Kevin Kertscher,
while we were discussing the premiere of the documentary film,
"The Finest Kind - The New Bedford Fishing Industry."
On August 13, 2017

Two of the nicest compliments I have ever had the pleasure of hearing

about my father, Captain Louis Doucette, Jr.

This book is dedicated to the following;

CAPTAIN LOUIS DOUCETTE, JR.

My father, and the mate of the F/V *Venus*, during a vicious nor'easter storm, while
fishing the Northern Edge of Georges Bank, on November 15th, 1962.
A New Bedford Fisherman for fifty years.

CAPTAIN LOUIS DOUCETTE, SR.

My grandfather, and the holder of the Carnegie Medal for Extraordinary Heroism, for his
role in the rescue of the crew of the six-masted schooner, the *Mertie B. Crowley*, on the
backside of Martha's Vineyard, in a nor'easter snow storm on January 23, 1910. His
lessons allowed my father to have the skill to bring the F/V *Venus* home,
after being "Hove Down at Sea," on Georges Bank.

AMABLE DOUCETTE

My great-grandfather, lost at sea while fishing on Georges Bank, in the year 1880.

CAPTAIN MAGNE RISDAL

And the crew of the *F/V Midnight Sun*,
They lost their lives (11 men total) battling the unexpected Nor'easter Gale
of November 14th & 15th, 1962, on Georges Bank.

CAPTAIN JOSHUA "SPUD" MURPHY,
ENGINEER HERBERT DOUCETTE,

My Uncles and their nine shipmates on the F/V *Doris Gertrude*,
They lost their lives (11 men total), in a nor'easter snow storm while fishing
Georges Bank, on January 13, 1955.

JOHN PENDERGAST

My sister's father-in-law swept from the deck of the F/V *Terra Nova*,
while fishing in heavy weather on Georges Bank,
in November of 1966.

"THE FINEST KIND"

EACH AND EVERY ONE OF THEM!

Prologue

<u>SETTING THE STAGE</u>

November 7th, 1962, a Wednesday, dawned clear and bright in the harbor of New Bedford, Massachusetts. There is a massive high-pressure system sitting off the East Coast of the United States, and it is in control of the weather from Maine to Florida. It's going to be a beautiful early November day with a high temperature of 46-degrees in New Bedford. Captain Thomas Larsen and Captain Louis Doucette, Jr., are busy preparing the F/V *Venus* to leave the dock at the D.N. Kelly & Sons Shipyard, in Fairhaven, Massachusetts. The *Venus* will be leaving shortly for a fishing trip to the Northern Edge of Georges Bank. Captain Magne Risdal is busy preparing the F/V *Midnight Sun* to leave the same shipyard. Captain Risdal is carefully monitoring the loading of the food for the trip because his regular cook, Hallvard Stoll, has been fighting off a bad cold and he has decided to take this trip off, to recover before the winter weather takes hold. These two boats are sister ships, both built to almost identical dimensions by the Harvey Gamage Shipyard in South Bristol, Maine. The *Venus* is two months old, and the *Midnight Sun* is two years old. These boats are both beautiful eastern rigged, pilothouse aft, wooden fishing boats, built by one of the top boat builders in the business. Gamage boats are built to be strong sea boats with an excellent track record of longevity and seaworthiness. Gamage boats are handmade by highly skilled Maine craftsmen. The *Venus* is rigged as a dragger to trawl for groundfish, and the *Midnight Sun* is rigged for scalloping, they are both top notch fishing vessels, and the captains and crews of both boats are friends.

On this same morning, Thomas Ewing III is a lawyer with the law firm of Debevoise, Plimpton, Lyons, and Gates in New York City. He is a young hard-charging attorney at one of the top law firms in the world. He is also an avid sailor, and he is the owner of a 30-foot, blue-hulled, sloop rigged sailboat, the *Kria*. He is busy this morning with his law career, but he is also busy contemplating a sail from Point Judith, Rhode Island to Essex, Connecticut, this weekend. His law associate and fellow Yale graduate, Attorney David Evans, has just agreed to act as crew on the *Kria*, for this weekend's sail.

The M/V *Captain George* is a 442-foot Greek-flagged cargo ship, and she and her crew have recently completed stops in New Orleans, Louisiana and Houston, Texas to take on cargo. The ship is in St. Mary's, Georgia this morning taking on a load of explosives to be transported to the oil drilling industry in Libya. She will be leaving St. Mary's, today and after another brief stop in Savannah, Georgia she will be bound for the Mediterranean Sea. The crew is looking forward to the trip east across the Atlantic, because after the delivery in Libya, they will be on their way home to Piraeus, Greece.

The schooners *Curlew* and *Windfall* are tied to the dock in Newport, Rhode Island, and they are preparing for a voyage to the Caribbean. They both plan to enter the winter charter trade in the Virgin Islands. The two crews are friendly, and they agree to an informal race to the Caribbean, with an intermediate stop in Bermuda, to keep things interesting over a long sail.

The USNS (United States Naval Ship) *New Bedford* (*AKL-17*), and her sister Camino Class cargo ship, designated as the USNS *AKL-43*, are both docked at the State Pier, in New Bedford, Massachusetts. They are taking on supplies for the United States Air Force - Early Warning Radar Detection Towers, known as "Texas Towers." They will be making a run out to re-supply Texas Tower #2, and Texas Tower #3, next week. These radar towers are erected offshore of the East Coast of the United States in international waters. They are designed to be our first line of early warning defense, should the Soviet Union launch an attack against the United States. We have just lived through the Cuban Missile Crisis, and the Cold War is very hot right now.

Captain William Fielder and crewman Louis Raulet of the F/V *Moonlight* are working on the boat in New Bedford, and they will be heading out to the Georges Bank fishing grounds tomorrow.

On this morning, John Isaksen is the mate on the F/V *Aloha*, his father Nils is the captain. Although he doesn't know it today, John Isaksen will be the last man to speak to the captain of another New Bedford scalloper, before she is lost with all hands.

Captain Hans Davidsen, of the F/V *Florence B.*, will be taking his scalloper out to the Southeast Part of Georges Bank tomorrow, to commence a fishing trip. In seven days, the *Florence B.* will amaze Captain Davidsen with her ability to shed water. On this day, he has no idea that the *Florence B.*, has submarine like capabilities.

Captain Albert Dahl, of the F/V *Monte Carlo*, is at his home this morning in Fairhaven, Massachusetts. He will be leaving for the fishing grounds on Saturday. He has no way of knowing it today, but he will soon be repeating the same word three times that all mariners dread, "Mayday, Mayday, Mayday." He also doesn't know that he will soon be leading the fight to improve the weather forecast for the fishing fleet.

Captain Edward Clark is the master of the 155-foot, Canadian cargo ship, the M/V *East Star*. He departed Havana, Cuba on October 24th, right in the middle of the Cuban Missile Crisis and the U.S. Naval Blockade of the island of Cuba. This morning, Captain Clark and his crew of twelve men, are battling a problem with the quality of the diesel fuel that they have on board. The *East Star* is somewhere north of the Turks and Caicos Islands and south of Bermuda. The M/V *East Star* entered and then left Cuba, during one of the most intense moments in world history, the nuclear weapon showdown between the United States and the Soviet Union. This morning he is squarely in the middle of the infamous Bermuda Triangle, and his ship is experiencing engine failure. November 7th, 1962 is not starting out to be a good day for Captain Clark, and things are going to get much worse.

Robert J. MacCharles is at the helm of his 30-foot ketch rigged sailboat, the *Islander*, and along with two friends, he is sailing somewhere south of Cape Cod. He is four days into a three-month vacation sail. His next intended destination is Bermuda. Captain MacCharles and the *Islander*, will never make it to Bermuda.

Within ten days, thirty-six men will be dead, and six of these ships ranging in size from 30-feet to 442-feet long will be lying on the bottom of the Atlantic Ocean. The remainder of the boats and men who survive the coming storm will never be the same, as they were, on this bright sunny Wednesday morning, in November of 1962.

PART I

THE SAGA BEGINS

NEPTUNE ISSUES A TEST
MANY WILL BE TESTED
NOT ALL WILL PASS

Chapter 1

<u>DID YOU SEE THE MOUNTAINS?</u>

It was a beautiful July summer day in the historic coastal town of Fairhaven, Massachusetts. I was visiting with my mother and father, as I was on vacation from my job in South Carolina. It was late afternoon, and the temperature was in the low 70's, with the summer afternoon southwesterly wind providing a nice comfortable breeze. This was a welcome relief from the heat of the Deep South which I had just left. We were sitting outside on the lawn, in Adirondack chairs, behind the freshly painted white picket fence. I was admiring my mothers' rose bushes that were climbing up the trellised gate. I was catching up on what had been happening in the family while I was away. My father mentioned that my nephew was out on his first fishing trip and was due in at any time.

Not long after, a car pulled up in the driveway of my brother's house, which was next door, and my nephew, Albert stepped out of the car. He was just home from ten days at sea on his first fishing trip to Georges Bank, needing a shave, and carrying a seabag full of dirty clothes. He was excited to see my dad, the "Old Sea Dog" of the family, who was now a recently retired offshore commercial fishing captain. Albert dropped his sea bag and bounded across the yard full of excited energy and shook hands with the both of us. He started talking about his fishing trip and how much he liked being a fisherman. My father told his grandson that he was happy that he enjoyed his first foray into the life of a commercial fisherman because it was necessary to like it if he was going to make fishing his life's work. Albert continued, giving us every detail of his fishing trip, my father had a sly smile on his face, and it was apparent to me that he saw some of his own thoughts and youthful optimism, reflected in his grandson. Albert was now the sixth generation of the family to venture out to Georges Bank to make his living. Then the old man asked him one question. When he asked this question, his facial expression changed, and I knew immediately, that my father's mind was flashing back to 3:26 a.m., on November 15th, in 1962.

"Did you see the mountains, Albert?"

My nephew looked at him like he was crazy. "What do you mean mountains, Grandpa?"

My dad said, "Sometimes there are mountains out there on Georges Bank, you'll find them, but most of the time they seem to find you! Did you see them?"

Albert said, "No, I just saw lots of water and lots of scallops."

The old captain said, "Well young fella if you stay with it, you'll see them soon enough. You'll know them when you see them, and you be careful out on deck when they show up!"

This was excellent advice since my dad spent fifty years fishing on Georges Bank and had seen the "mountains" that appear out on the ocean many times. He knew the danger better than most. But none were more dangerous than the mountainous seas that he faced on November 15th, in 1962.

Chapter 2

MOMENT OF CRISIS
ABOARD THE F/V *VENUS*

November 15, 1962 – 3:26 a.m.

"CAPTAIN LOUIE!
CAPTAIN LOUIE!
WAKE UP!!!"

My bunk is in the aft cabin of the F/V *Venus*. Jack Landsvik, the Engineer, is shouting at me to get up. I went off watch at midnight. I look at my wristwatch, and it's only 3:26 a.m. We've been at sea fishing on Georges Bank for seven days, and everyone is exhausted. Once we are on the fishing grounds, the boat operates 24 hours a day and all members of the crew work in shifts to keep the boat fishing continuously. You work sixteen hours out of every 24-hour day. I had been sleeping heavily, and even groggy I can tell the boat is moving wildly and Jack looks panicked. He's an experienced fisherman, and not much can rattle him. The weather report at 11:10 p.m. predicted winds at 35 to 45 mph and seas of 15 to 20 feet. We see that kind of weather all the time out on Georges. The movement of this boat tells me something far worse is happening topside.

"What's going on?" I ask.

"Cap, it must be blowing a hundred, and the seas are running 50 to 60 feet, and they're breaking, visibility is nil. We need you up in the pilothouse right now! We just blew out two pilothouse windows in a big breaking wave, and we're struggling. I think we're in a bad place on the bank. I think we're in shoal water; we must be down near the Cultivator. Please hurry Skipper, we're in terrible trouble!"

By the time Jack stops shouting I already have my gear on and I am slipping into my boots, moving towards the access ladder to the pilothouse.

BOOM!
CRASH!
CREAK!
SHUDDER!
GROAN!

I hear these sounds as my body is thrown through the air, from the starboard side crashing into the port side of the aft cabin of the vessel. These are the sounds of a boat in the throes of death. Jack and I are pinned to the port side bunk. The *Venus* is "hove down," and I can't get up because at this moment the port side of the hull is, in fact, the bottom of the boat. The *Venus* is lying on her side, and her keel is partially out of the water. Above all the noise, I can hear the engine revving loudly because the propeller is no longer biting into the sea, but instead, it is spinning in thin air. I've seen a lot of bad weather, but I've never been hove down before!

Please God, don't let another big breaking wave hit us right now because we will be finished. Come on Venus, get back up on your feet and give us a chance. I want to see my wife and kids again.

I know that I am in a fight for my life.

- Captain Louis A. Doucette, Jr.

Chapter 3

HOVE DOWN

The term "Hove Down" is a nautical term which describes a technique which was used to examine and repair the bottom of a ship's hull. If the equipment was not available to pull the boat completely out of the water to expose the ship's bottom for necessary maintenance, this was another means to complete the repairs or inspection. The technique of having the ship "Hove Down" was conducted while the ship was safely tied to the dock, in shallow water. By various means, the ship was hauled over on her side to expose the bottom of the opposite side of the ship. Shipwrights could then climb onto the now exposed bottom of the hull to complete an inspection or repair. When completed the ship was hauled over, or "Hove Down" on the opposite side, to complete the work for the now alternate exposed area of the ship's bottom. A vessel hove down on her starboard (right) side would have her port (left) side bottom exposed and vice versa. In this context, having a ship hove down was a predetermined event and was done relatively safely for the repair of the bottom of the hull.

This technique was used widely in New Bedford, Massachusetts during the era of whaling. Whaleships were very wide, and there were limited facilities available to haul them out of the water for repair. Whaling voyages often lasted several years, and it was imperative that the bottom of the ship be in perfect condition before embarking on a whaling voyage.

In summary, a ship that is in a hove down position has been flopped over on her side, and the bottom of the vessel is exposed and out of the water. Again, this was all done while the ship was safely in port and secured to a wharf.

A ship that is, "Hove Down while at Sea," is an entirely different matter, it is an unintended event, and it is very unsafe. It is often a prelude to the sinking of the ship and the death of her crew. A ship that is "Hove Down at Sea," has found herself in that configuration because of the force of the wind and the waves. This only happens when a ship encounters very heavy weather. It can also be referred to as, being knocked down, knocked down on her beam ends, or more familiar to most non-sailors as being capsized.

No ship's captain, or sailor, ever wants to be;
"Hove Down at Sea."

A NEW BEDFORD WHALER
HOVE DOWN FOR REPAIR
SAFELY TIED TO THE PIER

Now picture this scene one hundred and fifty miles from shore, in one-hundred-mile per hour winds, the wind shrieking through the rigging, making a noise that sounds like it emanated straight from hell. Big mountainous waves as tall as a five-story building smashing into the hull, anything not tied down being tossed about, including men, and you have a good image of a boat that has been;

"Hove Down at Sea"

Chapter 4

<u>GEORGES BANK</u>

Georges Bank is an extensive shoal area that lies about 150-miles due east of Cape Cod, Massachusetts. It encompasses an area of about 200-miles in length, and it is about 120-miles wide, at its' widest point. The bank resembles the shape of an egg. It has been one of the most productive fishing grounds in the world for groundfish and shellfish for a very long time. Approximately 12,000 years ago, this area was part of the North American land mass.

Scientists have determined that the earth has endured five periods that can be called an Ice Age. During one of these events, the water rose, and this area became an island. About 6,000 years ago, after another of these ice events, the water rose again and covered Georges Island with sea water. Georges Bank is essentially an island that has been flooded by the Atlantic Ocean. This explains the varying depths that are found on Georges Bank. You will discover depths of over one-thousand-feet very near other areas that have a depth of nine-feet. This shallow water of nine-feet is located about 120-miles from the nearest land. The varying depths and the proximity of the Labrador Current and the Gulf Stream all work to provide a wide variety of fish and shellfish at this location. This marine life is available for fishermen to harvest every month of the year.

NAUTICAL CHART OF GEORGES BANK

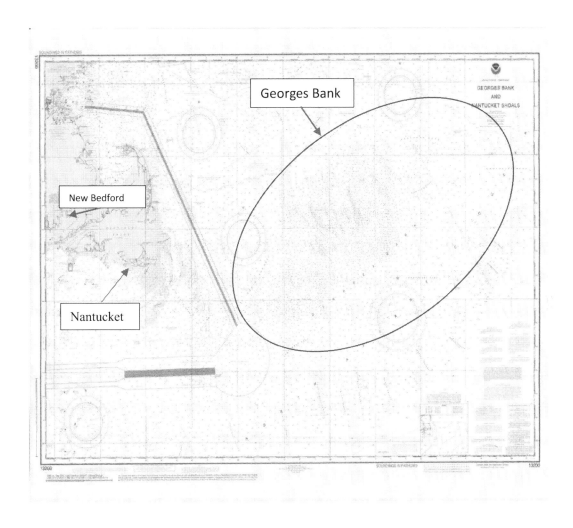

Chapter 5

NEPTUNE'S TRIDENT

While fishing anywhere on Georges Bank can be dangerous, one area is considered the most dangerous part of the bank, and this is the area that lies between the Cultivator Shoal and Georges Shoal. The water in this area is very shallow. There are points here that have a recorded depth of nine-feet under normal conditions, and as little as three-feet in storm conditions. The water boils through this area as it moves with the tide changes. Large breakers can be observed here like you would see at a beach during a storm. Fishermen have reported that at times you can observe the sea bottom, or what looks like a sandbar in this area. The first fishermen to routinely fish this area were from Gloucester, Massachusetts. These men became known as "Georges Men," and many of them lost their lives fishing in this area when a winter storm would brew up with northerly winds. It became well known that if you stayed in this area too long, and a storm with northerly winds hit, you were placing your boat and your men in extreme peril.

This area is defined by the Cultivator Shoal on the west side and Georges Shoal on the east side, with another, spoke of shallow water in the middle. These three shoals form a three-pronged configuration that resembles a pitchfork, or a trident, and this is the area that I have named "Neptune's Trident." This is not a name that I have ever heard used before to define this area; it is a label that I have coined for this story. It seems an apt description to me. This very severe storm has faded into history. Since this storm is sometimes referred to as the November of 1962 Storm, by those few, who have some knowledge, or remembrance of this destructive killer storm. I felt that a storm of this magnitude deserved a proper name and I have given it the name, "Neptune's Nor'easter."

The danger here at Neptune's Trident is both the shallow water and the shape of the shoals. These shoals form what is mostly a structure like a canyon. If a vessel gets into this area, and a storm brews up with northerly winds, it is almost impossible to escape.

This book is the story of a boat that got caught in Neptune's Trident and escaped, she was named the *Venus*.

NEPTUNE'S TRIDENT

GEORGES BANK

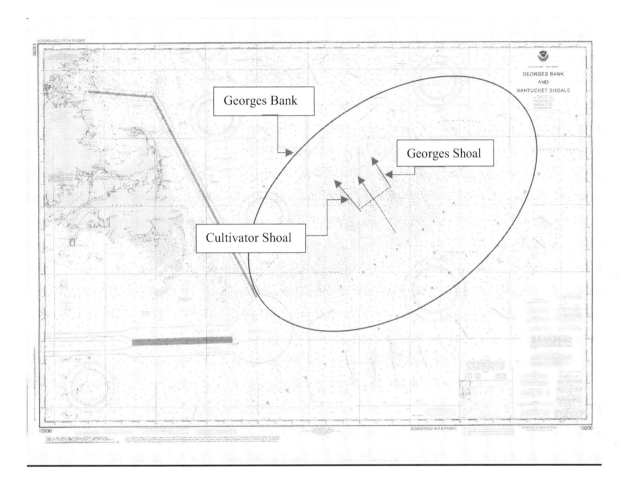

20

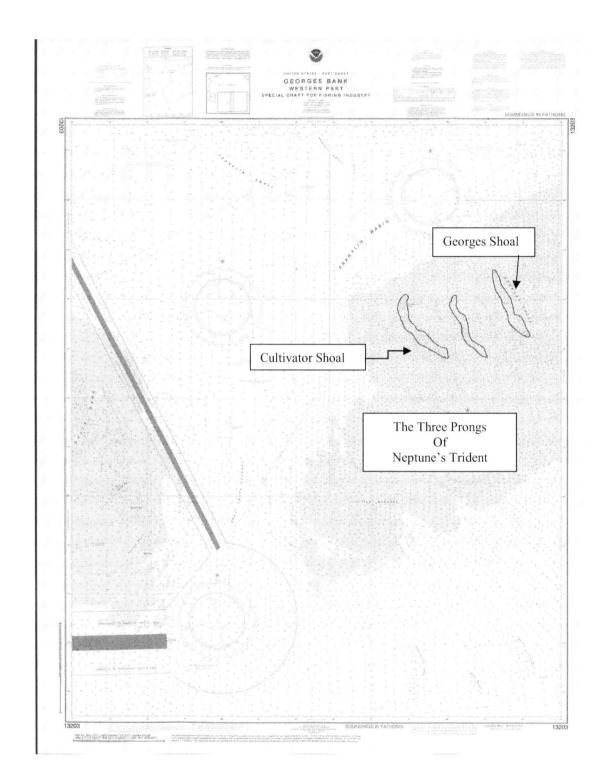

THE THREE PRONGS OF NEPTUNE'S TRIDENT

Chapter 6

BOMBOGENESIS

November 14 - 16, 1962

Extratropical Cyclone
Explosive Cyclogenesis
Extratropical Explosive Cyclogenesis
Weather Bomb
Bomb Cyclone
Bombogenesis

In November of 1962, the New Bedford fishermen did not know any of the above terms, and neither did the general public. In New England, we described storms in a few broad categories: Hurricanes, Nor'easters, Blizzards, and sometimes, a Nor'easter Blizzard.

The hurricanes were usually "named" storms. In New England, we had adequate warning that they were coming our way, because the Weather Bureau had been tracking them on their journey from the tropics, and then as they progressed up the East Coast of the United States. The weather forecast gave us time to prepare and make plans. This was not always true, and in 1938 my father encountered an un-forecasted hurricane of massive proportions while on the fishing grounds. But as time passed, the Weather Bureau became more accurate in hurricane forecasting.

Nor'easters were another matter, they came, and they went, and in New England, we accepted that they were a fact of life for our area of the globe, some were worse than others. My father weathered three hurricanes while at sea, and an untold number of nor'easters, gales, and other maritime storms over his fifty-year career. Dad would sometimes come home from a fishing trip and would comment that he had experienced a bad storm, sometimes the weather was bad at home as well, but often we had no idea. But to the fishermen of New Bedford, it was something that they expected, especially during the winter months, however unpleasant. Yet, in November of 1962, they encountered a nor'easter that was unlike any they had experienced before.

I often wondered to myself, why is my dad so obsessed with this one storm, knowing his extensive experience with heavy weather at sea? During my research, I came to understand why, and it can be answered with one word, Bombogenesis.

In the 1940's and 1950's, Tor Bergeron and other meteorologists at the Bergen School of Meteorology in Norway, began labeling some severe storms that rapidly developed and grew over the sea as "bombs," because they seemed to explode over the ocean. They noticed that these storms packed explosiveness that was unusual.

In the 1970's, the terms "Explosive Cyclogenesis" and "Meteorological Bombs" were being used by Professor Fred Sanders of the Massachusetts Institute of Technology (M.I.T.).

In the 1980's, Sanders and his team further defined a weather bomb, or what they began calling "Bombogenesis," as an extratropical cyclone, that deepens by at least 24 millibars, in 24 hours, at a latitude of 60 degrees. These storms were primarily a maritime weather event, and they formed in the mid-latitudes; therefore they were extratropical. In the Western North Atlantic, the most common development of this phenomena occurs within, or north, of the Gulf Stream.

In the year 2018, we hear these terms being regularly used by television meteorologists, and they always talk about the potential for a nor'easter to "bomb out," and the term "bombogenesis" is often used. Usually, this doesn't happen, but it sure gets these folks excited to talk about the possibility.

Hurricanes form and gain strength from the warm air in the tropics, which is the zone defined as the area of the globe between 23.5 degrees North latitude and 23.5 degrees South latitude.

Extratropical cyclones form due to horizontal temperature contrasts in the atmosphere across multiple weather fronts, in latitudes above the tropics. Therefore, they are considered extratropical or sometimes called post-tropical. Although their birth differs, the life of both storms can be similar in strength and destructiveness.

In 1962, if you had told my father, or any other New Bedford fisherman who was out in this storm on November 15th, that what they had experienced was a "Bombogenesis Storm," they probably would have shaken their head and thought you were mocking them, or just punched you in the mouth for acting crazy and stupid. But today, we know that this is in fact, precisely what they encountered.

Bombogenesis, also called Explosive Cyclogenesis, is defined as an extreme drop of a low-pressure system over a short period, and the latitude of the storm's position on the globe influences the force that is generated.

You often hear that a drop of 24 millibars, over a 24-hour period is the requirement for a low-pressure system to be defined as a "Bombogenesis Storm." However, this is not technically correct. Since it is latitude influenced, bombogenesis occurs as follows:

At 25-degrees latitude, it requires a drop of 12-millibars of barometric pressure, in any 24-hour period; to be defined as a bombogenesis event.

At 60-degrees latitude, it requires a drop of 24-millibars of barometric pressure, in any 24-hour period; to be defined as a bombogenesis event.

At 90-degrees latitude, it requires a drop of 28-millibars of barometric pressure, in any 24-hour period; to be defined as a bombogenesis event.

In summary, the higher you move up the globe in latitude, the higher the drop in barometric pressure required to create bombogenesis.

On Tuesday, November 13th, 1962, at 1:00 p.m., a low-pressure system began forming at 31-degrees latitude, off the coast of South Carolina to the west, and the island of Bermuda to the east. The recorded low-pressure was a mild 1008-millibars.

On Wednesday, November 14th, 1962, at 1:00 p.m., the low-pressure system was now located at 37-degrees latitude and was now positioned, 400-miles off the coast of New Jersey. The recorded low-pressure was now 992-millibars. It had dropped 16-millibars in 24-hours. At this latitude, a bombogenesis event occurs at something around 17-millibars, and this storm had fallen 16-millibars in the latest 24-hours. Explosive cyclogenesis had already begun to take place, and this was already a severe storm.

On Thursday, November 15th, 1962, at 1:00 p.m., the low-pressure system was now located at 41-degrees latitude, and it was now sitting directly over the Georges Bank fishing grounds. The recorded low-pressure was now 968-millibars. It had dropped 24-millibars in the latest 24-hour period. At 41-degrees latitude, a drop of 19-millibars would be required to be considered explosive cyclogenesis. This storm was now well past that requirement. This storm was now full-blown "Bombogenesis," no matter how you measure it. A weather bomb had now been dropped right on top of the fishermen who were on the Georges Bank fishing grounds, and to make matters worse, they had no warning that it was coming.

The intensity of this storm is the reason that the New Bedford fishermen of the time declared this storm to be the most severe heavy weather event of their careers. My father always maintained, that in his 50-year career, this was the only time that he thought he would be lost at sea. He declared that the three hurricanes and numerous other storms that he had weathered were not the equal of this storm.

The power and fury of this storm is the reason that the F/V *Midnight Sun* was lost with all hands.

In this story, we will follow the formation and development of this monster storm, which I have named Neptune's Nor'easter. In the Western Atlantic Ocean, this sea-storm reached out 1,000-miles from its' center to cause death and destruction to those who were unfortunate to be in its' path.

Forty-eight hours after this storm system left us, it brought additional death and destruction to the British Isles and Western Europe.

Bombogenesis
Neptune's Nor'easter
Georges Bank

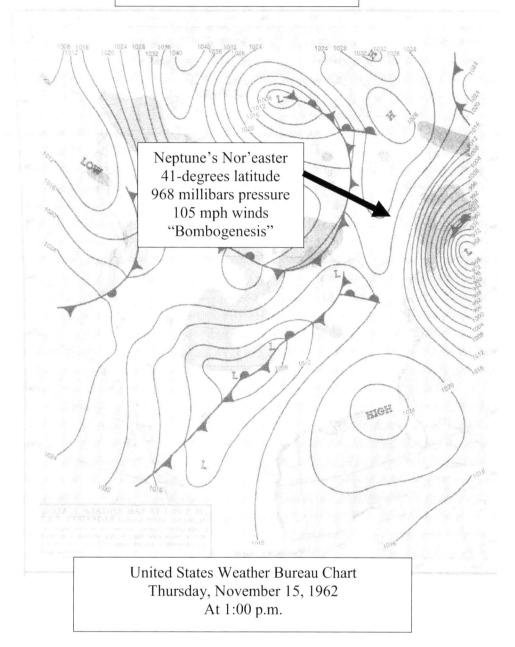

Neptune's Nor'easter
41-degrees latitude
968 millibars pressure
105 mph winds
"Bombogenesis"

United States Weather Bureau Chart
Thursday, November 15, 1962
At 1:00 p.m.

Neptune's Nor'easter

The Journey Up the East Coast

November 13 – 15, 1962

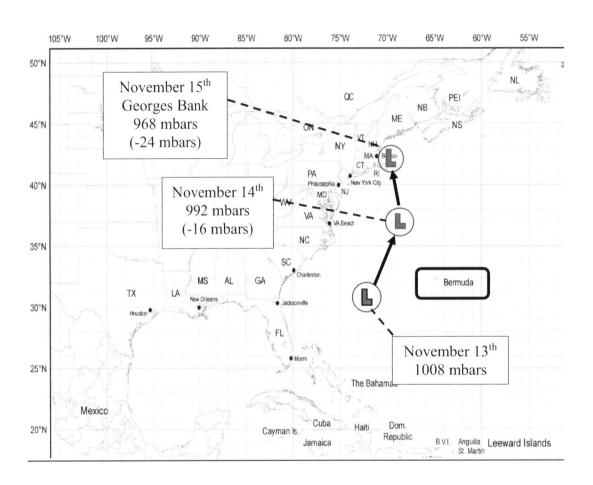

Notes:

1. All barometric pressure readings were taken at 1:00 p.m. for that day, from the official U.S. Weather Bureau Chart.
2. A drop of 16 millibars from November 13th to November 14th.
3. A drop of 24 millibars from November 14th to November 15th.
4. A bombogenesis storm was sitting over Georges Bank on Thursday, November 15, 1962.

Chapter 7

IMPORTANT DEFINITIONS

A few brief definitions and explanations are provided here, to assist the reader in understanding this story. These definitions are especially important for any non-mariner who may be unaware of these terms, and their meaning, or the location of these events.

THE "FINEST KIND"

Among the fisherman of New Bedford, Massachusetts, there is no higher form of praise than to label something as being, "The Finest Kind." Spend more than ten minutes among a group of fishermen, and you can be sure that you will hear it used. They apply this label to anything that they deem as being worthy of praise, and they use it on both animate and inanimate objects. I have heard it used in many ways, but here are a few examples;

To describe a very able captain, you may hear someone say;
"The Captain, he's the Finest Kind."

Or, to describe a new shipmate, someone may say;
"The new fella, he did a good job this trip, he's the Finest Kind."

You may hear a fisherman say when he is describing a fishing vessel;
"She's the Finest Kind."

If you're having dinner and you ask a fisherman;
"How's your food?"
If it's excellent, you would probably hear a reply something like;
"Yes sir, it's the Finest Kind of a meal."

Simply put, there is no higher form of praise from a New Bedford fisherman than to label anything with the description of being;

"The Finest Kind"

New Bedford and Fairhaven, Massachusetts

New Bedford is located on the south coast of Massachusetts, with a population of about 100,000 people, it is the sixth largest city in the state.

When you approach the New Bedford Harbor from offshore, you will notice that the harbor lies on a North to South line. The City of New Bedford is on the west side of the harbor, and the Town of Fairhaven lies on the east side. New Bedford and Fairhaven share an excellent natural harbor that has shaped the history of this area since its founding.

New Bedford Harbor - 1867

New Bedford Harbor – 2017

PILOTHOUSE or WHEELHOUSE

The pilothouse is a structure that is the control center on a fishing vessel. It houses the helm, or steering wheel, compass, engine controls, chart table, and all navigation equipment. On an Eastern-rig fishing vessel, it is located aft near the stern, and on a Western-rig fishing vessel, it is located forward near the bow. In the early days, the fishermen went to sea in sailing vessels, and as with most sail-powered vessels, the helm was located aft and was exposed to the weather. As fishing vessels transitioned to engine power, it made sense to add a structure to protect the man on wheel watch as is common on motor vessels.

F/V *Addie Mae*

My grandfather's fishing vessel the *Addie Mae* as she steams out of New Bedford harbor, with Fairhaven in the background in the year 1912. This picture is an excellent example of an early pilothouse that has been erected on a schooner-rigged fishing vessel.

THE FOC'SLE

FOC'SLE - Pronounced as, **FOHK-sel**.

The foc'sle is the area on the ship that contains the sleeping berths for the crew, and the galley where meals are prepared and served. In medieval times, this area had a raised structure above the main deck forward of the foremast to house the ordinary seaman. This is the reason that the service of an ordinary seaman was sometimes referred to as, "duty serving before the mast." This raised structure in the bow was named the forecastle. This nautical jargon for the crew's quarters has carried down through the years. The area of the crew's berths and galley, which on a fishing vessel are now generally located below deck in the bow of the boat, are now called a shorter version of the forecastle, it has become known, as the foc'sle.

VESSEL ABBREVIATIONS

F/V – designates a fishing vessel, such as the F/V *Venus*

M/V – designates a motorized vessel, such as the cargo ship M/V *East Star*

S/V – designates a sailing vessel, such as the S/V *Curlew*

Chapter 8

BACKGROUND & MOTIVATION

"We are tied to the ocean and when we go back to the sea,
whether it is to sail or to watch – we are going back from whence we came."

President John Fitzgerald Kennedy

I grew up in Fairhaven, Massachusetts, the son of a New Bedford fishing captain. My father grew up the son of a New Bedford fishing captain. The family's business address was Georges Bank, which is located about 150-miles off the coast of Cape Cod, Massachusetts. You get to this place of business by boarding a fishing boat in New Bedford, or Fairhaven, and riding it for something close to twenty-four hours to get to the fishing grounds. In 1962, you would then spend the next week to ten days working Georges Bank from the deck of that fishing boat. The work of the ship goes on twenty-four hours per day, with the crew working in shifts, in all kinds of weather, every month of the year. In a regular ten-day fishing trip, you will be awake and working for about 168-hours, or the equivalent of what someone ashore, working a standard 40-hour per week job, would work in a month. Once you have your catch, then you can head back to land and home. It's a relentless grind being an offshore commercial fisherman. The men that do it well are hard, tough men, of exceptional determination and stamina.

I did not follow my family tradition; I did not become a fisherman. At my father's urging, I pursued higher education. New Bedford has had three major industries that have dominated its history; Whaling, Textile Manufacturing, and Fishing. I spent my working life managing textile manufacturing plants. The duties of a mill manager and a ship captain are very similar in many ways. We are both utilizing machines and leading people to meet our objectives. We both bear the responsibility for everything that occurs under our command. The significant advantage that I had over my forebears is that the likelihood of my drowning while at work was almost zero. Unfortunately, this was not always the case for my fishing ancestors. My career has taken me all over the world, but I have always found myself being drawn to the ocean and my family's fishing heritage. In the end, I followed the pull of the sea and a new calling; I became the teller of the story.

My grandfather, at the age of twelve, left Nova Scotia and the only home he had ever known to become a crewman on a sailing ship. He spent the next fifty-four years making his living on the ocean. He had many adventures and experiences, including being awarded the Carnegie Medal for Extraordinary Heroism, for his role in saving the crew of the six-masted sailing ship, the schooner *Mertie B. Crowley*, on the backside of Martha's Vineyard at Wasque Shoals. He was sunk by a German submarine while swordfishing on the F/V *Progress* on Georges Bank. He survived the explosion of the F/V *Gleaner*, in 1919, while refueling with gasoline in New York City, an accident that resulted in the death of four of his crew, one of them being his brother.

My father made his first fishing trip at the age of eight, during summer vacation from school. By the time he was twelve years old, he could pilot a fishing boat, at night, back to Martha's Vineyard from Georges Bank. This required navigating the perilous and tricky shoals and currents on the backside of Cape Cod. He was being trained in seamanship and navigation by his father, just as many other Vineyard and Nantucket boys before him, had been taught by their fathers. It was a tradition of these islands to produce the next generation of ship captains. He weathered three hurricanes at sea, including the famous 1938 Great New England Hurricane, one of the most severe to ever to hit the mainland of the United States. Winds were clocked at 121-mph sustained, with gusts up to 186-mph, at the Blue Hills Weather Observatory outside of Boston. He lived through this hurricane, as a 27-year-old captain, while being caught offshore on the fishing grounds, in a 55-foot boat, the F/V *Sankaty Head*, which was owned by the legendary Captain Dan Mullins.

Due to the experiences of my father and my grandfather, our family has a wealth of sea stories. But the one story that my father told most often, and could not shake, was his story of encountering an unexpected nor'easter gale on November 15th and 16th, in 1962, on the Northern Edge of Georges Bank. He told this one over and over. The reason he couldn't shake it was because he thought he was going to die in this storm. He always said it was as close as he ever came, to being lost at sea.

In 2002, my father was still alive and was 91-years old. His mind and memories were as sharp as they had ever been at any time in his life. He was a great storyteller. My brother Al, who had fished extensively with my father, decided that we should get some of these stories on tape. My brother and sisters gave dad a tape recorder and taught him how to use it. He would sit in his home and tell these stories to the "machine." My father always called the tape recorder, "the machine." However, his memory was so good, that as he was recording a story, he often shot off into another story that happened to cross his mind, in the middle of telling the first story. He did a lot of jumping around in his narration. Over the years many people sought him out to tell them about his experiences with an eye towards writing a book. Nothing ever came of those attempts. As I sat down with his tape of this unexpected nor'easter that he encountered in November of 1962, I discovered why. All the details were there, but it was a disjointed narration. I knew right then, that if a book were ever written about any of his life, and especially this one experience that had made such an impression on him, it would have to be done by one of his children. We had all heard his stories hundreds of times, and we could understand when he was on track, and when he got off-track in the telling. We had heard them so often, that much to his annoyance, we would sometimes finish the narration for him. Like all kids do, we tended to downplay his attempts to continually tell his stories by saying, "Okay Pop, we know this one already, you've told us about this a million times." But we were taught to have manners and respect, and besides, he would not be deterred by our comments. We were kids, and he was a sea captain so the telling of his story would go on. Now I'm glad that he persisted as they were great stories, that made a lasting impression on me.

In December of 2004, a New Bedford fishing boat, the F/V *Northern Edge*, sank with the loss of all except one member of her crew. The loss of this boat and her name brought back many memories to me. It made me think about my family history and the amount of human loss and near-death experiences that my fishing family had experienced. While the F/V *Northern Edge* was lost on the Southwest Part of Georges Bank, her name stirred the memory of how I almost lost my father, on the Northern Edge of Georges Bank when I was 13-years old. I had some spare time, so I found my father's tape of the 1962 storm, and over a few days, I wrote about twenty-five pages of his remembrance. I knew he always wanted to see this story on paper. It was very brief, and not done all that well, but he loved it. It was probably the best gift that I ever gave him. He had me make copies of it, and he handed out some of them to his friends. I knew he was pleased. I wish he had still been alive for the writing of this book, but I have felt his presence many times during this four-year journey.

My father passed away on November 16, 2006, at age 95, fittingly 44-years to the day that he survived this storm. I gave the eulogy at his funeral, and in the tribute, I mentioned the Nor'easter of 1962. After the service, Captain Reidar and Mrs. Kirsten Bendiksen came up to give me their condolences. Mrs. Bendiksen told me that her father, Arne Edvardsen, was aboard the *Venus* on this trip with my father. She said that her father could never get over this experience either, as he too thought they would all perish in this storm. Kirsten said that her father would be sitting in his living room years later, watching television and he would start talking about this storm. She also told me that she and Reidar would routinely visit my father and that he had shared a copy of the story that I had written about the storm with them, and how happy my father had been with it. Kirsten then said to me, "When you write the book, I would like to have the first copy." I remember thinking, what book? I have thought of her words many times, as I've worked on this project, and they have sustained me in the effort. Mrs. Bendiksen, I plan to see that you get the first copy.

In this same storm, the F/V *Midnight Sun* was lost with all hands, eleven men in total. The *Midnight Sun* was a sister ship of the *Venus*. They were both built at the same shipyard in Maine, two years apart, but very close in dimensions and design. My father had been a friend of the *Midnight Sun*'s owner and master, Captain Magne Risdal. My dad had the highest respect for Captain Risdal, both as a man and as a very skilled fisherman.

When I started this project, I found home movies that the Risdal family has posted on the internet. I saw the man in those movies that was my father's friend. One of the videos showed Captain Risdal and his family at the launching of the *Midnight Sun*, in South Bristol, Maine, looking happy and proud with their new boat. One segment of this video captures Captain Risdal standing on the bow of the *Midnight Sun* proudly holding an American flag, it is a beautiful moment caught on film. A man who emigrated to the United States from Norway, fought as a United States Army soldier in World War II, worked hard to acquire a beautiful new fishing vessel, paying homage to his new country by displaying the stars and stripes, while also honoring his birth country by naming his boat the *Midnight Sun*. It is the story and dream of America, as it was in 1962. It was very sad for me, as I watched this happy moment in this good family's history, to know that they would experience the exact opposite emotions two years later.

In my research, I found a copy of an insurance case, that was heard in the United States District Court, in Boston, concerning insurance liability for the families of the lost crew. In the court's summary of the case, the blame for the loss of the *Midnight Sun* was placed entirely on Captain Risdal, which is not unusual, as the captain of the ship is the ultimate authority and the responsible party for all facets of the operation of any vessel. However, I found the judge's rendering of his decision mean-spirited. I feel that he personally attacked Captain Risdal, a man who was highly respected in the fishing community, and who was obviously not there to defend himself. I immediately knew after reading this summary that most, if not all, of the conclusions, were wrong and painted an unfair picture of Captain

Risdal. While I understand some of the tenants of Maritime Law that guided the judge, and I also understand that the surviving family members had no choice but to pursue this legal avenue to receive financial compensation, I do object to this court summary that is now available to anyone who searches Captain Risdal's name on the internet. It just isn't fair to have this type of negative report about the captain, lying out there on the internet without some rebuttal. As I watched the Risdal family movies, I was able to see Captain Risdal's image, and I felt that somehow, the captain and my father were encouraging me to write this book, to set the record straight. It's a wrong that should be made right.

The next item that motivated me to write this book was a need that I felt to present another view of the New Bedford and Fairhaven area, and the New Bedford fishing industry. There have been many bad things written about New Bedford, and if you were to believe even half of it, you would never set foot in our city. When I have read some of these things, it even sounds scary to me, and I know better. It often seems like New Bedford is portrayed as the modern-day equivalent of the famous seventeenth-century pirate city, Port Royal, Jamaica. A city which was known as "The Wickedest City in the World." There are no pirates walking up Johnny Cake Hill. You will not be accosted by Black Beard. Oh, I admit that like any seaport city in the world, we have our share of characters, scoundrels, scallywags, and serious criminals and thieves. But, if you are a casual visitor, they are not interested in you, they play in the background where the stakes are high, and you'll never see them, if you do see them, you'll never know that you did. I have been going down to the docks since I was a young boy, and like any other city, if you avoid the obvious trouble spots, and if you are respectful of others, you will have no problem.

New Bedford is an easy target for criticism, it is a city that dates to the founding of America, and during that long history, it has had ups and downs. Focusing on the troubled times, trouble spots, and some of our people who have lost their way is an easy way to write something to sensationalize your story. Do we have problems? Yes, of course, we do. This is true of almost every city in the world. I have lived from one end of this country to the other, as well as, in the United Kingdom over the past 47-years, and I feel qualified to declare that all areas, like all people, have their positive and negative points.

Commercial fishing is a rough life and fishermen are gone to sea for weeks at a time. It is hard to balance sea time, with home time, and inevitably some people get off course and lose their way. There are casualties, and lives are altered and lost on land, just as they are lost at sea, in the fishing community. But, most of the fishermen do their job and go home to their families when they get back, or they don't last.

I want to present another view of New Bedford; I want to highlight and show the positive side of fishing, and the men who go fishing but don't get written about. The men who go out and battle the odds to make their living. The men who go far out to sea and risk their lives to earn the right to call themselves New Bedford Fishermen. Over the last several years, I have made it a point to read every book that I can find, on fishing and fishermen, and I have found very little on the New Bedford fishing story. It's a story of discovery, tenacity, experimentation, adaptability, loyalty, courage, and I believe it is a story that deserves to be told. The men that you will meet in this story are not perfect men, like all humans they no doubt had their flaws, as we all do, but a true measure of a man's character is how he acts and reacts when faced with life and death circumstances. The story of this devastating storm highlights all the positive points of the men who go out to sea. This storm story and the challenges that it presented will give you a look into their world.

During the hey-days of whaling, New Bedford was the wealthiest city per capita in the United States. Whaling and the profits that it generated is why this city has such interesting and grand architecture from this period. Whaling voyages sometimes lasted several years and saw our ships visit every ocean and seaport on earth, and it is the reason why our city's population is so diverse. You will find surnames in New Bedford that hail from every corner of the globe.

There have been a lot of fine, hard-working men that risked, and in some instances gave their lives, to build the New Bedford fishing industry. Men like Captain Dan Mullins, the father of our modern fishing fleet. Captain Mullins brought the concept of trawling, to New Bedford from Europe. The beam trawling method was being used in England, while we were line fishing from dories and utilizing schooners. The trawling method, or dragger net fishing technique, was more efficient. Suddenly a boat caught in a week, what it took a month to do when dory fishing. The change to trawling propelled New Bedford into becoming a leading fishing port because our boats were now catching a more substantial amount of fish. This abundance of fish made fish buying a viable concept for New Bedford. Being able to sell their catch in New Bedford meant that the boats did not have to journey down to the Fulton Fish Market in New York City. Selling the fish at home, in New Bedford, reduced the downtime for our boats, and this meant that they could supply the market with even more fresh fish, by being out on the fishing grounds more days during the year.

The pioneers who first followed Captain Mullins lead into beam trawling were; Captain Lynch, Captain Avila, Captain Dutra, Captain Murley, and Captain Doucette, my grandfather. The "Old Timers," who began the run that would lead New Bedford to fishing prominence. These surnames reflect the diversity of our city, as you can hear the ancestry of, Ireland, England, Portugal, and France in these names. As Aristotle taught us; "The whole is greater than the sum of its' parts." The blending of ideas and knowledge demonstrates the theory that what makes America great, is this melting pot of cultures. In the early days of trawling, much of the gear needed was imported from Grimsby, England.

Not long after they began trawling, Captain Mullins and his disciples were fishing off Long Island, New York, and here they met the Scandinavians, who taught them about using otter trawl doors, instead of beams, to control the net. This was the beginning of the influx of the Norwegians to the fishing fleet of New Bedford. They brought their knowledge and experience, and this helped to improve the fleet even further. This is the reason why diversity is a good thing, and this diversity and blending of knowledge is something that was important in the past.

I will admit that by being a native of the area, my opinions may be slightly biased. However, I will offer in my defense, that while I grew up in the New Bedford area, in a fishing family, I have spent most of my adult life out of the city. I think that this gives me a snapshot view of how things have changed over the years in New Bedford, and how I can compare my hometown to my experience in other places.

First, and most important we have the ocean, its' presence dominates the area, and it is easily accessible to everyone. For my entire adult life whenever I have returned to Fairhaven, I always exit the interstate highway early, so that I can cross the harbor on the old swing bridge. This route allows me to see the fishing boats tied to the docks, and I always roll down the windows of the car, regardless of the season, or time of the day or night, so that I can smell the ocean. The ocean is in our blood.

I see positive signs of change as the waterfront area is now part of the National Park System. This past summer, I was impressed at how the National Park status has opened the waterfront to tourism, and I saw tour buses and tourists everywhere. I remember as a child visiting the Whaling Museum and there only being a handful of people visiting this magnificent museum. This beautiful building, loaded with exhibits and artifacts, including an 89-foot long model of the Whaleship Lagoda, the largest ship model in the world, and so large that you can walk her decks. She

sits in the middle of the museum with her sails set, in all her glory. I can remember
the thrill I got as a young boy walking her decks, and studying her rigging,
pretending I was at sea on some far-off ocean. Directly across the street, on Johnny
Cake Hill, you will find the Seaman's Bethel, with the preacher's pulpit in the
shape of a ship's bow, and cenotaphs attached to the walls honoring all the men
who have been lost at sea from our city, including two of my uncles and too many
of our friends. The Fishing Heritage Center is located just down the original
cobbled stone street that was walked by Herman Melville, and whalemen and
fishermen for more than two centuries. You will find restaurants that are serving
the freshest seafood that you have ever eaten, in various ethnic variations,
consistent with the diversity of our population.

Across the harbor, lies Fairhaven, my hometown. The first building that you see as
you cross the bridge is Fairhaven High School, a beautiful building featuring
Gothic architecture, often referred to as, "The Castle on the Hill," with views from
some classrooms of the harbor. The town center has additional buildings featuring
Gothic and Tudor influences; these buildings were donated to the town by Henry
Huttleston Rogers, a native of Fairhaven who amassed a fortune in the oil fields of
Pennsylvania. The town is also the location of Fort Phoenix, which guards the
eastern edge of the New Bedford Harbor, it was built in 1775, and saw duty in the
Revolutionary War, the War of 1812, and the Civil War. This fort is the location of
a naval cannon that was captured from the British, by an American ship on which
the legendary Captain John Paul Jones served, and it is known locally as, "The
John Paul Jones Cannon." Fairhaven is a beautiful New England seaside village.
There is much to see and learn from in our area of the world; it is more than it first
appears.

No, New Bedford is not perfect, far from it, but it is a city with a long history. It is
kind of like visiting your elderly grandmother's house, it might be a little dusty,
and out of order at times, but it is a hidden gem. Just look past the dust, and maybe
you'll see what I see.

I hope that I have presented a different view of New Bedford and Fairhaven, and
the fishing industry in this book. It seems to me that over the years, people have
blown into town, barely stayed long enough to have a cup of coffee, or more
probably a couple of stiff drinks, and then they feel qualified to pass judgment on
our home. Frankly, I'm a little annoyed by some of these negative comments from
people who have no real knowledge of who we are, and what makes us tick.

But we take motivation wherever we can find it, and these negative comments were motivation for me. If you say something about one of us, you are saying it about all of us. That's just the way it is, down at the docks in New Bedford. I see the writing of my book as an opportunity to present a different view, a favorable perspective, and a look into the courage and perseverance of the New Bedford fisherman. Another wrong to right, or perhaps in my case, another wrong to motivate me, to write.

As I researched material for this book, an underlying theme kept jumping out at me. This was the other loss that occurs when a ship and her crew are suddenly lost at sea. It is the loss on land that is rarely given the attention that it deserves; the loss felt and inflicted on the wives and children of the men who will not return home. While everyone is focused on the loss at sea, the pain and suffering of those left behind go on forever. I will try to highlight and provide some insight into the terrible pain and grief of those who are left behind, a pain that endures for the rest of their natural lives.

The last piece of the puzzle that fell into place, for me was the scope of this storm. I was thirteen years old, in November of 1962, when my father came home and talked endlessly about what had transpired on this fishing trip. I can look back now and realize how happy he was to be home and safe, but at that moment, I was somewhat oblivious to the enormity of the event. I did understand that he had survived a close call, but to me, at thirteen years old, my dad was bulletproof. In my mind, he was immune to being lost at sea, that might happen to other people, but not someone of his experience and skill. Only a 13-year old boy could be this naïve. I later realized how close he had come to death, but I still just had his view of the storm from the pilothouse of the *Venus*. When I researched this time-period, I was stunned. This storm was much more significant than I had understood. It was a monster that reached out over a thousand miles from its' center, and in today's dollars, it caused close to a million dollars in damages just to the New Bedford fishing fleet, not including the loss of one of the ports finest boats, the F/V *Midnight Sun*. The fleet took a terrible beating. This storm reached out and touched more than our fishing fleet. It caused havoc all over the Western North Atlantic and touched the lives of men from Canada, Norway, Greece, Italy, Belgium, Taiwan, England, Scotland and Ireland, as well as, Americans of various ancestry. It indeed had a global impact, and this weather system then carried over to the Eastern North Atlantic and caused additional death and destruction to the British Isles and Europe. Although my father had told me this story many times, I never realized the magnitude of this storm. Dad had told me the story from what he personally experienced, but not the totality of the carnage. In total, thirty-six seamen lost their lives in this storm, and six ships went to the bottom, on our side of the Atlantic. Only through exceptional maritime skill and a hefty dose of luck, was it held to those terrible losses. It very easily could have been 200-men and 21-ships lost. When I grasped how massive it was, and how it affected such a wide range of people, I was ready to move ahead.

It is my opinion that over the year's fishermen have not always been heard. This has been changing in recent times, as more people become aware of the life of fishermen, with books like the Perfect Storm, and television series like the Deadliest Catch. Also, by the work being done in organizations, like the New Bedford Fishing Heritage Center, in New Bedford, Massachusetts, aptly led by Laura Orleans, and in international locations like the Grimsby Fishing Heritage Centre, in Grimsby, England, the Fisheries Museum of the Atlantic, in Lunenburg, Nova Scotia, Canada, and the Karmoy Fishing Museum in Karmoy, Norway. If you are interested in preserving our fishing heritage, these organizations and others like them can always put your time, or donation to good use. They are determined good people, and they are doing great work to preserve and tell our fishing history, help them out if you can.

I hope you enjoy my father's story because this is a true story. We will follow the many facets of the forces at work on the men and boats that go far out to sea, to bring the rest of us fresh seafood. I hope that after you finish this book, the next time you dine on seafood, you will appreciate the effort and the risk that it took to bring it to you. Also, the next time you hear a television weatherman say, "We're all in the clear because this storm is moving out to sea," you'll realize that there are probably men out on that sea who are bearing the full brunt of the storm. They are not in the clear. They are most surely in the teeth of the beast, and they are trying their best to survive and come home. As many people have learned over the past few years, fishing is a perilous business. In New Bedford, we have known for a very long time just how dangerous it can be. Since the year 1910, we have lost over 350 men while fishing. This book is about a storm that nearly added my father, and ten of his shipmate's names, to that list.

This book is primarily written in the time of this storm. Fishing has always been a male-dominated business, and it was especially so in 1962. In this book, I refer to fishermen in the male vernacular, and to ships in the female vernacular. I mean no disrespect to the women, especially those that now work in the fishing industry. I had the pleasure of meeting and speaking with probably the most famous of that group last year, Captain Linda Greenlaw. After a brief conversation, I understood how she became a fishing vessel captain. I grew up around fishing captains, and the good ones exude confidence and competence, something that in the military is called "Command Presence." Captain Greenlaw has command presence in spades. I also raised three strong daughters of whom I am very proud. No gender bias is intended in this work.

Any mistakes in this work are all mine, and I accept the responsibility for any errors that you might find. Please accept my apologies, and I hope that my mistakes are few.

I have written this book from the point of view of the fishermen, and for this, I make no apologies.

Paul Doucette
Fairhaven, Massachusetts
Milledgeville, Georgia
Copyright, November 2018

Chapter 9

THE TROUBLE BEGINS:

ENTER THE S/V *KRIA*

Rhode Island and New York

November is a month of transition in New England, this is the time when winter begins to show itself, the temperature starts to drop, and the winds increase. The summer wind pattern of south and southwest wind begins to give way to northerly winds. Cold fronts develop and plunge down from the north, and warm fronts make their last journeys of the year from the warm south to the colder north. New England in November is often the place where these two weather fronts meet and collide, and the result is often spectacular, but it can also be deadly.

The 1962 hurricane season was mild with only five named hurricanes in the Western North Atlantic. However, as October was giving way to November, it appeared that Mother Nature was going to make up for the light hurricane season, by sending a succession of nasty low-pressure systems up the East Coast.

In November of 1962, Thomas Ewing III is a 33-year old lawyer with the prestigious law firm Debevoise, Plimpton, Lyons, and Gates in New York City. He is a graduate of Yale University, Class of 1951, and the Harvard Law School, Class of 1957. Debevoise and Plimpton are very selective in their recruitment of lawyers. They recruit and hire only the best candidates out of the best law schools in the country. Thomas Ewing is working at arguably the top law firm in New York City. Tommy, as he is known to his friends, is from a very prominent family.

His late father, Thomas Ewing, Jr., was the heir to the Alex Smith and Sons Carpet Company in Yonkers, New York. This company, which was founded in 1871, was a considerable force in the carpet industry for 83-years and employed thousands of workers. In 1929, Alex Smith and Sons were the largest carpet manufacturer in the world. Today, the area and buildings that it encompassed are designated as a national historic district. Alex Smith and Sons were the driving force and lifeblood of Yonkers, New York for close to a century.

Tommy's mother, Lucia Chase, was born and raised in Waterbury, Connecticut and she spent her summers in Narragansett, Rhode Island. She attended Bryn Mawr College in Philadelphia, Pennsylvania before the lure of ballet and New York City pulled her to her life's calling. She became a prominent ballerina and was to become known as the "Queen Mother of the American Ballet Theater." Lucia Chace Ewing was the force which through dedication, hard work, and the most essential accurate indicator of a person's commitment, personal money, but always out of love for ballet and what it should be, who kept the American Ballet Theater alive and a mainstay of ballet in the United States for years.

Tommy Ewing's future in November 1962 is unlimited. Tommy is destined to do great things. His potential to become an outstanding contributor to our society is off the charts. As a young lawyer at Debevoise and Plimpton, he is accustomed to dealing with problem situations, and having the opportunity and the responsibility, to make decisions which lead to resolutions. Tommy Ewing is an avid sailor and has been for most of his life. He attended a sailing school in Massachusetts as a young boy, and sailing became his passion. There was a tradition in his family with high skilled sailing. Tommy's first boat was a Lawley-15, a sloop-rigged sailboat, which he sailed and raced in Narragansett Bay, Rhode Island. The Lawley-15 was a one design sloop that was built by the George Lawley & Son Corporation in Boston. Lawley was one of the top boat builders in the world during this time, and they made everything from schooners to prams, but all of them to a very high standard. The Lawley shipyard built two America's Cup winners, the *Puritan*, and the *Mayflower*, these two boats won the America's Cup in 1885 and 1886 respectively. The Lawley-15 sloop was an excellent boat for a young man to learn the ins and outs of sailing, Tommy practiced, and he learned. As he grew, he regularly participated in the Newport to Bermuda races. He also completed an Atlantic cruise/race crossing to Sweden in a sailboat. Tommy Ewing was a skilled sailor with blue water experience. Sailing was not recreation to Thomas Ewing III, it was serious business, and he was knowledgeable and passionate about sailing and the ocean.

It is Friday, October 26, 1962, and Tommy Ewing is in his law office, and he has a problem that he is considering, and it is not a problem of the law. Tommy owns a 30-foot sloop rigged sailboat that is currently lying in Snug Harbor, Rhode Island. His problem is that the recreational sailing season has ended in this part of the world. November is closing in, and that means foul cold weather for the next six months. He needs to sail his boat, the *Kria*, from Point Judith, Rhode Island to Essex, Connecticut, to put her up in storage for the winter. It is a distance, of about forty nautical miles, and it should take about eight hours to complete the trip. He has his cousin, Basil Carmody, lined up to assist him as crew to sail the *Kria* to Essex. The problem is the weather is looking bad for this weekend, as a low-pressure system is bearing down on southern New England. He reluctantly calls off the trip due to the weather.

A week has passed, and it is now Friday, November 2nd, 1962. Tommy Ewing is again in his office in New York City. He has again made plans for this weekend to move his boat to her winter quarters. He has his cousin, still lined up to assist him on the sail. Tommy is checking the marine forecast for this weekend, and once more it isn't looking good. Another low-pressure system is moving up the coast with high winds. At the last minute, he calls Basil and says, it's a no go. He is getting anxious about this bad weather pattern because he knows the deeper he goes into November, the worse the weather will become. He is feeling the pressure to get his boat home and secure for the winter.

With his plans ruined for the weekend, he attends a party that his mother is throwing for friends and family. During the party, he laments his bad luck with the weather and his need to get the *Kria* to her winter storage boatyard in Essex, Connecticut. Basil is not available next weekend. Tommy asks his brother Alex to make the sail with him next Saturday, but Alex also has other commitments that he cannot break. First the weather, and now difficulty obtaining a crew for the run to Essex, the pressure is mounting.

Another week goes by, and it is now Friday, November 9, 1962. Tommy Ewing is back at his desk at Debevoise & Plimpton in New York City, with a million work-related problems to solve and complete. However, Tommy is distracted. He is checking the weather for this weekend because the pressure of securing the *Kria* for the winter is building. He is getting desperate to get his boat home. Tommy needs some good weather, and it is looking good, as a high-pressure system is sitting over New England. Finally, some good sailing weather, and even better this is a three-day weekend due to Armistice Day. The holiday will give him an extra day to accomplish the task if he should need it. However, he has a new boat related problem; he has no regular crew to assist him this weekend. His regular crew members have other commitments that cannot be broken. He finds a solution in his Debevoise & Plimpton law associate, and fellow Yale graduate, David Evans, age 28. Dave agrees to act as crew on the *Kria* this weekend. Now he can finally get the *Kria* to the shipyard in Essex.

But there is a problem!

A low-pressure system began forming at 1:00 a.m. this morning, over the panhandle of Florida, near Cape San Blas. The low barometric pressure was recorded at 996-millibars. In the early afternoon of Friday, as Tommy Ewing is making plans with Dave Evans to drive to Rhode Island, the weather looks great. High pressure and good weather are dominating the area from the Chesapeake Bay to the Canadian Maritimes. Everything finally seems right, and it's a go for the *Kria*. That low-pressure system is now near Jekyll Island, Georgia, and it's a small system that's bringing rain to the Carolinas. It doesn't seem to be anything to worry about if Tommy is even aware of it. If he is aware of it, he probably thinks the worst that will happen is they may encounter a little rain. It's a small system right now, but it's going to grow quickly, and it has a date with Captain Tommy Ewing, and the *Kria*, in Block Island Sound.

At 1:00 a.m., on Saturday, November 10th, 1962, as Tommy and Dave sleep in Rhode Island, that little low-pressure system is growing, and she is now in the Chesapeake Bay Area. She's pushing the high pressure out of her way, as another high-pressure area pushes up behind her, and speeds her travel up the East Coast. The little monster is on the move, she's looking for trouble, and she is stalking the *Kria*.

On Saturday morning, Tom and Dave make their way down to the Sanderstown Yacht club to board the *Kria*. They set about getting the boat ready to shove off for Essex, Connecticut. Edna Lindberg, the owner of the marina at Snug Harbor, Rhode Island, reported that the sky had been clear and the weather good when the *Kria* sailed out of Salt Pond, late Saturday morning heading south. The Coast Guard later reported that a strong wind had been blowing and the water was quite rough around noon, but probably not so bad that they would have turned back. This is especially true when you factor in the point that this was the first weekend of any decent weather in a month, and the pressure was on Tommy to move this boat. However, the Coast Guard also reported that by mid-afternoon they would have encountered gale force winds and exceptionally heavy seas, and this is precisely what happened.

A careful analysis of the weather charts for November 10, reveals that by mid to late afternoon the *Kria* probably ran directly into a Triple Point Frontal Low-Pressure System. This is the exact point where a warm front meets with a cold front and creates the third point, the occluded front. This collision of weather fronts is the classic Triple Point weather scenario, and wind shear at this triple point can be massive. In fact, this is precisely the weather pattern that tornado chasers look for in the Plains States, as these conditions often spawn a tornado. Unfortunately for the *Kria* and her crew, she sailed directly into this type of weather system.

Around 4:30 p.m., the Lighthouse Keeper at the Watch Hill Lighthouse in Rhode Island, spotted the *Kria* sailing under only her jib, a short distance offshore. She seemed to be sailing under control, but the fact that she was moving under only her jib, means that she had reduced sail area to a minimum. Reducing sail area is a storm tactic to keep a sailboat sailing under control, what sailors would call, "staying on her feet." The lighthouse keeper then noticed that the *Kria* was heading too far south, and she was heading towards the dangerous Watch Hill Reefs. Although it was almost dark, the full moon meant that the man on duty could still observe the boat staying on the same course, and she had moved a half mile further. Then the lighthouse keeper observed that the running and stern lights went out. A light blinked directly at the lighthouse several times, this alarmed him and caused him to leave his post to call the nearest Coast Guard rescue station, at New London, Connecticut. When the lighthouse keeper returned minutes later, he could still see the light. He assumed that the boat was proceeding slowly toward the entrance into Little Narragansett Bay and Stonington Harbor.

This assumption was to be proven wrong!

Two Coast Guard cutters from New London arrived within twenty minutes, and searched the surrounding waters for several hours, but found nothing. Since there had been no report of a missing boat, it was assumed that there had been no accident, and consequently, no further search was ordered.

In looking at this accident today, fifty-six years later, it seems that the *Kria* encountered an explosive weather event. I believe that she ran directly into a Frontal Triple Point Low-Pressure System, at a time when her course would have placed her beam to the sea. The direction that they would have been sailing to clear Watch Hill would have been west, or some point of the west, on the compass. The wind was blowing from a northerly direction, which would have placed the *Kria*'s starboard side directly at the wind and the waves. The fact that the lighthouse keeper observed her sailing under her jib only confirms that she was experiencing heavy weather. His observation of the *Kria* heading too far south, and heading towards the dangerous Watch Hill Reefs, also proves that she was fighting for her life. The Watch Hill Reefs are marked very clearly on the charts for this area. It is marked with navigation buoys and the passage is known as the "Watch Hill

Passage." Tommy Ewing was a skilled sailor who sailed this area for most of his life, and it is evident that he was a highly intelligent man. Captain Ewing was heading south because he had no choice, he was probably trying to get stern to the seas, this being an attempt to survive the massive waves. Turning the boat before the wind may have been his only chance, because, with only his jib flying, Tommy may have had trouble rounding up into the wind, to take the seas head-on. Even if he could have turned into the wind, he would have limited sea room before hitting the beach. The *Kria* was trapped, with danger on all sides, and she was struck with massive wind shear in a position that offered them no viable alternatives for escape. It would seem, that the *Kria* probably hit the reef and broke apart. The light that the keeper saw was perhaps a flashlight beam from the crew, who were in the water.

No one knew the *Kria* was missing, and no search was conducted on Sunday. No search was conducted on Monday, which happened to be Armistice Day, now known as Veterans Day.

Late Tuesday morning, November 13th, 1962, someone from the Debevoise & Plimpton law office, called Tom's mother, Lucia Chase Ewing. They asked if she had heard from Tom because neither he nor Dave had shown up at the office that morning. Since this was very unlike them, they were beginning to get worried. They knew that Tom and Dave had planned to sail the *Kria* to Essex over the weekend. Everyone hoped that they were just delayed and that they would soon show up at the office and they agreed to keep in touch.

The Coast Guard and Navy were both contacted shortly after noon. After checking various marinas along the line of sail, the *Kria* was officially declared missing. Since it was mid-November, there was not enough daylight left on Tuesday to send out planes. At the end of Tuesday, all that was known was that the *Kria* was missing, but no wreckage had been reported along the beaches. Alex Ewing, Tommy's brother, called Bayard Ewing, his uncle, in North Kingstown, Rhode Island, to alert him that Tom and his boat were missing. Bayard contacted his friend, and a man who he had run against twice for the United States Senate, Senator John O. Pastore from Rhode Island, to solicit his help. Senator Pastore contacted the Navy and arranged with the Naval Air Station at Quonset Point, Rhode Island, to begin an air search at dawn.

In New York, friends and associates at Debevoise and Plimpton, worked all night to organize a second search party, based out of New York. Lucia and her niece, Deidre, went to Tom's apartment at East 74th Street in New York City, and they arranged to maintain a twenty-four-hour presence at the apartment, in the hope that Tom would turn up alive and well.

By Wednesday morning, November 14th, a coordinated search was underway. Coast Guard ships and planes, Navy ships and aircraft, including the submarine Sablefish, and a private airplane with Alex Ewing, Bayard Ewing, and a cousin, Irving Sheldon all aboard, were all searching the line of sail. At the end of Wednesday, there was still no trace of the *Kria* or her crew.

The search was expanded on Thursday, November 15th, with two additional airplanes. Fishing boats were alerted by the marine telephone operators in both Boston and New York to be on the lookout for a 30-foot blue hulled sloop, with a crew of two, missing and presumed lost. The Oceanographic Institute and Laboratory in Woods Hole, Massachusetts, provided details on currents and identified possible areas to search carefully. The shoreline of Block Island and Fishers Island were being searched, as well as, the entire coastline from Watch Hill, Rhode Island to Essex, Connecticut, by people on foot. At the end of Thursday, there was still no trace of the *Kria*, or her crew. The Coast Guard and Navy were being taxed to the limit on this day because another low-pressure system had caused all hell to break loose in the offshore waters of the Western North Atlantic.

Late Friday afternoon, as the search continued, some gear including a sou'wester hat, with the name Ewing stenciled in the band, and pieces of a sailboat washed up on the shore at Sandy Point, near Stonington Harbor in Connecticut. Alex Ewing proceeded to the scene to inspect the articles that had been found. Alex had the heavy burden of having to confirm that these items were from the *Kria*, and it was now sure that his brother, Thomas Ewing III, and his friend and work associate, David Evans, were presumed to be dead. The horrible storm had claimed her first two victims.

On Saturday, November 17th, 1962, a Memorial Service was held at St. James Church, in New York City, for Thomas Ewing III and David Evans.

On November 30th, 1962, the body of Thomas Ewing III came ashore on the north side of Napatree Point.

A small private service was held, and Thomas Ewing III was buried next to his father and his grandfather, in the family plot, in Yonkers, New York. Shortly after the service, Lucia Chace Ewing made a trip to Rhode Island, to talk to the lighthouse keeper at the Watch Hill Lighthouse, who had first reported seeing the *Kria* in the throes of the November storm. Lucia spent most of the summer of 1963 in Rhode Island. Often late in the afternoon, she would drive down to Watch Hill and sit on the lawn next to the lighthouse and stare out into the sea. It was her way of coming to grips with the loss of her eldest son. For the first time in her adult life, she had no interest in ballet. That summer, she threw herself into the building of a summer cottage next to her property, with a view of the ocean, in memory of Tommy. She filled the cottage with furniture, pictures, and other memorabilia, from Tom's New York City apartment. She maintained this cottage, and made it available to Tom's friends, as a summer place that they could use. She named the cottage, "Moonraker," the name of Tommy Ewing's Lawley-15 sloop, that he had sailed and raced as a boy in Narragansett Bay.

Two fine young men were gone. Two Ivy League-educated lawyers, practicing and learning their profession at one of the top law firms in the world, were no longer with us. It was a tragedy to all concerned, and to our nation, as these are the type of men who would have gone on to accomplish great things. They were taken in the prime of their lives, by the unrelenting and unforgiving forces of nature. We can gather some measure of what the world lost when, Thomas Ewing III and David Evans were taken by this storm, by looking at the life of Tom's younger brother Alex, and the life that he lived.

Alex Ewing would go on to lead an exemplary productive life. He was a graduate of Yale University, and he would go on to become a journalist, author, founder and general director of the Joffrey Ballet Company, cattle rancher, founder and president of the Foundation for American Dance, and chancellor of the University of North Carolina School of the Arts. Most importantly he was a devoted husband and father. An accomplished and full life indeed. He was described as kind, and generous, a motivator to all around him, a renaissance man, and a great contributor to our society. I am confident that his brother Thomas Ewing, and David Evans would have led similar productive lives. Alexander C. Ewing passed away in Winston-Salem, North Carolina on December 27, 2017, he was 86-years old.

The lesson that the loss of Thomas Ewing III and David Evans leaves for all of us who go down to the sea, but especially for recreational boaters, is that a healthy respect for the ocean and Mother Nature is paramount. The problem is that most recreational boaters have a day job, which helps fund their boating and sailing passion. The pressure of work responsibility and time limitations has contributed to bad decisions many times in boating accidents. In 1962, Captain Tommy Ewing did not have the benefit of the detailed weather analysis systems that we have today. We will see how this comes into play as a significant problem for the rest of the boats in this story. However, in looking at how this accident took place, time pressure was a contributing factor. Mr. Ewing was no doubt a hard charger and a skilled, confident sailor, but he was also under pressure to go this weekend. He had experienced a series of delays, and he saw this weekend as his best chance to move his boat. No one is stronger than Mother Nature when she is showing her bad side. How I wish Tommy would have waited, or just found a shipyard in Rhode Island to store his boat for the winter. I wonder what he and David Evans might have accomplished in their lives.

Captain Thomas Ewing III, Esquire
Mr. David Evans, Esquire

Rest in Peace
You Men of Yale

This low-pressure system was the opening round in the fight that was coming. This opening salvo was part of a one-two combination of severe weather. These two weather systems would join and interact causing this week to be a terrible week for mariners. This first low-pressure system, which I have named, "the *Kria* Low," would continue heading north from Block Island Sound, but it would move slowly and then stall over the Canadian Maritimes. In this position, it would continually send northerly winds down into New England waters, and this would assist in building big seas, as it waited for the next larger low-pressure system to come up the coast. Together they would join forces for some of the worst marine weather the area had seen in more than fifty years. This system would extend out one-thousand-miles, from some of the lowest pressure ever recorded in New England waters, for November. On November 12th, as the search for the *Kria* was getting underway, the elements required for another low-pressure system were forming off the western tip of Cuba. At this point, the beginnings of the next low-pressure system were imperceptible to even the most seasoned weather observer. But, it was a weather system that was going to move fast and grow fast. This system would stay over the water and follow the Gulf Stream for its entire journey up the East Coast; it was going to be a real beast and a freak of nature.

Neptune was annoyed, and his temper was showing!

United States had a surplus of Liberty Ships, and to assist some maritime nations in rebuilding their economies; many were sold. Greece, a country with long maritime history, purchased 526 Liberty Ships, including the *McCrackin*, and she was eventually renamed and re-flagged, as the M/V *Captain George*.

In November 1962, the M/V *Captain George* was 442-feet in length, and she is rated as a 7,188-ton cargo ship. The crew consists of twenty-five men, who are Greek nationals. The crew is looking forward to the trip east and returning home to Greece, after unloading their cargo in Libya.

On November 3rd, 1962, the M/V *Captain George* left New Orleans, Louisiana, and then made stops in Houston, Texas, St. Mary's, Georgia, and finally Savannah, Georgia, before heading northeast on her crossing of the Atlantic, bound for Tripoli, in Libya. Her cargo of explosives is scheduled to be unloaded in Tripoli for use in the oil drilling industry.

The cargo is made up of sulfur, flour, and rice, as well as, explosive materials. The explosives are 12,000-pounds of nitro-carbo-nitrate (NCN) in bags, and 4,000-pounds of dynamite and blasting caps. The NCN is stored in Holds #2 and #3, forward of the bridge. NCN is used as both an explosive and as a fertilizer. The explosive dynamite and blasting caps are stored in Hold #5, the hold furthest aft on the ship, along with barrels of oil. The M/V *Captain George* is loaded with a dangerous combination of chemicals. Flour and sulfur are both capable of creating explosive dust. NCN is known to be highly explosive and has been the cause of many horrific accidents, not to mention the dynamite, blasting caps, and oil, all stored together in the aft hold. These chemicals are stored in the confined space of the ship's cargo holds. The *Captain George* is a floating bomb, and she is about to encounter a weather bomb.

As the ship leaves Savannah, Georgia bound for her Atlantic crossing, the crew is not aware that they will be sailing directly into a storm of extremely low pressure, with hurricane force winds, and seas of 30 to 60-feet in height. As they run their course northeast towards Bermuda, they are caught in the grips of a terrible gale. On Wednesday night, November 14th, 1962, shortly after 10:00 p.m., they are in trouble. As the ship battles hurricane-force winds and large waves, the ship is rocked by an explosion. The cargo they are carrying is dangerous, and they no doubt suffered an impact explosion, due to the heavy rolling and pounding of the ship into the stormy seas. The blast was followed by the outbreak of a fire, in Hold #4, and this is where most of the sulfur is stored. They don't know it yet, but their fate has been sealed, they are sitting on a chemical bomb, a sulfur fire is raging down below, and they are in the grips of a terrible storm. Without the large, storm-tossed waves, this event may never have happened.

Captain Karamezis realizes the serious implications of this sulfur fire and issues orders to address the emergency. He knows that if they cannot get this fire under control, and if it spreads, the ship will be blown out of the water. He immediately dispatches a four-man firefighting team to Hold #4, to fight the fire. He knows that he must get this sulfur fire suppressed. He next sends men to Hold #5, and he instructs them to remove the explosive material from this hold and to throw it overboard, all while the ship is rolling and pitching in the raging storm. The firefighting team is experiencing great difficulty in Hold #4; the burning sulfur is producing sulfur dioxide fumes, which are fatal to humans. They are losing the fight, and Captain Karamezis now instructs the radio operator to send out an SOS message.

At 10:34 p.m., on Wednesday, 11/14/62:

The M/V *Captain George* sends out the following SOS message;

"SOS…SOS…SOS…,
Position is 37 degrees, 15 minutes North, x 60 degrees, 45 minutes, West,
Explosion and Fire…Require Immediate Assistance…Require Immediate
Assistance."

The Coast Guard receives this message and immediately puts rescue assets into motion. Request for assistance is broadcast out to all vessels in the area. At this moment the Coast Guard is waking up to the realization that they have multiple problems tonight. They have inshore assets working on the hunt for the S/V *Kria*, and now they realize that they have issues offshore, as well. They are beginning to receive calls for help from a schooner in distress near Bermuda, and two U.S. Navy cargo ships are experiencing difficulties, as well as, numerous fishing boats on the always treacherous Georges Bank. Things are showing signs of an overload on the assets of the Coast Guard. Two large Liberian flagged tankers, the SS *Trinity Navigator*, and the SS *Virginia* are near the M/V *Captain George*, and they alert the Coast Guard that they are heading to the reported position of the Greek cargo ship. In the best tradition of sailors everywhere, they race to the scene to offer any possible assistance.

The U.S. Navy directs the submarines, USS *Torsk,* and USS *Cutlass*, to proceed at the fastest possible speed to the area of the M/V *Captain George*, and to render all possible assistance.

The Coast Guard and the Navy prepare to send airplanes to the scene, to locate the *Captain George* and to assist in the rescue effort. The Coast Guard diverts the USCGC *Mendota* to the scene, after the naval ship, the USS *Compass Island* takes over rescue efforts for the schooner *Curlew*.

Upon hearing the first SOS message, Captain John Forder, the pilot of a British Overseas Airways Corporation (BOAC) jetliner bound from New York to London, diverts from his flight plan and proceeds to the last reported position coordinates of the M/V *Captain George*. At 2:25 a.m., three hours after the first SOS message, Captain Forder finds the cargo ship. Captain Forder was quoted as saying; "The first thing that I saw was a light. We started down. There was the ship, wallowing in the white-topped water. The whole aft area was on fire. I started circling and calling. We received no reply on the distress frequency. One of our navigators was able to read the Morse Code that the ship was transmitting. They were asking for a confirmation of their position, and they were asking when would help be arriving. We radioed an SOS from our aircraft to the Coast Guard and reported that we had located the sinking ship. Storm clouds were hampering our view from the air. We could see that the entire aft section of the ship was involved in smoke and flame. She was underway because we could see her wake. But, as we circled, she seemed to slow down. There was too much smoke, and too many broken clouds, to see the men on the deck. Giant waves were pounding the ship. It was a terrible scene. It gave us such a feeling of helplessness."

Captain Forder, the BOAC (now British Airways) aircraft pilot, stays on station for three-hours flying over the ship. He relays messages from the *Captain George* to the Coast Guard, and he pinpoints the exact location of the ship for the rescue assets that are racing to the scene. After three hours, he is satisfied that rescue assets are about to arrive. He then turns his aircraft, loaded with passengers, and heads back to New York. He has expended a great deal of fuel circling the *Captain George* at low altitude, and he does not have enough fuel left on board, to continue his flight to London.

Captain Karamezis was in communication with the BOAC aircraft and reported to Captain Forder that; "He would not abandon the ship until absolutely necessary." He thanked Captain Forder for his efforts and said that it gave his crew hope that

56

their plight was known to others, as they battled the fire, toxic fumes, and the sea. Captain Forder estimated that seas were ranging from 30 to 60-feet in height. What a heroic act, that this 40-year-old British pilot undertook, to come to the assistance of the M/V *Captain George*. A beautiful display of courage to help others who were in distress.

Captain John Forder
Aircraft Commander
British Overseas Airways Corporation
"The Finest Kind"

At 11:30 p.m., Wednesday, 11/14/62;

At this time, the fire was eating at the sulfur, and the acrid sulfur dioxide mix was curling out of the hold and blowing across the deck while being whipped by the strong winds. Toxic fumes were hindering the firefighting effort of the crew. Captain Karamezis issues another message. The *Captain George* radio room sends another message to the Coast Guard;

"Expect explosion to go up any minute. Help!"

Then two minutes later;

At 11:32 p.m., Wednesday, 11/14/62;

Facing a losing battle against the sulfur fire, the master of the M/V *Captain George* is gravely concerned that the fire will soon get to the explosives in Hold #5, and he sends another message to the Coast Guard requesting helicopters to remove the crew. His request is denied because his position is too far away from any available rescue helicopters, and they would not be able to reach his position, and then return safely before running out of fuel. This was at a time before the refueling of helicopters in-flight was routinely available.

With no hope of getting off the ship anytime soon, the crew continues to fight the fire. They also manage to pull more of the most dangerous cargo to the stern of the ship and throw it overboard.

At 11:48 p.m., Wednesday, 11/14/62; The radio operator sends the following message; "Putting cargo over the side. Conditions are getting worse."

At Midnight, Wednesday, 11/14/62

Another message; "Activating automatic Alarm."

The radio operator has set the automatic radio distress alarm in motion.

At 12:47 a.m., Thursday, 11/15/62;

The radio operator sends; "Explosives jettisoned from aft. Looks more promising now, the only explosives aboard are now forward of the bridge."

The explosives forward of the bridge, are Nitro-Carbo-Nitrate (NCN), which is stored in both Hold #2 and Hold #3. This chemical is as dangerous as the explosives that were stored in Hold #5, and there is a tremendous amount of it in these two holds.

At this point, the crew believes that they have the situation under control, but then the fire flared up again. This was due to the heavy rolling of the ship which was moving the smoldering cargo around in the hold. As the cargo moved and was becoming exposed to more air, the added influx of oxygen gave the fire new life. It is now impossible to reach the explosives in the forward holds. The sulfur dioxide fumes are curling out of Hold #4 and blowing across the deck, and the crew is helpless to stop it. Seawater is getting into the hold and further feeding the sulfur fire, and it is now raging out of control.

At 4:10 a.m., Thursday, 11/15/62;

Radio operator sends; "Unable to enter the radio shack due to the sulfur fumes. Please hurry, I am tuning the automatic "Gibson Girl."

The "Gibson Girl" is an emergency, hand-cranked, distress radio with limited range. From this point on, the remaining messages will be relayed from the M/V *Captain George* to either Coast Guard aircraft, or the tanker *Virginia*, and then they will be re-relayed to the Coast Guard Rescue Headquarters.

At 5:30 a.m., Thursday, 11/15/62;

The radio operator sends out the following message;

"The #4 Hatch is on fire. We are unable to extinguish the sulfur fire. The captain is afraid that the fire might spread to the #5 Hatch where oil is still stored, or to the explosives forward. Attempting to make a course for Bermuda. Crew morale is still high. All the crew is well, but we are taking on more water, tanker *Virginia* is standing by."

At 10:19 a.m., Thursday, 11/15/62;

The SS *Virginia* relays a message to the Coast Guard, from Captain George Karamezis, the master of the M/V *Captain George*, declaring that he has ordered the crew to abandon ship.

It is at this point that crewman George Anthis finds his younger brother, who is also a crewman on the ship. There are two large lifeboats on board the vessel, both rescue crafts are amidships, one on the starboard side, and one on the port side. George Anthis tells his younger brother that they must split up. He advises his brother to get in the starboard lifeboat, which is on the leeward side and should, therefore, be the easier boat to launch, and he will get in the port side lifeboat, on the windward side. He tells his brother that by splitting-up this will increase the chances that one of them will make it home to their family in Greece. They agree to the plan, embrace, shake hands, wish each other luck, and run off to their respective lifeboats.

Then came a period when the abandon ship appeared to be impossible. Weather conditions of high winds and seas were making it difficult to launch the two lifeboats. The *Virginia* then attempted to come alongside the *Captain George*, but the waters were too rough. The captain of the *Virginia* reported to the Coast Guard that he had suffered some damage to his ship in the attempt, and he could not try it again without imperiling his vessel. It was now up to the crew of the *Captain George* to launch their lifeboats and make their way to the *Virginia*, or the *Trinity Navigator*, both of whom were standing by waiting.

At 3:58 p.m., Thursday, 11/15/62;

The first lifeboat that was attempted to be launched was the port side boat, on the windward side of the ship. This boat was considered the more difficult of the two lifeboats to launch because the hurricane force wind was directly hitting this side of the ship. Only five men were working on the windward lifeboat; the other twenty crew members had made their way to the other boat, which was thought to be the easier boat to launch. In lowering the port side lifeboat, 54-year old crewman, Stelios Paschalides, lost his balance and tumbled into the sixty-foot seas. He clutched desperately to the side of the lifeboat, and his shipmates struggled to hold onto him, while also trying to stay in the boat themselves. The lifeboat came briefly under the lee of the *Captain George*, and this reduced the wind and pressure on the lifeboat, and after five minutes of terror, Paschalides shipmates were able to haul him into the boat. As she left the lee of the *Captain George*, the lifeboat was then immediately swallowed up in the massive waves, and the tankers lost sight of the boat and the five men aboard. After about thirty minutes, the lifeboat reappeared, swirling madly out of control, but with all five men still aboard hanging on for dear life. The lifeboat was now very close to the *Trinity Navigator*, and her crew was trying to maneuver their large ship up to the small rescue craft. On a catwalk of the *Trinity Navigator*, the First Mate was directing the rescue effort of his ship. The crew of the *Trinity Navigator* were all Taiwanese nationals. A massive wave broke over the catwalk, and it threw First Mate T.T. Lu onto the deck twenty-five-feet below. The wave bounced him against the deck and the side of the superstructure like a rubber ball. Miraculously, Mate Lu survived this fall, and then the crew of the *Trinity Navigator* was able to get a line to the lifeboat, and they then extracted all five men to the safety of the tanker.

At 4:30 p.m., Thursday, 11/15/62;

Now with darkness creeping in, it is now or never for the remaining crew of twenty-men still aboard the *Captain George*. They are finally able to launch the second leeward lifeboat. This boat was also swallowed up in the fifty-foot seas, but several times it got close to the rescue ships. Both ships made passes at the lifeboat, to rescue the occupants, but they failed in those attempts.

At 6:20 p.m., Thursday, 11/15/62;

The lifeboat was now only fifty-yards away from the *Trinity Navigator*, and it appeared that the remaining twenty-crew-members would be saved. However, a massive wave of approximately sixty-feet broke over the lifeboat and caused her to capsize, throwing all twenty-men into the sea. The *Virginia* was then able to retrieve two of the men alive. The other eighteen-men were in the water fighting for their lives. An Air Force plane dropped a life raft, but to no avail, as the wind grabbed it, and it spun far away from the helpless men in the water. The last view of these men alive, was of them all in life jackets, holding on to one another, as they crested a giant wave, and then disappearing as they slid down the back side of this fifty-foot monster. They quickly vanished from sight, and they had no flashlights, or strobe lights, to signal their position. Coast Guard planes circled the scene and fired off flares, to illuminate the area. These planes were soon forced to leave the scene due to running low on fuel. Another Coast Guard plane came on station, but no further sighting of the eighteen men in the water was made. Upon daylight, a twenty by thirty-mile search box was flown to look for possible survivors. None were found.

At 3:28 a.m., Friday, 11/16/62;

The two tanker captains gave up the search due to the heavy seas and gale force winds that were endangering their ships. The two ships, with five survivors on the *Trinity Navigator*, and two survivors on the *Virginia*, were riding out the storm and drifting to the west, toward the United States mainland. The captains reported that they were still experiencing 60-mph winds, and they informed the Coast Guard that they could not change course, due to sea conditions. The *Trinity Navigator* and the *Virginia* arrived in Paulsboro, New Jersey, on the evening of Sunday, November 18, 1962.

The United States Navy Submarine, USS *Torsk*, remained on scene and continued searching for the eighteen missing men.

On Saturday, 11/17/62;

The search for the eighteen-men continued with little hope. The search team now consisted of six planes, the USS *Torsk*, and the USCGC *Mendota*. The search area now encompassed an area of 2,600 square miles. It was reported this morning that the weather has improved in the area, as the winds have calmed, but seas are still running high. Later in the day, an aircraft spotted a capsized lifeboat, and bodies in the water, approximately 260-miles northeast of Bermuda. There was no sign of anyone being alive.

On Sunday morning, 11/18/62;

The Coast Guard assets on the scene of the wreck reported that the superstructure of the M/V *Captain George* had burned away and that the decks were white hot. This was followed by a massive explosion, and the *Captain George* then sank into the sea, approximately 300-miles Northeast of Bermuda, at 36-degrees, 48-minutes North and 61-degrees, 23-minutes West.

Tuesday, November 20, 1962;

The USCGC *Mendota* arrived in Bermuda with the bodies of three of the missing crew members from the M/V *Captain George*. The Coast Guard spotted three other bodies, but those bodies vanished into the sea before they could be recovered. The *Mendota* also spotted five life jackets, bobbing in the water among the bodies, and the overturned lifeboat. The three recovered bodies had been badly mutilated by sharks. The remains of the other fifteen men were never recovered.

THE FIVE SURVIVORS
RESCUED BY THE *TRINITY NAVIGATOR*
Sunday, November 18, 1962
Paulsboro, New Jersey

Left to Right,
Antonius Arapis
George Anthis
Costas Veletzas
Themis Patzatzis
Stelios Paschalides

George Anthis is second from the left, and he has just been informed that his brother did not survive. His grief is sadly evident on his face in this photograph. It was said that he blamed himself for his brother's death, by sending him to the starboard lifeboat. He, of course, had, in fact, sent his younger brother to the lifeboat that had the better chance of surviving this tragedy. The other four crew members are obviously happy to be alive. Stelios Paschalides is on the far right, and he is the man who was in the water for five minutes before his four shipmates were able to pull him into the lifeboat.

DIAGRAM OF A LIBERTY SHIP

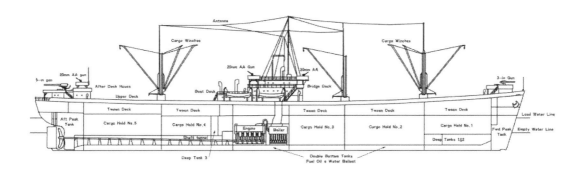

Hold #2 and #3 – NCN, Sulfur, Flour, & Rice
Hold #4 - Sulfur
Hold #5 – Dynamite, Blasting Caps, and Oil

Neptune's Nor'easter had now claimed another eighteen-men, and the total now stands at twenty-men lost, and two-boats sunk, a 30-foot sailboat, and a 442-foot ship. It was not over yet. It was going to get worse.

Rest in Peace

You Modern Day Argonauts

A WWII Liberty ship that was sold to Greece and converted to a commercial cargo ship, shown dockside in Piraeus, Greece. This is a sister ship of the M/V *Captain George* and this is a good example of what she would have looked like before she was lost in Neptune's Nor'easter.

Chapter 8

A SCHOONER RACE TO THE CARIBBEAN

Curlew and *Windfall*

On Sunday, November 11th, 1962, two classic wooden schooners left Mystic, Connecticut, in a stiff breeze of 25 to 30-mph from the northwest, bound for Bermuda. A low-pressure system ("the Kria Low"), had passed through the area the day before and the wind was still up, but not enough to delay these two schooners from leaving port. In fact, this was just the kind of wind that these schooners were built for, and the captains anticipated making good speed toward Bermuda. The plan was to make a stop in Bermuda and then continue to the Caribbean, where they both intended to enter their boats in the winter charter trade. They were the 65-foot *Curlew* and the 56-foot *Windfall*. The boats both had pedigrees which originated in the craftsmanship of Maine built schooners. These two boats were both built in the 1920's, at the Fred F. Pendleton Shipyard, in Wiscasset, Maine. The *Curlew* was designed by the famous naval architect John Alden of Boston, Massachusetts. The *Windfall* was designed by the prominent naval architect William Hand, Jr. of Fairhaven, Massachusetts. The boats had spent some days in Newport, Rhode Island with final fitting out for the journey, and all being schooner men they became friends. They agreed to conduct an informal race to the Virgin Islands, to keep things interesting, on what was going to be a long trip.

As the boats cleared Montauk, on the eastern tip of Long Island, New York, they began to separate. The larger stay-sail-rigged *Curlew* was faster than the traditional gaff-rigged *Windfall*. The last sighting that the crew of the *Curlew* had of the *Windfall* was that evening, just before sunset. The boats communicated by radio a few times, but soon they lost all contact. They expected to catch up with each other in Bermuda.

The Story of the "Magical" *Curlew*

Sailors like to talk about and assign a personality to their ships. The human and the ship that he sails on are inextricably linked. The human depends on the ship, and the ship depends on the human. They both need each other to function and to survive their shared journeys on the sea. Sailors talk to their ship sweetly when she is sailing well, and they scold and curse her when things are going badly. It's an emotional relationship. In the mind of a sailor, they sometimes love, and they sometimes hate, the ship that they are sailing on. In their imagination, the ship takes on a life, and she is almost a living breathing creature to him. They also always refer to their ship in the feminine vernacular, such as; "She's a good ship," or "She's a beauty." As strange as it sounds, this is how sailors fall in love with their ship. Sailors will tell you that a good ship seems to have an identity, a persona, something akin to a soul. If they have endured an ordeal at sea, such as during a battle while at war, or coming through a dangerous storm, the sailors aboard that ship will start to say; "She's a lucky ship," or "She's a magic ship." If ever there was a magic ship, it most certainly would have to be the schooner *Curlew*. Even Hollywood couldn't dream up a story like this one. The *Curlew* is simply, as the fishermen in New Bedford would say, "The Finest Kind."

The *Curlew* was built in 1926, at the Fred F. Pendleton Shipyard, in Wiscasset, Maine, from a design by the naval architect John Alden. The Pendleton Shipyard had a long reputation of building some of the most beautiful schooners on the water.

John Gale Alden was born in Troy, New York, in 1884. He was always fascinated by boats, and his family took their summer vacations in Rhode Island, where he was surrounded by, and enjoyed Narragansett Bay, the sights of the local fishermen, and the many sailboats of all sizes and configurations. This environment fueled his passion, and when he was not messing around in boats, he was doodling and drawing boats.

At eighteen years old, he enrolled at the Massachusetts Institute of Technology (MIT) in Cambridge, Massachusetts, to study naval architecture. He apprenticed under Starling Burgess, and Bowdoin B. Crowninshield, two of the leading naval architects of their time.

In 1900, his family moved to Dorchester, Massachusetts, where the Boston fleet of Grand Banks fishing schooners were docked. He would spend hours studying and drawing the lines of these schooners and talking to the fishermen about their boats. These conversations and his drawings would be the basis for the future designs that would make him famous.

In the winter of 1907, he undertook a voyage that would complete his education and inspire his later work. The fishing schooner *Fame*, which was owned by the Eastern Fishing Company, had to be returned to Boston from Newfoundland. The crew had all come down with smallpox, and they were in quarantine, and unable to sail the fishing schooner back to Boston. Alden was offered the job of retrieving the schooner *Fame*, and he accepted the assignment. He put together a crew of five men, only one of them, having extensive schooner experience. On this voyage, Alden encountered a nor'easter gale with 70-knot winds, and the schooner also became burdened with ice. After having completed this offshore winter trip, and after having had time to reflect on the lessons that he learned from making this trip, Alden made it his priority to design boats that would be resilient and stable in heavy seas, and that could be sailed single-handed, if necessary. This would be his trademark, a boat that would be graceful, but also designed to be able to take the worst that the sea could throw at her. Alden was quoted as saying; "I was very much in love with a vessel that sails on her bottom, not on her beam ends." The design genius of John Gale Alden was never more apparent than in *Curlew*, as her history will attest.

The schooner *Fame* was lost at sea the following year, on May 26, 1908, when she was run down by the steamer *Boston*, in heavy fog at night, off the coast of Maine. The steamer saved only two of the twenty-two fishermen aboard the fishing schooner. The other twenty men all perished in the accident, as they were below decks sleeping when their schooner was run down. One of the lost fishermen, Peter Doucette, was a distant relative of mine, and a native of Tusket Wedge, Nova Scotia, Canada.

The schooner *Curlew* was built for Charles Andrews, a member of the New York Yacht Club. She was initially designed as a standard schooner, with a gaffed foresail, and it was intended that the *Curlew* would be used as a cruising boat. However, she was fast, and Charles Andrews' son, Richard Andrews, began to enter her in long distance races. During the 1930's she raced in the New York Yacht Club's ocean cruising class. She was a regular participant in the Newport,

Rhode Island to Bermuda races. The *Curlew* competed with the fastest schooners of her day and held her own.

In 1937, the *Curlew* was sold to William Jay Schieffelin Jr., the great-grandson of William H. Vanderbilt. The new owner converted her to a staysail schooner, which was the preferred configuration for competitive racing schooners. Mr. Schieffelin moved her home port to Ashville, Maine. *Curlew* had found her way back home, to the State of Maine. New canvas was ordered from England, and the *Curlew* now sported sails from the loft of Ratsey & Lapthorn, the leading sailmaker in the world in 1937. Nothing but the best for *Curlew*!

That was about to change; Uncle Sam was going to come calling!

While *Curlew* spent her first fourteen years running with the rich and famous, she was now getting ready to shift gears with a changing world, and she would soon find herself preparing for the coming war. World War II was on the horizon, and *Curlew* was about to join the military. On January 31, 1940, the *Curlew* was sold to the United States Coast Guard, for the sum of one dollar. She was assigned to the United States Coast Guard Academy in New London, Connecticut. Here she served as a training vessel for the cadets who would go on to become the officers and future leaders of the Coast Guard. *Curlew* also saw service with the Coastal Picket Force, as a submarine patrol vessel, searching for German submarines, known as U-Boats.

After the war, on January 8th, 1951, *Curlew* was transferred to the United States Coast Guard Recruit Training Center in Cape May, New Jersey. Here she spent nine long years and was used to teach basic seamanship to new Coast Guard enlisted recruits. *Curlew* had now moved from the spit and polish of the Academy to the grind of the enlisted ranks. She was now being used, and tended to, by the least experienced sailors in the U.S. Coast Guard. In late 1959, the Coast Guard surveyed *Curlew* and declared her beyond economical repair. *Curlew* was then de-commissioned on May 26, 1960, and she was no longer in the service of her country. Like an old warhorse, she was deemed too old, at 35-years, and was no longer needed by her country. *Curlew* was being put out to pasture. But, this magic ship would have none of it, and she waited patiently for her next reinvention. She had been rode hard and put up wet by the Coast Guard, but though bowed, she was never broken. The *Curlew* is a "Sea Dog" that doesn't know the word quit.

Curlew only had to wait six months. On November 7th, 1960 in a sealed bid auction, *Curlew* was purchased from the Coast Guard for 3,000 dollars ($24,000 in 2018). The new owners were Mr. Robert Gervasoni of Trenton, New Jersey and Mr. Sam Fiorello of Yardley, Pennsylvania. *Curlew* was in bad shape when they received her. She had broken loose from her mooring during Hurricane Donna, and she had lost her bowsprit and foremast in the storm. In addition to this damage, the Coast Guard had stripped her, including removing her engine. The new owners arranged for a tugboat, and they towed *Curlew* to the Stoneman Shipyard, on the Maurice River, in Delaware Bay, New Jersey. This is a trip of about thirty nautical miles. Once at the shipyard, the owners discovered that *Curlew* had been taking on water during the tow, and they also found an open seacock. Fortunately, the seacock was fouled with seagrass. It was a miracle that *Curlew* didn't sink during the tow. Once again *Curlew* wouldn't give up, she just kept going. Her bowsprit may have been broken, but her spirit was completely intact. That spirit was going to be tested to its limits soon.

Over the next year, the owners spent countless hours working on *Curlew* with the help of the Stoneman Shipyard. The schooner was slowly but surely being brought back to her former glory. A new Ford marine diesel engine was installed. The cabin sole was covered in linoleum, and Mr. Gervasoni decided to recover the cabin sole with teak, as it was when she was originally built. Fittingly, for a ship that had served on U-Boat patrol during the war, the teak for this project came from a yacht that was being scrapped at the shipyard. That yacht had previously been owned by none other than Adolf Hitler, and she was taken as war reparations by the United States. To the victor goes the spoils!

Curlew was now ready, and the owners sailed her up to the Essex Yacht Club in Connecticut. It was in Essex that they met a young Englishman, Captain David Skellon, who had extensive blue water sailing experience with multiple ocean crossings, and experience in the Caribbean charter business. Captain Skellon was hired to be the new captain of the *Curlew*. The mission was to take her to the Caribbean and enter the charter business. *Curlew* was going to work; she was getting a job!

Before heading south, *Curlew* went on a shakedown cruise to Newport, Rhode Island. Here they met up with another schooner, the *Windfall*. The two schooners left Newport bound for Bermuda, but the weather kicked up, (the Kria Low), and they ducked into Mystic, Connecticut. Due to the delay, Bob Gervasoni had to abandon the trip to Bermuda, because he had some pressing matters at work that could not wait. He planned to fly to Bermuda later, and meet the *Curlew* for the second leg of the run down to the Virgin Islands.

The crew of *Curlew* now consisted of;

Captain David Skellon, of London, England
Mate Ed Lowe, from Maine
Owner Sam Fiorello, of Yardley, Pennsylvania
John "Spider" Slim, of Bordentown, New Jersey
William Colby, of Bordentown, New Jersey
James O'Neil, of New Britton, Connecticut

On *Curlew*, the passage started out routinely for an early November voyage. On Monday, November 12, 1962, Armistice Day, the wind died out, and the schooner was required to use her auxiliary diesel engine to make progress. The sea was very confused and agitated from the "Kria Low."

On Tuesday afternoon, the wind picked up and came from the southeast with rain squalls.

On Wednesday morning, the wind was northerly and was now blowing 50-knots. Trouble started to develop as the heavy wind carried the gallows frame away. The braking screw on the propeller then failed, which kept the propeller shaft from turning, and then the packing box around the propeller began to leak. The leak was becoming so bad, that the bilge pump, which was powered by the engine, was barely able to keep up with the incoming water. Several halyards then failed and separated, and there was some sail damage. The Captain gave the order to strike all sails, and *Curlew* was now running before the wind, heading south under bare poles. This means that she had no sails set, and she was being propelled south, by the power and force of the strong winds.

3:00 p.m. – November 14, 1962 – Wednesday

Captain Skellon took the wheel for his one-hour wheel watch. Within ten minutes he was soaking wet, as the seas were breaking over the stern of the *Curlew*. The water was warm as they were in the Gulf Stream, and the winds were still increasing. Things were complicated by sailing in the Gulf Stream, which is always challenging. The Gulf Stream originates in the Caribbean, and it moves in a northerly direction up the East Coast, before arcing northeast toward the coast of Britain and Europe. Now the *Curlew* was encountering winds out of the north, and the Gulf Stream also flows in a northerly direction, which creates opposing forces. Wind blowing from north to south, and the current running south to north, and this sets up a collision of powerful forces. This is a recipe for very rough large seas and agitated sea conditions, or what sailors call a "confused sea," and this makes the ocean a very nasty place. There are a few places on the world's oceans that are known to be extra dangerous, and one of them is being in the Gulf Stream with hurricane force winds from the north. The captain thought that the wind would diminish by morning, and despite the blow and the system failures, *Curlew* was moving well through the rough seas. It was a testament to her exceptional design as she rode these big waves. John Alden had recently passed away, but he still must have been proud of *Curlew*.

When the captain came off watch and went below to get some rest, he was surprised to see how bad things looked in the cabin. All the bunks were soaking wet, as sea water was cascading down through the main hatch, bilge water was sloshing around the cabin floor, and cans of food were rolling around on the sole of the cabin. The captain rallied the men below to clean things up, as best they could, and then he turned in to get some rest. Before turning in, the captain decided that only he and the mate, would take the helm and steer the boat during the night in this bad weather, and he lengthened the wheel watches to two hours.

1:00 a.m. - Thursday – November 15, 1962

The *Curlew* sped through the night heading south in the fierce northerly wind, with no sails up, fighting the mountainous seas. On the second morning watch, the fore headstay parted. This was caused by a monster sea which almost ripped the mast out of the boat. The whip of the mast by the force of the sea parted the forestay. The wave carried *Curlew* in its' momentum and caused the boat to broach. The *Curlew* was capsized, and she laid on her side for almost three minutes. Slowly, the schooner righted herself from her, hove down position. Captain Skellon thought she was going to sink, but *Curlew* would not allow it. At this point, the captain called all the members of the crew topside. The captain then carefully crawled forward on the deck and tightened down the main fisherman halyard, which was still shackled to the bowsprit. This added a little strength to the damaged rigging. The broach was caused by the speed of the boat, and the opposing forces of the wind and the water that were colliding and getting out of synch with the boat. The captain correctly assessed that he had to slow down the speed of the vessel, as *Curlew* plunged down the backside of the giant waves. He needed to gain some control of the boat, or this was going to happen again. At this point, the captain decided to employ the storm tactic of setting a sea anchor. Under the existing conditions of heading south, before a northerly wind, known as "running before the wind," he decided to set a sea anchor that is known as, "trailing warps." To accomplish this technique, the crew broke out some three-inch line (rope) and made one end secure to one corner of the stern, and then they began playing out the line, while attaching whatever they could find to the line, to aid in creating more resistance or drag, such as life rings, and even some old canvas sails. The line was then made fast to the other side of the stern, and this created a large loop, which acted as a speed brake by adding drag to the boat. This tactic was successful in slowing down the speed of the boat by about two-knots. This reduction in boat speed made a big difference in the feel of the helm. Satisfied that everything was now under control, the captain went below and turned in for some needed rest.

7:00 a.m. – Thursday – November 15, 1962

A giant wave broke over the full length of the schooner and caved in the main cabin skylight. This skylight was protected by the ten-foot-long dinghy, which was turned upside down covering the skylight, and the dinghy was lashed to the deck. The wooden dinghy was smashed to pieces by the force of this wave, and the broken dinghy and broken skylight, including the seawater, came straight down into the cabin through the opening. Captain Skellon was thrown from his bunk during this incident, and he was pinned against the hull by the sea water. For about three minutes he tried to get up but could not. There was now eighteen-inches of water in his bunk. This breaking wave grabbed the owner and attempted to throw him overboard, but when it curled, it washed him back into the cockpit, and in doing so, Sam was smashed into the wheel. The force of his body slamming into the wheel broke five of the eleven spokes of the wooden wheel. The scene that the captain found, when he finally made his way back topside, was that of Mate Lowe carefully bringing *Curlew* back on course, with a severely damaged wheel. Control of the wheel, to steer the boat was paramount to their ability to survive. Captain Skellon noticed that the outer ring of the wheel was moving about three or four-inches, before the center of the wheel moved at all. This was a severe complication as the wind was now blowing 75 to 80-knots, and the seas were 60 to 70-feet high. Somehow, the mate was bringing *Curlew* back on course. They all wondered how long the broken wheel would hold together.

At this point, the captain went below and switched on the radiotelephone to the distress frequency, so that he could issue a "Mayday Call" to the Coast Guard, but he had to wait because the frequency was tied up in numerous other "Mayday" calls. Once the channel cleared and it was his turn, Captain Skellon issued his "Mayday" call for *Curlew*, and he estimated his position as being 80-miles (NW) northwest of Bermuda. Within ten minutes, the Bermuda Coast Guard replied to the captain's "Mayday" request. Over the next two hours, with the aid of aircraft and other ships, the position of the *Curlew* was fixed, as 60-miles east-northeast (ENE) of Bermuda.

12:30 p.m. – Thursday – November 15, 1962

A Coast Guard plane came roaring over *Curlew* and made radio contact. The aircraft asked the captain his status, and he replied, "Critical." The airplane then broadcast out the position of *Curlew* and asked any ship in the area to render assistance. There was now more than two feet of water covering the cabin sole down below. The plane was circling very low, and it announced that they were going to drop a life raft. Before Captain Skellon could reply, *Curlew* broached again, and she was hove down, with her mast in the water. This allowed more seawater to flood into the cabin, through the damaged skylight. Amazingly, *Curlew* fought her way back up, and she got back on her feet, but there was now three-feet of water covering the cabin sole. The plane was circling *Curlew* very low, and now the Coast Guard aircraft did drop the life raft, but the crew missed picking it up by inches. The Coast Guard airplane now announced that the USS *Compass Island* (U.S. Navy) was thirty miles away, and she was coming to render assistance.

2:00 p.m. – Thursday – November 15, 1962

Here comes the United States Navy to the rescue, in the form of the USS *Compass Island* (AG-153), under the command of Captain Charles Allen Dancy. Here the "Magical" *Curlew* again displays her magic touch. Of all the ships that could come to assist *Curlew*, the *Compass Island* has several interesting qualifying traits. First, she is a large ship, 563-feet in length, a beam (width) of 76-feet, she draws (depth) 26-feet of water and displaces 18,000 tons, with a crew of 234-United States Navy sailors aboard. She has been outfitted with stabilizing fins, to reduce her roll in heavy seas. Second, her mission in the U.S. Navy is classified as a navigational research test and missile tracking vessel. This means that she is equipped with the most modern and advanced navigational equipment available. If the *Curlew* could pick a ship to come to her aid and assist her in her trek to the safety of Bermuda, she could do far worse. The *Compass Island* is a large, capable, state of the art, United States Navy Ship, with a highly trained and competent crew, with the very best navigational equipment and navigators in the Navy aboard this ship. Here's the next part which is right out of Hollywood. The USS *Compass Island* is named for an island in Penobscot Bay, Maine, which is only 40-miles from Wiscasset, Maine, the birthplace of the *Curlew*. The magical *Curlew* is reaching out to her Maine connection for help. A ship named for an island in Maine, coming to the rescue of a Maine built schooner, it makes you wonder!

The *Compass Island* steamed up to the *Curlew*, as close as possible, to view and gauge the condition of the schooner and her crew. Captain Skellon was now in constant communication with the *Compass Island* bridge, and he checked and confirmed his course with the navigator. Once the course was confirmed as being correct, Captain Skellon then gave orders to organize all safety equipment, in case they would need to abandon ship and have any chance to be recovered by the *Compass Island*. Lifelines, life jackets, flares, flashlights, emergency rations, dye markers, and shark repellent, were all secured and made ready, along with the life raft. Captain Skellon then took the helm to relieve Mate Lowe. Now back at the wheel, the captain was feeling the full strength of the storm. He was immediately struck by the size of the waves, which were now like giant square blocks of seawater, with their crests being blown off by the hurricane force wind into white foam spray. The seaworthiness of the Alden designed *Curlew* amazed the captain, who was a very experienced blue water sailor.

4:00 p.m. – Thursday – November 15, 1962

Two hours had passed since the arrival of the *Compass Island*, but to the crew on *Curlew*, it seemed like two days. During this time, they experienced more wind and massive seas, and they were hoved down twice more. They were hanging on solely due to the knowledge that they were slowly making progress towards the safety of Bermuda, and they were under the company of the United States Navy. Captain Skellon then turned the wheel back over to the mate, and he rechecked that all the members of the crew were in the cockpit. He next checked that everyone aboard had all of their safety equipment in place. Now confident that everyone could get off the schooner, with a chance of recovery by the *Compass Island*, he went back down below to man the radiotelephone, and to consult his navigation charts. He left the companionway hatch open a couple of inches to give himself a chance to escape if the worse happened. After multiple knockdowns, this was a distinct possibility. The *Compass Island* was giving the *Curlew* course corrections to navigate her through the current that sets north of Bermuda, and around the shoals that guard the island. The water was now waist high in the cabin, and it was sloshing back and forth with every movement of the schooner.

The crew was experiencing extreme fatigue as they had little to eat over the last three days. They had mostly eaten lifeboat rations with rum, to sustain themselves. However, by sunset, they took encouragement that they were only twelve miles away from the safety of Bermuda. The seas were now at least 70-feet in height, as they approached the reefs that guard the island. As it was getting dark, the captain switched on the running and spreader lights, and he asked the *Compass Island* if she could close the distance between the two ships. The Navy captain agreed to close the gap, and he assured Captain Skellon that he had four lookouts on the bridge, with binoculars, and that they could easily see the *Curlew*'s lights. Captain Skellon consulted his large chart of Bermuda, that was soaking wet, and he asked the *Compass Island* to navigate him through the shoals and banks on the west side of the island, by keeping *Curlew* on the 500-fathom line. The crew on *Curlew* could occasionally catch a glimpse of St. David's Head Light, about two miles off the port beam, and this raised their spirits and determination to fight on. Slowly, *Curlew* made her way around the southwestern tip of Bermuda, and by now being on the south side of the island, she had gained the lee of the island, and this helped shield the schooner from the northerly wind. This position helped to reduce the size of the seas and ease the movement of the schooner. Morale of the crew was rising as the end of the ordeal seemed close at hand. Captain Skellon gave the order to haul in the trailing warp sea anchor and to put the engine in gear. As the seas continued to diminish, thanks to the shielding of the island, *Curlew* was brought onto a course of ENE through the power of her engine, to make a course for St. George's Harbor. Spirits were high, but they were all exhausted. The throttle was brought to full revs, and the Ford engine pushed *Curlew* along at 10-knots.

10:00 p.m. – Thursday, November 15, 1962

Curlew was now at the southeastern tip of Bermuda and could now clearly make out St. David's Head Light. After taking a hand bearing and consulting with the *Compass Island*, Captain Skellon gave the order to swing the schooner to port and to make a new course to the north to reach St. George's Harbor, which was approximately two miles away. *Curlew* was now attempting to run dead into the northerly wind, and she progressed slowly, but after a quarter of a mile, she came to a dead stop, despite having her engine at full revs. They could not make any more headway against the sea and the hurricane force winds. *Curlew*'s attempt to proceed north, dead into the wind, was unsuccessful. Safety so close, but unable to reach it.

Captain Dancy then suggested that he proceed forward and have *Curlew* follow and utilize the size of the Navy ship, as a sea and windbreak, for the schooner. A gallant attempt was made but failed. The *Compass Island* could not maintain steerage at the slow speed, that was *Curlew*'s maximum speed, in these conditions. The *Compass Island* was now ahead of the *Curlew*, and she announced that they intended to circle around for another attempt. As soon as, *Curlew* came clear of the shelter of the Navy ship, they were hit with the full force of the storm, and *Curlew* was driven backward a quarter of a mile, even though her diesel engine was wide open. At this point, Captain Skellon ordered the mate to back down the engine, because he feared that the banging of the schooner into the short and choppy seas was beating the yacht to the point that they were probably going to sink the *Curlew*.

At this point, Captain Skellon recalled; "The Bermuda harbor pilot boat called and announced, that they were standing by at the Spit Buoy and asked, "Do you need us to put a pilot on board your vessel?" I was sure that they had no real idea of the conditions outside of the harbor, and the condition of the *Curlew*. I thanked them, but I declined the offer."

The *Compass Island* now attempted another approach to the *Curlew*, from the port quarter, but got too close, and *Curlew* had to bear away quickly as the massive ship was finding itself in water too shallow for her size. The two ships only missed colliding by three-feet, a very close call. However, *Curlew* fell in behind the *Compass Island* again and followed her lead. *Curlew* was now just 400-yards from the "Spit Buoy," which is the initial approach to the St. George's harbor channel. At this point, the Navy ship had to bear away again, exposing the *Curlew* once more to the full force of the storm conditions. This was as close as they would get, to making Saint George's Harbor. For the next two-hours the Navy ship and the schooner would try every technique they could think of, to make the harbor, but to no avail. Each, and every attempt failed, and now *Curlew* was rapidly losing ground to the storm.

1:30 a.m. – Friday – November 16, 1962

Captain Skellon and Captain Dancy now discussed the possible alternatives over the radiotelephone. They agreed that the only course of action to take now, was for *Curlew* to turn and run back to the south side of the island and try to gain some shelter from the wind. Their thinking was that under the shelter of the lee of the island, it might be possible to anchor, or even beach the *Curlew*. If the schooner could continue to hold together, they could wait until dawn and then review their options in the light of the day. Captain Dancy concurred, and the *Compass Island* approached *Curlew* on her weather side, to aid the schooner in the rounding of the southeastern tip of Bermuda. If they could get past the southeastern tip of the island, and head west for a short distance, they could gain the protection of the southern lee of the island. The storm conditions would not allow it, and *Curlew* could not shorten the distance between her position and the island. It was now apparent that with the hurricane force winds from the north, *Curlew* would never get close enough to the land to win the protection of the lee of Bermuda.

A discussion took place between the two captains, about running *Curlew* back offshore. The Navy passed on a weather report that the current weather conditions would continue for at least another twenty-four hours. The *Curlew* crew was distressed at not being able to gain the safety of the harbor and morale plummeted with the failure. The prospect of going back offshore was not something that they wanted to experience again, as it looked like a certain death sentence. At this point, Captain Skellon asked Captain Dancy for any suggestions. The Navy captain replied, "Abandon ship while you can!" This was excellent advice from a professional United States Navy officer, and captain of a state-of-the-art warship. Captain Dancy had watched the *Curlew*, and her crew, put up an incredible fight. Now it was apparently time to throw in the towel and end this fight. The fighter was clearly out on her feet. Captain Dancy was an unemotional witness to this gallant effort, but he was not emotionally attached to *Curlew*, so his vision was not blurred. It was clear from his perspective that this fight was over. *Curlew* was not going to make it. The saving of human lives was now the priority. Captain Skellon and owner Sam Gervasoni had to concur, *Curlew* had fought hard, but she would soon sink. The decision was made to abandon ship. It was a sad moment for the gallant schooner, whose crew was now going to leave her. Captain Dancy radioed his intentions to heave-to and bring the *Compass Island* broadside to the wind. The sailors then secured a cargo net to the lee side of the ship. It was now up to the crew of the *Curlew* to get the schooner close to the *Compass Island*, and then scamper up the cargo net to safety, all in big seas with hurricane force winds, in the dead of night. The crew all took a swig of rum to fortify themselves for a daring escape. Captain Skellon directed Mate Lowe to bring the schooner alongside the navy ship, as close as possible. On the first attempt, they came too close to the stern of the *Compass Island*, and nearly fouled her propeller. As the stern of the *Compass Island* fell from a wave, it snapped off the *Curlew*'s bowsprit like a matchstick. Mate Lowe went full reverse on the engine and came back for another attempt. Getting aboard the *Compass Island* was their only chance to stay alive. This time, Mate Lowe from the State of Maine, brought this Maine built schooner in perfectly and made a perfect landing up to the side of the ship. *Curlew* was now nudged up to the side of the *Compass Island*, but as the two ships were rising and falling with the waves, *Curlew* was going up and down at least ten feet. The crew began to scramble up the cargo net to safety immediately. Captain Skellon made sure that all members of the crew were off the deck of the schooner, and then he began his ascent up the cargo net. At this same time, the foremast and shrouds were carried away with a loud crack. The rub rail, stanchions, and the cat rail, all exploded into a shower of splinters. Galvanized steel wire from the shrouds was flying everywhere, like whipping deadly snakes. Even though he was a tall, thin, young man, in very fit condition, the experience and toll of the last three days had left Captain Skellon exhausted, and he could not negotiate the final six-feet of the cargo net on his own. Three U.S. Navy sailors came over the rail and grabbed the captain, and with the help of other shipmates, they physically hauled him aboard. The mainmast and shrouds then slammed into the exact spot where the captain was stuck, just moments before. A few seconds longer and the captain would have been impaled by the shrouds and spreaders of the rigging. Once Captain Skellon was on deck, a head count was made, and it was realized that John "Spider" Slim was not onboard the ship. Spider in his haste to get clear of the *Curlew* did not wait to reach for the cargo net, he jumped upon a large fender that had been put over the side by the sailors, to cushion the landing of the *Curlew*. Being a former tree surgeon, Spider attempted to scale the fender securing line, hand over hand. He made it halfway up the side of the ship, before sliding back down exhausted from the effort. Spider was later quoted as saying; "I figured they would have to haul the fender back on board anyway, so I just sat on the large fender and held on." As my brother, a former U.S. Navy Boatswain's Mate, hammered into me many years ago, a vessel properly operated does not leave fenders hanging over her side, while underway. This is a good tip for recreational boaters if you want to look like an amateur, leave your fenders hanging over the side while underway. You see it all the time, and I've watched my brother shake his head in disgust, every time he sees it. The United States Navy does not steam her vessels underway with fenders hanging over the sides. So, Spider guessed correctly, and he was hauled aboard, with the fender, by the deck crew of the *Compass Island*.

It was now 2:15 a.m. and all the crew were rescued and safe. A sad and dejected crew said goodbye to the magical *Curlew*, sure that she would soon sink. The Navy agreed, and the *Compass Island* disengaged and left *Curlew* to go on her own. *Curlew* was now a "Ghost Ship," still afloat for the time being, but with no crew aboard. The gallant schooner was now on her own, in the teeth of hurricane force winds and 70-foot seas.

The crew of the *Curlew* were now being cared for, and looked after, by the United States Navy. First, they were all hustled off to the *Compass Island* "Sick Bay," to be checked out by the medical staff. After being cleared by the ship's doctor, getting the men comfortable was the next order of business. They were all hungry, exhausted, and soaking wet, so it was showers and dry clothes, then on to bacon and eggs with coffee and brandy, before turning in for much-needed sleep. Everyone slept solidly for a good twelve-hours before rising for more food and coffee. For three days, the crew of the *Curlew*, lived a life of luxury, courtesy of Captain Dancy and the United States Navy.

Then on the third day, a Coast Guard airplane that was searching for any survivors of the M/V *Captain George*, and the schooner *Windfall*, spotted the *Curlew* still afloat and making her way as a "Ghost Ship" at sea. Again, *Curlew* just will not quit! The "Sea Dog" is alive and can there be any doubt that this "Magic Ship" is one of a kind. How did she keep going after three days adrift in hurricane conditions? It was a testament to the design genius of John Gale Alden and the boat building skill of the Fred F. Pendleton Shipyard. John Alden passed away, on March 3rd, 1962, in Florida, eight months before his *Curlew* would find herself in this terrible storm. How did *Curlew* survive on her own for three days at sea, with no crew? Here's a theory; perhaps the spirit of the man, whose middle name was "Gale," came to the helm of this "Ghost Ship" to guide her through this Nor'easter Gale. One of his design tenants was to build a schooner that could be sailed single-handed, if necessary. Whether you believe in this kind of thing, or not, it certainly makes you wonder.

Captain Dancy also informed the owner, Sam Fiorello, and Captain Skellon, that the tugboat, "*Bermudian*," had put to sea, from Bermuda, with the stated intention to salvage the *Curlew*. Since *Curlew* was now without a crew on board and was unmanned on the high seas, she was fair game and could be claimed as salvage by anyone who boarded her. When the owner and captain relayed this news to the rest of the crew, they all agreed to ask Captain Dancy to put them back aboard *Curlew*, to block the tug from claiming the salvage rights to the schooner. The three days of rest for the crew had recharged their spirit, and they were all up to the challenge of re-boarding their *Curlew.*

Once more, the USS *Compass Island*, named for an island in Maine, to the rescue of this Maine built schooner. The Navy set a course at top speed to the vicinity of the reported position of the *Curlew.* Using her state-of-the-art radar capability, the *Compass Island* soon had a position fix on *Curlew*, and they also had a position fix on the tugboat *Bermudian*. Now, Captain Dancy contacted the captain of the *Bermudian*, to assert his authority over the situation, and he informed her captain that a United States Navy warship was in the process of placing the rightful United States citizen-owner, aboard a United States documented vessel on the high seas.

The tug replied that *Curlew* co-owner Bob Gervasoni had hired them and that he was in fact, onboard the tug. Bob had flown to Bermuda as planned, and he was awaiting the arrival of the *Curlew* when the storm struck. He then received word that the crew had to abandon ship and that the USS *Compass Island* had rescued them. When Bob further discovered that *Curlew* was found still afloat, he contracted with the Bermuda Board of Trade to hire the *Bermudian*, to recover the schooner.

The *Compass Island* and the *Bermudian* rendezvoused at midnight, on Sunday, November 18th, 1962. The crew now faced the hazardous task of jumping from the *Compass Island* to the tugboat, over a six-foot gap between the ships. The weather had improved, but a large swell still prevailed. Everyone made the jump and completed the transfer without incident. The *Compass Island* then confirmed the coordinates of the position of *Curlew* for the *Bermudian*, and then the USS *Compass Island* steamed off, bound for New York and the Brooklyn Navy Yard. The Navy crew was overdue for leave, and a change of command ceremony was scheduled. Captain Dancy was moving on to another assignment, and this adventure would be his last mission as the commander of the USS *Compass Island*. Quite a way to go out. A magnificent display of a United States Navy Captain, coming to the aid of his civilian countrymen. Well done captain, you and the officers and men, of the USS *Compass Island* displayed the finest tradition and ability of the United States Navy.

The United States Navy,
Second to None,
Then and Now,
"The Finest Kind!"

At dawn on Monday, November 19th, a tow line was made fast to *Curlew*, and the *Bermudian* began to tow the barely floating yacht toward Bermuda. After nine hours, they entered St. George's harbor. The hull now had over five feet of water over her cabin sole. Everything below was smashed and ruined.

The owners and the crew were severely shaken up by this experience. Funds were limited, and repairs were made as best they could. Captain Skellon secured some scuba diving equipment and made a dive to examine the hull. He found all her seams, and fastenings in good order. *Curlew* was then pumped out, and she was towed to the harbor at Hamilton, Bermuda. The owner's resources were pretty much expended, and most of the crew had to move on to find other paying assignments. Captain Skellon left Bermuda sometime later and returned to England.

Curlew was then detained in Bermuda for six-months, as a legal battle took place with the tug operator, who demanded $35,000 ($275,000 in 2018), in salvage fees. This was finally settled for $3,500 ($27,500 in 2018) after the tug operator realized that the owners were in no position to meet his demand.

Once *Curlew* was put back into reasonable shape the plan was to take her to Puerto Rico, and then on to Yacht Haven Grande, in St. Thomas, the U.S. Virgin Islands, to enter the charter trade. The owners now needed *Curlew* to start earning some money. On the way, Curlew encountered another storm off the Carolinas but came through it all unscathed. The owner, Sam Fiorello, was now the captain of *Curlew*. Once they reached St. Thomas, they found a long list of boats awaiting charter parties, and a boat rotation system in place at Yacht Haven, this placed *Curlew* at the back of the queue as the last boat in. Captain Fiorello then took *Curlew* to some of the other Caribbean islands in search of work.

In September 1963, Hurricane Flora hit the island of Tobago, with sustained winds of 120-mph. *Curlew* broke loose from her mooring during the storm and went aground on soft coral. Again, she survived, and after some repairs were made, the owners sailed her back to the Trenton, New Jersey area, where they made further repairs and sailed *Curlew* for about two years.

Curlew was now about to open a new chapter in her history; she was about to transition from the Atlantic Ocean to the Pacific Ocean. *Curlew* was sold to new owners, who were from California, and they sailed her to their home waters of San Francisco Bay, via the Panama Canal. Five years later, *Curlew* was sold again, and she made her home port in the Los Angeles area. During the next ten years, she made a trip to the South Pacific and received extensive repairs in New Zealand. Her next owner worked her in the inter-island charter business in Hawaii. In 1985, Curlew was again sold, and her new owners completed an extensive rebuild of the schooner. Curlew now met the very stringent United States Coast Guard safety requirements for carrying passengers for hire. Her home port was moved back to Southern California at Long Beach.

In July of 2002, *Curlew* was sold to Captain Robert A. Harrison, Jr., of Newport Beach, California. Captain Harrison had been searching for a schooner to buy for over ten years, never finding the one that exactly fit his requirements, and his eye. Here the "Magic Ship" *Curlew*, works her magic once more and finds her way to catch Captain Harrison's eye. It was meant to be, a true schooner man, and a deserving schooner find each other. Captain Harrison has completed numerous repairs and upgrades to *Curlew*, and all at a considerable cost, and she is once again, the thing of beauty that sprung from the mind and genius of John Gale Alden.

Here is the good news, this magnificent schooner is still going strong, at 92-years old this year (2018). *Curlew* has been down many times, but she always manages to land on her feet, and she has done it once again. *Curlew* can be found today at her home port of Dana Point, California. This magic schooner is all, "Shipshape and Bristol Fashion," at the Dana Point Wharf. Now a grand old lady of the sea, she is available for charter. You can have the privilege, of enjoying a sail along the magnificent coast of Southern California, on the schooner that would just never quit. What could be better than that? In my opinion, absolutely nothing! She has survived many adventures over her ninety-two years, and she has a rich history to fascinate any lover of ships and the sea. *Curlew* is a true testament to the era of the great schooners and the design-genius of John Gale Alden.

The magic ship has worked her "magic" once again, and she has found her way to her captain and savior, and I for one, am so glad for *Curlew*. The old sea dog who never quit is now in the capable hands of an outstanding sailor, and someone who loves his ship.

Captain Robert A. Harrison, Jr.
I applaud and salute you, sir!
As we would say in New Bedford,
You, Sir, are "The Finest Kind"

The Story of *Windfall*

Another beautiful classic wooden schooner, built in Maine in the 1920's, at the same Fred F. Pendleton Shipyard in Wiscasset. In 1962, *Windfall* hailed from South Freeport, Maine, the home of the famous L.L. Bean Company. When you think of Maine, you think of the images that you see in the L.L. Bean catalog when it shows up in your mailbox. You think of lobster dinners, clambakes, the rugged rocky Maine coastline, thick pine forests, parents with their children and their Golden Retriever enjoying a secluded beach all romping in the surf, and of course the lobster boats, with lobster pots stacked all over the docks. Last, but not least, you think of magnificent classic schooners with their sails full, and a "bone in her teeth." This last image is the schooner *Windfall*, with her bearded captain, a pipe clenched in his teeth, at the helm, driving *Windfall* hard and close hauled. That captain is William A. Rogers, known to all, as Captain "Cheever" Rogers, schooner man.

This…is Maine!

I wish this story had a happy ending, but unfortunately, the schooner *Windfall* was lost in Neptune's Nor'easter, of November 14th and 15th, in 1962. Five young men were taken by the forces of nature, along with a beautiful boat, all sent to the bottom of the sea. This is also the story of two women in South Freeport, Maine, suddenly left behind with a total of five young children to raise on their own. These women never forgot their husbands and the boat they sailed on, and for the remainder of their lives, they celebrated a church service every year in November. The yearly service became known as, "*Windfall* Sunday." This is the story of a mother on the other side of the Atlantic, in England, anxious for news of her son. Finally realizing that he has been taken from her just as her husband, a Royal Air Force pilot, was taken from her during World War II. Two men she loved, taken far too early in their lives. The heartbreak and tragedy of it all is hard to bear.

William A. Rogers was born and raised on Long Island, New York. He picked up the nickname of, "Cheever," to differentiate him from his dad who was also named William. His father was a surgeon and chief of staff at a hospital in Flushing, New York. The family had a house near the water, and sailing was something that they enjoyed. Dr. William K. Rogers went off to World War II, where he found himself running a field hospital at a place called Anzio, in Italy. Anzio was a slaughterhouse for the Allies, and Dr. Rogers saw too much, and it changed him for the rest of his life. When he returned from the war, he had enough of practicing medicine. The doctor needed to escape from the pressure of being a surgeon, and he found a new purpose in Maine. He bought a boatyard with a partner in South Freeport, and the family left Long Island and moved to a new life, in the State of Maine.

Cheever joined the Navy to fulfill his military obligation. While he was on leave from the Navy, visiting his parents in Maine, they introduced him to a young woman named Pat who would become his future wife. When Cheever was discharged from the Navy, he tried several jobs, but none of them seemed to be his calling. He decided to enroll at the University of Maine, in Orono, and soon he became the captain of the university sailing team. By the time Cheever graduated, his family had grown, and he and his wife now had three children. He loved being on the water, so he and a friend tried lobstering, but it didn't work out. Cheever was working various jobs, but he couldn't settle on any of them, he was still searching for his calling.

In 1960, his calling came right up and found him. He was hired to be the captain of the *Optimist*, a 57-foot steel-hulled ketch. The owner desired to enter the *Optimist* in the winter charter service in the Caribbean. Cheever put together a crew to sail *Optimist* south to the Caribbean. The crew consisted of his father, "Doc" Rogers, Phil Murray, a television announcer in Portland, Maine, and Carleton "Cotty" Barlow who was 19-years-old. They left Maine in October of 1960, and Cotty Barlow in an interview recalled; "We had thick fog heading out until we reached the Gulf Stream. Five or six-days into the trip we ran into hurricane type conditions, and we got bashed. The high winds blew out the sails, and the boat was rolling 55-degrees with the mast spreaders almost touching the water." They were running before the wind under bare poles. Cheever played out a line from the stern, and tied items to the warp, to increase the drag, and this was a technique to slow the boat down, as she surfed down the back side of the massive waves. After this adjustment, even with no sails up, *Optimist* a heavy steel-hulled boat was still making seven knots of speed. When asked how Captain Cheever Rogers performed in this crisis, Cotty replied; "He was magnificent. He was my hero." Assistance came from a British freighter that spotted them off Bermuda and helped them make it to St. George's Harbor, on the island of Bermuda.

Cheever spent the winter of 1961 working the charter trade in the Caribbean, as the captain of the *Optimist*. The Caribbean in 1961 was not as commercialized as it is now. Cheever had to hustle to keep paying customers on the boat. It was difficult, but he preferred it to the shore side jobs that he had tried. Cheever was back on the water, and he could see that the concept of charter boats was growing. It looked like an opportunity to get in on the ground floor doing something that he loved. The truth was, the charter business was a struggle. Finding clients was always a problem, and no clients meant no money. In his first year with the *Optimist*, this was the reality. He began referring to the *Optimist* as a dog to sail, heavy and slow, she became known as the "Iron Whore." Here we have that example of a sailor hating his ship when things are going badly.

In the spring of 1961, Cheever returned to Maine with the intent to buy a boat. He had a different idea about the perfect type of boat for the winter charter trade in the islands. He needed something that looked the part, something salty, and he knew what that was, he needed a schooner!

Cheever set off to find financial backing so that he could secure a schooner. He found his backer and went looking for the boat, and he discovered that boat in *Windfall*, a 56-foot schooner, built in the 1920's at the Fred F. Pendleton Shipyard in Wiscasset, Maine. *Windfall* was built from plans by William Hand, Jr., the designer of the famous Arctic exploring schooner *Bowdoin*, which is now a National Historic Landmark. William Hand, Jr. was a prominent naval architect, who in 1920, established his design and boat building business in Fairhaven, Massachusetts. He designed many different types of vessels, including schooners. A collection of his designs resides in the archives of the Massachusetts Institute of Technology (MIT).

Windfall was a genuine classic schooner, and she was gaff rigged. Her hull was painted white. She had been working the charter trade out of Miami, and the Bahamas. She had gone through updates in 1954 and 1955, a new engine, updated electronics, including a radiotelephone, as well as, new rigging and sails. She could accommodate six guests. It looked like the perfect boat to start his charter business. It seemed ideal, six months in the Caribbean, then back up to Maine in the summer, and charter *Windfall* off the Maine coast for the next six months. It seemed to be the perfect plan.

The truth was, that as beautiful as *Windfall* appeared, she was eating money. She needed to be made, "Shipshape and Bristol Fashion," to attract well-heeled guests. That took time and money, both of which are always in short supply when you're young and trying to establish a new business. The charter business was very competitive during these years. Somehow Cheever and the *Windfall* made it through the winter, and then it was back to Maine to reunite with his family. A young family with a dream!

The family spent the summer working on the boat with everyone pitching in to improve the schooner. Wooden boats that are forty plus years old require constant attention. Jonathon Rogers, Cheever and Pat's son, recalled this time saying; "Dad always made it fun around the boat. It was work, but it seemed like fun and an adventure. There was never any yelling or screaming. I idolized my father; he was the best sailor you could ever imagine."

As the fall of 1962 approached, the captain began assembling a crew for the run south to the Caribbean, and what all hoped would be a successful season. The mate and navigator was John Schwarz, a close friend from South Freeport, who was also an artist. Cotty Barlow was scheduled to be the next member of the crew, but he decided to return to college. Cotty recommended his close friend for the job, and 19-year old, Peter Van Ness, from Princeton, New Jersey was hired in Cotty's place. Robert Bockins signed on as the cook, and he was from Jamestown, Rhode Island. The final member of the crew was Aulliston Baird, age 20, from Inverness, Scotland. Aulin had come to America looking for adventure and a change from the expectations that followed him in the United Kingdom. A gifted artist, he had completed his studies at the prestigious Stowe School in England, but he was not interested in going on to university. Aulin was different; he was an artist and a free spirit. He loved to hunt and fish on the family estate in Scotland. He was not interested in following the career path that was expected of young British upper-class gentlemen. Working in an office at a desk, was something he could not even contemplate. He came to America to work on the farm of a family friend for the summer and then figured he would see where that might lead. It led this 20-year-old Brit to the deck of the schooner *Windfall*. After signing on, Aulin began to grow an Abraham Lincoln-style beard, just like the one that his skipper sported.

Windfall left South Freeport on Saturday, November 3rd, 1962, which was a late start. The delayed start was necessitated by the fact that Cheever wanted to be home for Halloween so that he and his wife could take his children out "Trick or Treating." Pat later said that she felt guilty for pushing him to leave later than he would have liked. It was now time to go, and *Windfall* sailed out of South Freeport heading south to meet her fate. Pat said that she and others connected to the boat watched it sail away until they couldn't see *Windfall* anymore. They were gone, but to the assembled family and friends who watched from on shore, they had no idea that they would never see *Windfall*, or her crew, ever again.

The plan was to sail to Newport, Rhode Island, and then over to Block Island, before running a course to cross the Gulf Stream on the way to Bermuda. They encountered some heavy weather along the way, and they dropped into Mystic, Connecticut along with the schooner *Curlew*, who they had met up with in Newport. The two schooners and their crews bonded in Newport, and they planned to race to Bermuda, and then on to the Virgin Islands. *Windfall* and *Curlew* were now linked forever, and they were headed into a test that would see only one of them survive.

We do not know precisely what happened on *Windfall* but based on the description of what transpired on the *Curlew*, and the storm tactics that Captain Rogers employed previously in a strong storm in this area with the *Optimist*, we can draw what are probably very close assumptions. No doubt, Captain Rogers would have attempted to slow down the speed of *Windfall*, as she surfed down the back side of mountainous seas. He would have turned to the storm tactic of rigging a sea anchor of trailing warps, just as he had successfully employed on *Optimist* two years before, and just as Captain Skellon was doing on *Curlew*. The *Windfall* was no doubt overpowered by the severity of the storm, just as happened to the *Curlew*. I would suspect that she was taken down by the large breaking seas and she was hove down. If another massive breaking wave hit her in this vulnerable position, she probably then broke up and sank.

On Thursday, November 15, 1962;

The Belgian flagged tanker, the SS *Stad Gant*, reports to the U.S. Coast Guard that they have spotted five men in the water, floating on what appears to be wreckage, approximately 300-miles off Cape Hatteras, North Carolina. The captain of the *Stad Gant* reports that weather conditions are so extreme that he could not get close enough to execute a rescue. He further advises that he cannot turn his ship, due to the heavy weather, without imperiling his vessel. The fact that he sighted five-men, the exact number of the crew on the *Windfall*, and the location of the sighting, rule out that these men could have been survivors from the M/V *Captain George*, and point to these men being the crew of the *Windfall*. If the tanker spotted these five men desperately clinging to life, then these men no doubt saw the tanker. Can you imagine the emotions that the crew of the *Windfall* felt, as they watched this large ship sail away?

<u>On Sunday, November 18, 1962</u>;

An anonymous report is filed that five-men were spotted floating on wreckage approximately 100-miles east of Cape Fear, North Carolina. The Coast Guard sends a plane from Elizabeth City, North Carolina to investigate, but the aircraft is unable to locate anything, and cannot confirm the sighting. If true, it would indicate that the crew of *Windfall* were hanging on to life, a full four-days since encountering the storm.

<u>On Friday, November 23, 1962</u>;

Eight days after the storm first hit, a Coast Guard plane spots a body, two spars and rigging floating on the ocean. The Coast Guard dispatches the USCGC *Cherokee* to the scene. No bodies were recovered, but they do recover three doors and part of a wheel. An air and sea search covering 15,000 square miles is conducted northeast of Bermuda, with no further trace of *Windfall*, or her crew.

The search is finally called off by the Coast Guard, but Pat Rogers still clings to the idea that they are still alive. She has convinced herself that they lost the use of the sails, engine, radiotelephone and that they were somewhere drifting. Pat held onto this idea for some time. This feeling is not unusual for the spouses of sailors who have been lost at sea. They have just vanished, and you have no closure.

I witnessed this lack of closure first hand as a child. In January of 1955, I was five-years-old when the F/V *Doris Gertrude* was lost at sea. Two of my uncles were on this boat. My father's sister, Evangeline Doucette Murphy, was the wife of Captain Joshua Murphy. To me, I knew them as, "Uncle Spud," and "Aunt Vangie." They were both great people. Their home was a short distance from our house, and our families were close, as both my uncle and my dad, were New Bedford fishing captains. My mother did not drive, so when my father was out fishing, which was about seventy-percent of the time, my Aunt Vangie was our lifeline as she was our transportation. In fact, on the night that I was born, my Aunt Vangie drove my mother to the hospital. We didn't make it to the hospital in time, and I was born in the car, so my Aunt Vangie was physically present when I entered the world. Aunt Vangie had an outgoing personality, and we all loved her, because she was always laughing, and you felt happy and safe when Aunt Vangie was around. She was a rock. I have very fond memories of my Aunt Vangie. Our world was turned upside down in January of 1955 when the F/V *Doris Gertrude* was overdue from her fishing trip. The Coast Guard began an extensive search, but neither the *Doris Gertrude* nor any of her crew was ever seen again.

I have a very vivid memory of sitting with my mother and my Aunt Vangie, at her Cape Cod style home on Gilbert Street, in Fairhaven, Massachusetts, waiting for some word on the fate of the *Doris Gertrude*. My cousins, Josh and Michael, were not home, as they have been sent to school. I can still see it in my mind, Aunt Vangie sitting in her rocking chair, with the telephone close by, hoping that it will ring with good news, but knowing deep down that too much time has passed. She is crying, and my mother is trying her best to comfort her. Aunt Vangie is waiting for her daily phone call update from the Coast Guard. I am only five-years-old, so I am trying to be quiet, and I have some five-year-old concept, that I am witnessing my first tragedy. Finally, the phone rings, and it is the Coast Guard. Vangie is listening and then she is asking questions of the Coast Guard official on the phone. She soon hangs up, sits back in her rocking chair, and lets out a frustrated sigh. Now my aunt is crying, and she is looking at the phone, and now she is angry with the Coast Guard. She is saying; "They tell me to wait, they are doing all they can. I need to know what happened! What do they expect me to do, sit here and twiddle my thumbs?" I have been very quiet up to this point, but my five-year-old mind wonders, how do you twiddle your thumbs? My brain causes my mouth to blurt out; "Aunt Vangie, how do you twiddle your thumbs?" Even at five-years-old, I realize immediately that I have asked an inappropriate question at the wrong time. I can sense that I have made a mistake. My aunt looks at me and very calmly demonstrates the technique of twiddling one's thumbs. I have never forgotten that moment. What a beautiful person my Aunt Vangie was, here she is consumed with worry and grief, and she composed herself enough to answer a silly question from a five-year-old boy. It would have been easy for her to scream at me at that moment, and looking back I would not have blamed her, but she recognized that I was a child and that I meant no disrespect. I have never forgotten her for it. I have always held a fondness for my Aunt Vangie, as she, my mother, and I, had two special personal experiences, my birth in the car, and my learning how to twiddle my thumbs. Josh, your mother, was the best, and I regret that I never told her, and your brother Michael that, so I'm saying it to you now. She was a great lady, and I miss her.

Also, on the *Doris Gertrude* was my father's brother, my Uncle Herbie. He was another larger than life personality. Always the center of attention, ever the life of the party. He always had a grin on his face. He survived World War II, where he was a U.S. Navy Seabee in the Pacific, and came home only to die too young, fishing on Georges Bank. Uncle Herbie was the engineer on the *Doris Gertrude*. Herbie usually was on my father's boat. Uncle Spud had been having some engine problems, and my father and Spud agreed to have Herbie transfer over to the *Doris Gertrude* for a few trips, to help work out the engine issues. This trip was scheduled to be Herbie's last trip on the Doris Gertrude, after this trip, he was expected to go back to my father's boat.

I have a memory of my Uncle Herbie coming into our house, talking a mile a minute and laughing. My sisters have a memory of my Uncle Herbie, before he had children of his own, coming to our house late on Christmas Eve, to wake them up and tell them that Santa Claus had come. My brother has many memories of Uncle Herbie, while fishing. Uncle Herbie did not sweat the small stuff, minor irritants were no big deal to a man who regularly risked his life, both as a fisherman and as a U.S. Navy Seabee during World War II. I have a photograph of my Uncle Herbie working on an engine, down in the engine room on a fishing boat, and I have kept it on my writing desk during the writing of this book. This photograph of my uncle has inspired me during this project. He left a wife, and three young children, Herbert Jr., Jacqueline, and Phillip.

Just as Pat Rogers and Jean Schwarz were left with five young children to raise in Maine, in 1962, my Aunt Vangie and Aunt Dora were left with five young children to raise in Massachusetts, in 1955. The sea had taken their husbands without a trace. The lack of closure is the most painful part; there is no body to bury, no grave to visit, no finality, just questions, and wonder. Just as Pat Rogers was convinced that *Windfall* and her crew were drifting somewhere on the ocean, my aunts had similar thoughts. They both clung to the idea that Spud and Herbie, would suddenly come walking through the front door. For the longest time, they both hung on to the notion that maybe the boat was sinking, and that they got picked up by one of the Russian fishing boats that were all over Georges Bank, at that time. Or perhaps, the Russians just decided to kidnap them all, and that they had been taken back to Russia, where they were being held against their will. In 1955, we saw the Russians and their communist way of life as being the cause of every bad thing that happened, and this was no different. We saw commies behind every tree. The role of the Soviet Union in the disappearance of the *Doris Gertrude* was a concept that my aunts held on to for a very long time. My father thought that they probably got run down by a large ship, because the weather was heavy with snow and zero visibility, and they had been fishing near the area that all the large vessels took on their way to and from Europe, known as the "Steamer Track." This is the problem when men are lost at sea, and no bodies are recovered; there is no real closure, lots of theories and lots of speculation, with no real definitive answers. This is the other side of men lost at sea. It is the side that is not always given enough light, as we always focus on the ships and sailors who are lost, but the loss back on land is just as tragic, and it lasts for the rest of the lives of those people who are left behind. To my five cousins, two of whom are deceased, I regret that I have never said this to you, but I am sorry for your loss, God bless you all!

Finally, in December of 1962, the Coast Guard brought in three men who were familiar with the schooner *Windfall*, to examine the debris that was recovered by the Coast Guard Cutter *Cherokee*. They were Hunter Lewis of Plainfield, New Jersey, Carl Winters of Houston, Texas, and David Janes, the brother-in-law of the *Windfall*'s captain. They all positively identified the debris as coming from the schooner *Windfall*. A photograph of the *Windfall*'s wheel was examined against the damaged wheel that was recovered, and it was an exact match.

Rear Admiral, R.M. Ross, USCG, wrote to Pat Rogers on December 31, 1962; "From the evidence available in the case, I believe that a reasonable inference may be made that the five men on the *Windfall* perished at sea. I regret that more hopeful information cannot be given, and desire to express my sympathy to you in this tragic event." This letter from the Coast Guard was as much closure as Pat Rogers and Jean Schwarz were going to get.

For those left behind, the agony, grief, and questions of why continued. The South Freeport community and their friends, neighbors, and church tried as best they could to embrace Pat Rogers, and her three children, and Jean Schwarz and her two children.

Notes and cards from family and friends came in the mail. One letter showed up in Pat Rogers' mailbox from England. Upon opening the letter, Pat discovered that it was from Gelda Sladen, the mother of Aulin Baird. In the letter, she said; "I have been through this all before, nineteen years ago, when Aulin's father was reported missing from a bombing mission during the war. I waited eighteen months at that time with no news. Cruel though the news proves to be, it is better to know, than the agony of uncertainty, and alternate hope and despair. She said that Aulin was very much like his father, which added to her love for him. She said that she knew the inexpressible agony and loneliness of losing a husband, but she knew that Pat would find the strength to go on for her young children, as Sladen had done twenty years before." Gelda went on to say; "They were all doing what they wanted to do, and if it is God's will that their time is up, then they go, and that is something we cannot and must not fight against. "The strength of this woman is impressive, reaching out from across the ocean to comfort Pat Rogers, as she was grieving for her lost son. Offering advice that is so on point, that it bears repeating. "They were all doing what they wanted to do, and if it is God's will that their time is up, then they go, and that is something we cannot and must not fight against." This advice given by just anyone would be easy to dismiss, given by someone who had to endure this type of pain twice herself, gives it complete credibility. Absolutely the right advice to anyone who has experienced a senseless loss, but not so easy to give this type of advice, and it is not so easy to take, and execute this advice. A fine display of courage, determination, and empathy, all while enduring overwhelming grief herself. The strength and clear-headedness of this British woman are why there will always be an England. A perfect example of; "Head high and stiff upper lip." We do not know what transpired in the last hours on *Windfall*, but with a mother like Gelda, I feel sure that Aulin Baird acquitted himself well, and battled to the end. Gelda Sladen, a credit to her British Heritage.

Fortunately, Pat Rogers was another strong woman. She also found the strength to go on with her life. Pat remained in South Freeport; it was her home. It was the perfect place to raise her children. She gave back to her community in many ways over the remainder of her life. She became a member of the Freeport School Board, and she was a strong advocate for education. She was also passionate about the environment, and she loved animals.

Pat Rogers remained close to Jean Schwarz and her family. The two wives came up with the plan for a church service, which would become known as "*Windfall* Sunday," in their church. They celebrated the memory of the *Windfall*, and her crew for fifty-years until they both passed away.

The storm has now claimed five more lives and another vessel.

The total is now twenty-five-men, and three-vessels lost.
A 30-foot sailboat, a 442-foot ship, and a 56-foot schooner.
It was not over yet, it continues!

Captain William "Cheever" Rogers, South Freeport, Maine
Mate John M. Schwarz, 37, South Freeport, Maine
Peter Van Ness, 19, Princeton, NJ
Alliston A. Baird, 20, Inverness, Scotland
Robert Bockins, Jr., 31, Jamestown, RI

Rest in Peace
You Schooner Men

Chapter 9

<u>**ANY PORT IN A STORM**</u>

In the New Bedford and Fairhaven recreational sailing community, we have many great destinations that are within an easy reach of a day sail. These range from destinations on Cape Cod, Martha's Vineyard, Nantucket, and the Elizabeth Islands. Inevitably, in the summer when sailors are getting ready to leave the dock, someone will always ask; "Where are you headed?" This question is asked partially out of curiosity and partly for safety reasons. If in the unlikely event that you are overdue returning, then someone will know where to start a search. If you say Cutty Hunk, then someone will almost always say; "Don't miss it, or you'll end up in Portugal." I've heard it dozens of times, and everyone responds with a chuckle, and some reply like; "We'll be careful, but if we're not back in a couple of weeks, call the Portuguese Coast Guard." Cutty Hunk is the last island in the Elizabeth Island chain, and there is nothing between it and Europe. If you missed Cutty Hunk Island and kept going, you just might wind up in Portugal. This chapter has a similar ring to it, as three men from New England left Boston and set a course for the island of Bermuda. They never made it to Bermuda, but they did survive a very dangerous ordeal at sea, and eventually landed in a very different location. The story of the ketch *Islander* and her crew sounds amusing on the surface, but what they endured before they finally reached dry land was not funny in the least, and they were fortunate to escape with their lives.

Three men decided to take an extended vacation and sail south. Robert J. MacCharles, age 32, from Milton, Massachusetts, is the owner and captain of the *Islander*, a 30-foot ketch-rigged sailboat. The other members of the crew are George Griffiths, age 37, from Quincy, Massachusetts, and Jack Wiseman, age 22, from Nashua, New Hampshire.

The *Islander* and her crew left Boston on November 3rd, 1962, with the intended destination of Bermuda. On November 11th, they are approximately 500-miles south of Cape Cod, when they run into a storm (the Kria Low). The waves build to 40-feet in height, and the *Islander* is capsized. The boat righted herself, but in doing so she was dismasted, and she received considerable damage. The engine was dead, and despite all efforts, it could not be restarted. For thirty-six-hours, the *Islander* and her crew drifted out of control in heavy seas. The crew tried to salvage whatever hadn't been lost overboard in the knockdown or had been ruined by the salt water that they had taken aboard when she was capsized. They now had no sail power, no engine, no radio, and no way to communicate with anyone to report their predicament. One of the essential items that they did manage to salvage was a flare gun and twelve distress flares. This flare gun would prove to be their most important possession.

After a short respite, another storm, Neptune's Nor'easter, was brewing and the seas started to grow even larger. It was looking bad for the crew, as the *Islander* was taking on water faster than they could keep it out, by hand bailing. The crew had fired off two of the twelve flares that they had, and they were relieved to find that the flare gun worked, but also dismayed that no one came to their aid. No one responded because no one was in their vicinity to see the distress flares. They were very alone in the deep ocean.

This second storm was coming on strong on the night of November 14th, when the men sighted a large ship underway in mountainous seas near their position. They fired off the third flare, and then another, and watched the ship intently hoping that she had seen their distress signal. After a few minutes, they fired another flare. They now had six flares left in their arsenal. So far, every flare they had fired had worked, but this did not mean that the flares that remained would do the same. They observed the ship, knowing that this might be their only chance for rescue. They discussed what their strategy should be, knowing that they had to make this ship see their distress signal. If they used all their flares and were not seen by this ship, then they might be doomed. They instinctively knew that this was a life or death moment. They also knew, that if they did not fire their flares at the right time, the crew on watch aboard this ship might be facing an angle where the flare would not be seen. The tension on board the *Islander* was at a peak. The three men knew they were in serious trouble and this encounter might be their only chance to live. Then they saw the ship alter course, and she seemed to be heading in their direction. They immediately fired off another flare and watched and waited. The ship continued to come in their direction, and they could see her size and realized this was a large cargo ship. They fired another flare, and the ship signaled back with her whistle and lights, they now knew that they had indeed been seen, and they would be rescued.

The rescue ship turned out to be the M/V *Aireo*, an Italian flagged cargo ship, commanded by Captain Leonardini. The captain sprung his ship into action to come to the aid of the *Islander* and her crew. In an incredible display of seamanship and control of his large ship in heavy seas, Captain Leonardini, then brought the M/V *Aireo*, right up alongside the S/V *Islander*. However, as he brought his ship up close, a massive wave hit her, and the *Aireo* was slammed into the starboard side of the sailboat. This collision damaged the *Islander*, and stove in her starboard side, and the ketch now started to sink fast. All three crew members of the *Islander* now had no choice but to jump into the storm-tossed seas, as the *Islander* was disappearing from under their feet. After a few minutes, the crew of the *Aireo* hauled Captain MacCharles, and then Jack Wiseman, aboard the cargo ship, exhausted but unhurt. As the crew was busy saving MacCharles and Wiseman, the third member of the crew, George Griffiths, was drifting away in the darkness. Griffiths was quoted as saying; "The lights of the ship were getting fainter. I kept calling and yelling in the hopes that they would hear me. I thought this is it; I'm going to be lost at sea." The *Aireo* and safety were now more than 400-yards away from Griffiths, and he was sure he was doomed. Suddenly, the ship turned and started back in his direction. The Italian crew on the deck of the *Aireo* had heard Griffiths shouting, as his voice was carried by the wind. It was a miracle that he could be heard over the noise of the wind and the waves. The conditions had to be just right, and the crew on deck had to be very alert to hear this man. Clearly, it was not Griffiths' day to die. Captain Leonardini maneuvered his ship carefully, and they found George Griffiths drifting in the towering seas, in his life jacket. He had been in the water alone, for close to an hour.

The three men had lost everything in the sinking of the *Islander*. They only had the clothes on their backs and their life jackets, but they had their lives. After determining that the three men were unhurt, the Italians secured some dry clothes and made the three Americans comfortable aboard the *Aireo*. The captain arranged to feed the rescued men, and then he let them get some sleep for the rest of the night, as they were exhausted.

The next morning, Captain Leonardini had the men delivered to the bridge, as the *Aireo* was navigating her way through this unexpected storm. The captain informed the New Englanders, which due to the position of the storm, and because he had a cargo to deliver, that it would be impossible to take them back to the United States. Captain Leonardini informed them that they would have to ride along with the *Aireo* to her next scheduled destination.

The next scheduled stop was…Copenhagen, Denmark!

So here are these three New Englanders, who left Boston with the idea of taking a vacation to the warm weather of the Caribbean Islands, and they are now headed to Denmark in late November. After what they had endured, they were quite happy to be alive and glad to be heading anywhere, and of course, they were very grateful to Captain Leonardini and his crew for saving their lives.

Upon reaching Denmark, Captain Leonardini contacted the American authorities. Eric Lundahl, the American Consul in Copenhagen, took the men under his wing and issued them new passports, arranged for suitable clothes, provided some emergency money, and booked them passage back to the United States on an American ship. They arrived back in New York City on December 17th, 1962, in plenty of time to celebrate the holidays, and give thanks for their close escape from death. The *Islander* unfortunately never made it home, and she rests on the bottom of the Atlantic Ocean.

This storm takes another vessel.
The total is now twenty-five men and four-vessels.
A 30-foot sailboat, a 442-foot ship, a 56-foot schooner, and a 30-foot Ketch.
It continues to grind on!

Rest in Peace
The ketch *Islander*

Chapter 10

THE M/V _EAST STAR_

The Cuban Missile Crisis is on,
and Cuba Strikes Back at the Canadians

In October of 1962, the Cold War between the United States and the Soviet Union is raging, and it is dangerously close to becoming a hot war. Premier Nikita Khrushchev has decided to place intercontinental ballistic nuclear missiles in Cuba. President John F. Kennedy has taken a stand that this will not pass, and he uses the Monroe Doctrine, as the basis for a naval blockade of Cuba. This is known as the Cuban Missile Crisis, and it is as close as the United States, and the Soviet Union, ever came to all-out nuclear war. The blockade of Cuba began on October 16, 1962, and was lifted on October 28, 1962, after Russian cargo ships were given orders by the Kremlin to turn around, and to bring their cargo of missiles back home to Russia.

Into the middle of this crisis comes Captain Edward Clark, age 61, the master of the 155-foot, 644-ton, Canadian cargo freighter, the M/V _East Star_. The white-haired, Captain Clark is from St. Josephs, Newfoundland, Canada, and has been a ship's master for 34-years. He is an experienced mariner, and like most Newfoundlanders, he has spent his entire life on, and around the ocean. Captain Clark and his crew of twelve-men have drawn the unenviable task of transporting a Russian traveling circus from Quebec, in Canada to Havana, Cuba right in the middle of the U.S. Naval blockade of the island. Somehow, they complete the delivery of the circus, and they are anxious to leave Cuba, before a possible American invasion. It is widely known, that the United States has massed troops, from the 82nd and 101st U.S. Army Airborne Divisions, as well as, Marines from Camp Lejeune, in South Florida, and they are prepared to make an amphibious, and airborne attack, if necessary.

After taking on fuel for the return trip to Canada, Captain Clark gets permission from the U.S. Navy to leave Cuba, on October 24th, 1962. Captain Clark now sets a course to the Turks Islands, to take on cargo for transport to Halifax, Nova Scotia, in Canada.

The M/V *East Star* was built in Sweden in 1930, she is 155-feet in length, has a 27-foot beam, draws 18-feet of water, and displaces 644-tons. She was sold to a Norwegian firm in 1938 and was owned by Norwegian shipping companies until 1962, when she was sold to the Canadian firm, Sumarah R.V., from Halifax, Nova Scotia. She is a 32-year-old small cargo freighter, in November of 1962.

Shortly after leaving the Turks and Caicos Islands, on a direct course to Nova Scotia, the ship begins to have problems with the fuel for her diesel engines. They had taken on 18-tons, and 88-gallons of diesel fuel in Havana, but now the engines are sputtering and failing, and it becomes apparent that about 15-tons of the fuel that they purchased in Cuba are nothing but pure water. They have been sabotaged by the Cubans. The captain takes actions to conserve fuel by reducing speed, and he uses what little fuel remains to power the lights and the radiotelephone equipment. He is unable to raise anyone on the radiotelephone to report his plight.

On the evening of November 7, 1962, Captain Clark gives the order to cut the engines and to raise the distress flag, as he is out of fuel, and out of any other options. They are now at the mercy of the elements, and they drift with the wind and the Gulf Stream for nine-days, before they run right into the middle of Neptune's Nor'easter, with hurricane force winds, and 60-foot seas. During the nine-days that they are drifting, the captain reports that five other ships came in view, and none of them responded to the distress signal that was being flown from the mast. The vessel wallows helplessly through days of severe heavy weather, and she begins to founder. Large breaking waves are completely swamping the ship. The #1 Hold in the bow becomes full of seawater, and the ship is now listing more than 25-degrees. Finally, on Friday, November 16th, the ship looks like it is in imminent danger of sinking. Captain Clark reluctantly gives the order to abandon ship. The crew abandons ship into one lifeboat with ten men, and a raft with three men and they spend the next 22-hours surrounded by sharks. One crew member reported that the sharks were so close, that their fins were scraping the sides of the raft, all while drifting in the Gulf Stream, 130-miles from Bermuda.

On Saturday, November 18th, a Coast Guard airplane on a search mission for any possible survivors of the M/V *Captain George* spots a flare. Upon closer investigation, the *East Star*'s crew has been found, although the Coast Guard had no idea that they were missing. The *San Gaspar*, a large British Tanker of 32,000 tons is in the vicinity, and she responds to the Coast Guard call for assistance. The M/V *San Gasper* is soon on the scene, and they rescue Captain Clark and the crew of the *East Star*, thirteen men in total, without incident.

Surprisingly, the M/V *East Star* is still barely afloat, and she is taken in tow by the *San Gasper*, with the hope of bringing the ship to nearby Bermuda. After a few hours, this proves to be impossible, as the *East Star* begins to list more heavily, and she is cut free. Very shortly after that, she founders and sinks, approximately 155-miles, north-northeast (NNE) of Bermuda, at 33 degrees, 19 minutes North, and 63 degrees, 40 minutes West, another victim of Neptune's Nor'easter.

The questions involving the fate of the *East Star* remain to be asked. A Canadian company has lost a ship, and thirteen Canadian nationals have just narrowly escaped this ordeal with their lives. The question is why? Why was the *East Star* sabotaged in Havana? Canada had always traded with Cuba in non-military supplies. However lately, with the implications of the missile crisis, and the threat of all-out nuclear war, the Canadian government has sided with the United States and was firmly not in favor of Soviet ballistic missiles being placed in the Western Hemisphere. Was this an act of sabotage, a small strike back at Canada from the Castro regime, or was it a simple act by the Cuban dockworkers to show their anger, toward foreigners? It has been only nineteen-months since the CIA backed the invasion of Cuba, at the Bay of Pigs. Emotions are running very hot against Americans and foreigners in Cuba. In either case, it still seems strange that they would take out their frustrations on the Canadians. The Cubans real beef was with the United States. Maybe this was as close as they could get to Americans, so they took it. After all, Canada has always suffered from the, "almost like Americans," syndrome and this illustrates in another way, the tension that existed in 1962, between the Soviet bloc and the West. It highlights the reason why the U.S. military was reluctant to evacuate the radar towers that were in place off the United States mainland, in international waters. In 1962, we hated them, and they hated us, and the world was worse off because of it. People not mixed up in the rivalry were brought into harm's way, like the M/V *East Star* and her crew of Canadians.

Nothing good ever comes from hate, a lesson the world still needs to learn in 2018.

The storm takes another ship,
the total is now twenty-five-men and five-vessels lost.
It is not over!

Rest in Peace
M/V *East Star*

PUERTO RICO

The storm was reaching out in all directions from its' center and generating gale force winds with heavy seas. Two people are killed, ten people injured, and five-hundred people are driven from their homes in Puerto Rico. The streets in San Juan were flooded, along with massive power outages across the island.

Captain Moses Lockward, the skipper of the Dominican flagged freighter, the M/V *Gold Star*, reported that; "Waves off the coast of Puerto Rico were the worst that I have encountered in my 30-years at sea".

PART III

"HOVE DOWN" ON GEORGES BANK

As the storm was raging all over Georges Bank, individual battles for survival were being fought by all the boats that were out on the famous fishing grounds this day.

Two New Bedford fishing vessels would be "Hove Down," during this storm and return home to tell their story. Most probably, this also happened to a third New Bedford fishing vessel, but she never returned home to tell her tale.

The following are stories of nine New Bedford fishing vessels and two U.S. Navy ships that had the bad luck of being out on Georges Bank, in this unknown severe storm, that I have named Neptune's Nor'easter.

Chapter 11

THE HISTORY OF GEORGES BANK

"Georges Bank is one of the roughest places in the world to fish."

Wesley George Pierce

One hundred nautical miles northeast of Nantucket Island, and one hundred nautical miles due east from Chatham, Massachusetts, lies Georges Bank. Chatham is located at the elbow of Cape Cod. The fishermen who work this bank and know it best, simply, but respectfully, refer to it "Georges." To the men who risk their lives fishing this bank, there is only one place called "Georges," and it is to the New England fisherman, what Fenway Park is to baseball. It is the major leagues of East Coast commercial fishing.

Georges Bank is the most prolific fishing ground on the East Coast of the United States. It is a prime breeding ground for fish and shellfish. This bank is part of a series of shoals that begin with the Grand Banks, off the coast of Newfoundland and Labrador, in Canada and these shoals extend down the coast of North America past Nova Scotia, and Maine, and continue down to Massachusetts. Georges Bank is the most southern shoal area of this chain. Georges is oval shaped and resembles the shape of an egg; it is approximately 200-nautical miles long and 120-nautical miles wide in the middle. The sea floor of Georges Bank is more than 300-feet higher than the sea floor of the Gulf of Maine, which lies immediately to its north. Georges Bank occupies an area that is larger than the size of the entire State of Massachusetts.

Just who was the first man to sight Georges Bank is unknown. Probably the Norsemen saw evidence of these shoals on their early journeys to this area. The first Europeans to discover and work the North American fishing grounds were the Basques, from Northern Spain. The Basques had access to salt, and they developed a salted cod business that was so lucrative, that they kept the location of these fishing grounds a secret for five-hundred years. The Basques know how to keep a secret.

In 1497, John Cabot was on a voyage of discovery for King Henry VII of England, and he was amazed to find close to a thousand Basque fishing vessels working the Grand Banks. Cabot named this place New Found Land and claimed it for the English King.

In 1524, the Italian explorer, Giovanni da Verrazzano, sailing for France, discovered Georges Bank and named it Armelline Shoals. Verrazzano chose this name for its symbolism, as Armelline was the name of a man who was known to be an evil Papal tax collector. When Verrazzano viewed the currents and breaking waves this far from land, he perceived it as a dangerous and evil place, and he gave it the name of an evil man.

In 1602, the English lawyer, explorer, and navigator, Bartholomew Gosnold, made basic charts of this area. He renamed these shoal waters, St. Georges Bank. He also named and defined the locations of Nantucket Island, Martha's Vineyard Island, Cape Cod, the Elizabeth Islands, and the Great Round Shoal Channel.

In the early days of the colonization of America, Georges Bank was defined from Gosnold's crude charts as a place of great danger, and it was therefore avoided. There was no real need to venture out to Georges Bank, as it was well offshore of the mainland. All that was known, from those few who had ventured close to this area, was that you could observe large breakers flying up in the air as you would see during a storm pounding onto a beach, a scary thing to witness this far out to sea. Of more immediate concern to the inhabitants of this region, was an understanding of the shoals and currents that were closer to Cape Cod, and the islands of Nantucket and Martha's Vineyard.

The wealth of the early settlers was mostly dependent on what they could harvest from the sea. Chief among the bounty from the sea was the ability to catch and harvest codfish from the ocean. Cod was so crucial to the prosperity of the people of Massachusetts that to symbolize its' importance, a five-foot-long, hand-carved wooden model of a codfish was commissioned by the State Senate. This carving became known as the "Sacred Cod," and it was hung over the gallery of the House of Representatives chamber in the Massachusetts State House. It was elevated in that hall to remind all who saw it, of the importance of the codfish to Massachusetts. Even today, it is still there to oversee the work of the elected officials of the state.

As the need increased to catch more fish to feed and power the growing population of this region, fishermen began to venture out into the dangerous waters of Georges Bank. Those fishermen who had boats large enough began to work the bank from the deck of their boats. To expand their catch, they developed the dory fishing process. They next started to build schooners to utilize the speed of this type of vessel. This was important to allow them to get to the fishing grounds, and then after filling the boat, to get back to the market quickly with fresh fish. The speed of the schooners allowed the market to move from salted fish to fresh fish. The fishermen were on a mission to build faster sailing schooners, and they added more sail area to make their vessels go faster. This need for speed also created danger, as these schooners sometimes became victims of the balance between speed and safety.

The fishermen found an even greater abundance of fish on Georges Bank than they had ever imagined. The fish were larger than the same species of fish that they caught in other areas, and this was an indicator of the superior habitat that Georges Bank provided to the marine life. They also found danger in abundance as well, and many men died attempting to fish Georges Bank, as they contended with storms and the shoal waters. The fishermen from the port of Gloucester were the first to develop the Georges Bank fishery. The men who ventured out to Georges Bank from Gloucester became known as, "Georgesmen." It was a name of respect for the bravery that these men displayed in fishing this hazardous location.

In the 1800's, a total of 3,436-men were lost at sea fishing from the port of Gloucester in schooners, many of them on Georges Bank. Gloucester paid a terrible price to open this fishery. During the Civil War, a man from Gloucester was statistically safer in the Army, than if instead, he stayed at home and worked as a Georges Bank fisherman.

Also, during this period the country was growing, and trade with Europe was becoming more important to America. Georges Bank was a significant danger to the trans-Atlantic ships that were journeying to and from Europe. It was now imperative that better navigational charts be provided for both the trans-Atlantic shipping interests, and the fishing industry.

In 1821, fully 219-years after Gosnold provided a basic definition of the size and location of Georges Bank on his crude charts, President Monroe authorized the Commissioner of the Navy to survey Georges Bank and the surrounding areas. The stated purpose of the survey is to establish the extent, position, and peculiarities of these shoals. The justification for this survey was based on the far-reaching importance of this information to the commerce of the United States.

This survey determined that four major shoals existed on Georges Bank, and between these four shoals, the water depth ranged from 15 to 35-fathoms. West and north of the shoals the water ranged from 90 to 160-fathoms, and east and south it increased to 2,000-fathoms, where it then dropped off the Continental shelf to the bottom of the deep sea. The area of lowest depth was comprised of three long narrow spits, which are now known as Georges Shoal and the Cultivator Shoal. At one position on Georges Shoal, it was found to only have a depth of three-feet, under certain tidal conditions.

This low depth is a point that is very hard to explain to non-mariners. It is hard to imagine, that at a distance, of more than one-hundred-miles from Cape Cod the water is only three to nine-feet deep. Theoretically, you could jump out of a boat and stand with water just up to your waist. This trick is not actually possible, due to the fast currents and breaking waves at this location. It sounds crazy to the layman, to think that this far out to sea the water is only three to nine feet deep, but it is a fact.

Due to the extreme low depth of the water on this part of the bank, and the varying depths surrounding this location, the tide runs rapidly through the area of Georges Shoal and the Cultivator Shoal. The sea is attempting to push through a restriction. As the tide sets, it must pass from deep water through an area of shallow water. It creates something close to the image of pouring water through a funnel, or more technically, it creates a "venturi effect." On the eastern edge of these shoals, it creates a spectacular visual event. On a westerly set of the tide, large breakers are formed reminiscent of what you see when waves break onto a beach during a storm. When the tide is setting eastward, it causes a waterfall effect which pours through Georges Shoal in a cascade of foam. This phenomenon can be seen from some distance.

The clerk for the survey of 1821, concluded that it was not possible to complete a definitive survey of Georges Bank. He stated that due to the rapid changes in weather at this location, time was not available to complete such a detailed study. Due to these constraints, the decision was made to define the boundaries of Georges Bank, and leave it at that. This would be an effort to protect the trans-Atlantic shipping interests, and to provide as much information as possible to the fishermen, but the fishermen would have to proceed under the knowledge that they would develop on their own, through trial and error. The error is often resulting in their death. The fishermen were considered expendable. The clerk concluded his report by saying; "I do not believe a more perfect survey can be made, as the main shoal cannot be penetrated safely." He is saying that this area of Georges Bank is too dangerous to chart in accurate detail. This is the beginning of a long history of the American government turning their back on the Georges Bank fishermen. This would not be the last time that the fishermen were cut loose by their government, 197-years later, it is still happening.

In 1821, the fishermen from Gloucester, Massachusetts, began going to Georges Bank to fish for cod and halibut. Only a few dared to go at first, but the fishing was too good, and by 1835 there was a large fleet of Gloucester boats fishing at Georges Bank.

In his excellent book, titled "Going Fishing", first published in 1934, longtime fisherman, Wesley George Pierce, described Georges Bank as follows; "Georges Bank is one of the roughest places in the world on which to fish, more especially so during the winter months, for then fierce gales, with snowstorms prevail, and many vessels have been lost with all hands. In a single storm, on the night of February 24, 1862, 15-Gloucester vessels and 123-men were lost, leaving 71-widows and 140-fatherless children to mourn for their loved ones who would return, no more. There are several very shoal spots on the Bank: Cultivator Shoal, Georges Shoal, and several others which always break during a heavy gale, and woe betides the vessel that drifts onto one of these shoals, for she is very likely to be lost with all her crew."

Wesley George Pierce, spent his life as an offshore commercial fisherman, following his father into the business. He was from Maine, and he made his first trip to Georges Bank at the age of fifteen. He fished everywhere on the East Coast from Labrador and Newfoundland on the Grand Banks, out to the Flemish Cap, the Gulf of Maine, Georges Bank, and south to the Carolinas, in his life as a fisherman. He was born in 1869, and his career moved from sailing on schooners and dory fishing, to the movement to engine driven vessels and the transition to draggers. He had seen and done it all, and he aptly described the dangers of fishing on Georges Bank.

However, these "Georgesmen" from Gloucester were catching a lot of fish. In 1875, Captain Solomon B. Jacobs, in the schooner *Samuel R. Lane*, landed 123,000 pounds of large cod in Gloucester. So, the fishermen put aside their fears of the treacherous Georges Bank, and equal streaks of competitiveness, courage, confidence in their seamanship abilities, and yes, greed kicked in, and off to Georges they went to get that big trip of fish.

These same motivations would find my father on the Northern Edge of Georges Bank in 1962, in an extra-tropical cyclone, one-hundred-years after 15-Gloucester schooners and 123-men perished, in the exact same spot on Georges Bank. This dangerous area near Georges Shoal and the Cultivator Shoal is the location that I have named, "Neptune's Trident."

In 1931, the Coast and Geodetic Survey of the Department of Commerce made another survey of Georges Bank. This survey was much more detailed than the previous studies, and it provided much-improved information to all mariners, and especially the fishermen who depended on this area for their livelihood. This survey discovered three great underwater valleys that had been carved out during the glaciers of the ice age. Finally, mariners had a better understanding of the many different depths and topography of Georges Bank. This improved detail would assist them in navigating the bank that is so beset with treacherous currents, menacing shoals, and enveloping fog. Finally, the government provided a much-needed service to the Georges Bank fishermen. But, the government's real true motivation to conduct this survey, was a need that was highlighted by World War I, and the experience of modern naval warfare, especially the advent of submarines. The government wanted to know more detail about the coastal waters in the event of the outbreak of another war. The war drums were already beating, and soon World War II would be a reality. It was not really about the safety of the fishermen. The government has always viewed fishermen as being expendable. The fishermen of America represent a small portion of the population, so their importance to the federal government is often overlooked. The fishermen have learned over many years not to expect much from the government, and many times they feel that when the government finally comes to help, things usually get worse. This long history is why most fishermen have an adverse reaction when approached by government officials. Many fishermen are descendants of fishermen, and the history of events that have happened in the past is often passed down orally along many generations. These stories contain tales of storms encountered, boats that they sailed on, humorous events, and most importantly slights, insults, and wrongs, that are never forgotten.

An understanding of the topography of Georges Bank is the key to the telling of my father's story on the F/V *Venus*. Under the best of conditions Georges Bank is a dangerous place, but under severe storm conditions, the danger increases exponentially with the intensity of the weather. The most hazardous part of Georges Bank is the shoal area of Georges Shoal and the Cultivator Shoal. This is the area that the survey of 1821, could not penetrate but confirmed that the water level could be as low as three-feet under some conditions.

This place of extreme danger on the bank, was where my father and his shipmates on the *Venus* were located on the night of November 14th, 1962. At 3:26 a.m., on November 15th, the *Venus* was somewhere in-between the Cultivator Shoal and Georges Shoal, with 105-mph winds from the north, and the tide setting to the north. In a fishing vessel that required ten feet to float, they were dangerously close to a place that only supported nine feet of water under the best of conditions, and as little as three feet of water under severe storm conditions. The combination of high winds and shallow water was the reason why my father thought that this was his day to die. The *Venus* could not be in a more dangerous location on Georges Bank, while under these storm conditions. As a captain of any vessel must do, he did not voice his thought to the crew, that this might be their last day alive.

Chapter 12

THE NOR'EASTER COMES TO GEORGES BANK

"There's a Jesus lot o'wind that blows on Georgie's Bank."

Captain Woody Bowers
New Bedford Fishing Captain
Native of Nova Scotia, Canada

We first saw evidence of this storm on land, on the afternoon of Wednesday, November 14th. In New Bedford, we experienced strong winds and some minimal flooding. But as you moved east the intensity of this storm was more apparent. Provincetown, Massachusetts, at the tip of Cape Cod, recorded 90-mph winds and waves estimated at being 40-feet high. On Martha's Vineyard, a 30-foot boat moored in the harbor at Oak Bluffs was swamped and sunk. On Nantucket Island, it blew down fences, twisted television antennas, and flooding was experienced as massive waves invaded the beach front. The Martha's Vineyard and Nantucket Steamship Authority canceled all scheduled service to the islands and issued a statement that service would not resume until Saturday, November 16th. The Eastern Airlines scheduled flight from New Bedford to Nantucket and Martha's Vineyard was aborted by the pilot after experiencing strong crosswinds at both airports. The pilot then altered his flight plan and returned to the New Bedford airport where he made a successful landing. The thirteen passengers on the flight were put up at the New Bedford Hotel, and airmail that was on the plane was returned to the New Bedford Post Office. The flight was then scheduled to leave New Bedford at 9:00 a.m. the next morning, but this was also canceled due to the high winds that were still in the area. This flight did not get out of New Bedford until Friday, November 16th, 1962.

Meanwhile, parts of Maine received over a foot of snow as this storm, and the "Kria" low, teamed up with another cold front coming down from Canada. However, the brunt of this storm was thrashing along offshore. Today, this would be recognized by meteorologists, as an Extratropical Explosive Cyclone with Cyclogenesis, Bombogenesis, or just as a Weather Bomb. In 1962, the meteorologists at the U.S. Weather Bureau in Boston initially denied it even existed.

On the afternoon of November 14th, the storm center was now located 300-miles ESE (east-southeast) of Boston and was moving slowly towards Nova Scotia,

Canada. This expected path would put the nor'easter on a course to put its most dangerous rotational side, right over the fishing grounds of Georges Bank. Any fisherman on the bank was going to get clobbered by this beast. The worst part was that there was no warning to the fishing fleet that this storm was coming. The national weather service was in the dark, and unfortunately, the fishermen were in the dark right with them. To the forecasters at the Weather Bureau, it was a mistake; an error made at work. To the New Bedford fishermen out on Georges Bank, it was a matter of life and death. Eleven very experienced and capable fishermen paid for this mistake with their lives.

The United States Weather Bureau issued Gale Warnings from Eastport, Maine, to Block Island, Rhode Island, for north to northwest winds of 35 to 45 mph, for November 15th. However, wind gusts of 105 mph were being reported from the northeast.

The following will highlight the intensity of this unknown storm in relationship to other extreme weather events that have occurred in the Western North Atlantic;

1938 Great New England Hurricane – **941 mbar** – The losses from this hurricane were, 564 dead, 1,700 injured, 8,900 homes and buildings destroyed, and 2,600 boats destroyed. Two New Bedford fishing boats, the F/V *Arial* and the F/V *Charles Carlson* were lost with a total of nineteen fishermen lost at sea. This hurricane is rated as one of the top ten worse hurricanes to ever hit the mainland of the United States, and the worst to ever hit this far north.

2012 Super Storm Sandy – **946 mbar** – Massive destruction.

1954 Hurricane Carol – **955 mbar** – This storm led to the decision to build the New Bedford Hurricane Barrier due to the widespread destruction.

1991 Hurricane Bob – **984 mbar** – Hurricane Eye passed directly over New Bedford.

1991 The Perfect Storm – **973 mbar** – 75 mph wind – The storm made famous by the book and the movie.

1962 Neptune's Nor'easter – **968 mbar** – 105 mph wind – Bombogenesis.

The above data is an attempt to quantify the intensity of this storm in relation to other known extreme weather events. This is important, because later in this story we will uncover efforts by the United States Weather Bureau, and a United States District Court Judge, to downplay the severity of this storm.

Neptune's Nor'easter never received a great deal of attention. It was a remarkable story in New Bedford, and it received some national and international coverage for a few days, and then it was forgotten. It had impacted the New Bedford fishing fleet in a big way, and the men who survived this storm never forgot this experience, and they prayed that they would never experience anything like it again.

Chapter 13

THE PROFESSIONALS ON GEORGES BANK

USNS *NEW BEDFORD AKL-17*
and
USNS *AKL-43*

THE PROFESSIONAL LICENSED MARINERS

USNS *NEW BEDFORD*
AKL-17

Along with the fishermen on Georges Bank during this storm, there were others, including two cargo vessels that are designated as United States Naval Ships (USNS). This identifies these ships as being the property of the United States Navy, and they are staffed by professionally licensed mariners, who are known as the United States Merchant Marine.

During World War II, the demand for shipping to move material around the country and the world was enormous. Part of the reason that the allies were victorious was due to our industrial might and our ability to move our production output to places where it could do the most good. A vital component of this delivery system was sea transportation. To this end, the United States built many cargo ships during the war. Probably the best known were the Liberty Ships that could carry large amounts of cargo across oceans, such as the previously covered M/V *Captain George*. A lesser known series of cargo ships were the light cargo ships, which were built for the U.S. Army to move troops and supplies, thus freeing up the Army's dependence on the Navy. These ships were mainly 177-feet in length and were known as Camino Class light cargo ships. After the war, the Navy took over control of these ships from the Army, and they were then designated as United States Naval Ships (USNS). Navy ships are identified as USS or USNS. The designation of United States Ship (USS) is given to ships that are warships, and they are crewed and operated by U.S. Navy personnel. The ships that are designated as USNS are owned and controlled by the Navy, but they are crewed and operated by civilian professional mariners.

The USNS *New Bedford* (*AKL-17*), and the USNS *AKL-43* were Camino Class Supply Freighters owned by the U.S. Navy, and they were tasked with the duty of transporting supplies and U.S. Air Force personnel, out to the Texas Towers.

On November 15, 1962, in the height of the storm, the USNS *New Bedford* reported to the Coast Guard that she was disabled with a broken steering cable. She requested a Coast Guard Cutter to standby, in the event, that her steering cable could not be repaired at sea. Captain Sixto Manqual reported that he was in no immediate danger, so the Coast Guard concentrated their efforts on the F/V *Moonlight* and the F/V *Monte Carlo*. The steering cable was repaired by the crew of the *New Bedford*, and she proceeded on her own back to port, without any other difficulties.

The USNS *AKL-43* was offshore during Neptune's Nor'easter, and she received extensive damage above deck. The starboard boom was broken in the center of the boom. The port boom was torn loose from its' moorings on the deck, and both booms had to be lashed to the deck of the ship. These booms are used to lift heavy cargo on and off the ship, and they are made of 5/8-inch tubular steel. The *AKL-43* arrived back at the State Pier, in New Bedford, shortly before dawn on the morning of Friday, November 16, 1962. A man on the pier saw the damaged booms, and yelled up to a crewman; "How are you doing?" The reply was; "We are lucky to be alive."

The *AKL-43* left New Bedford on Wednesday, November 14, at 4:00 a.m., for a trip to Texas Tower #3, which was located on Nantucket Shoals near the Nantucket Lightship. The weather report which they received before leaving New Bedford said; "40 to 50-mph winds through early Thursday morning, diminishing after 7:00 a.m., to 15 to 25-mph with 18 to 24-foot seas."

At 2:00 a.m., on Thursday, November 15th, Captain Jack Salmon reported his position as five miles from Texas Towers #3, and conditions as follows; "An approach to the Tower is impossible due to the weather conditions. I then ordered the ship to heave-to and wait for the weather to ameliorate. At 11:00 a.m., four hours after the weather report predicted the storm to have diminished, the conditions were winds of 60-mph, gusting to 78-mph, with seas running 30 to 38-feet. I was jogging the ship slowly into the wind to stay in place. The ship was rolling between 38 to 45-degrees and several times she rolled as far as 52-degrees. The storm blew at peak intensity, from 11:00 a.m. to 3:00 p.m., and snapped both booms early. The booms had to be secured and tied down before they damaged the structure of the ship. The wind sucked an inflatable life raft right out of its container, where it then inflated and blew away. Under these severe weather conditions, the crew had to go out on deck and corral these booms, which were whipping around in the hurricane force winds. All of this while the ship was pitching and rolling violently in this severe heavy weather, in the middle of the night. The ship carries a crew of 26-men, all of whom are professionally licensed mariners."

Captain Jack Salmon further said; "I was never in any doubt of the ability of our ship to pull through the storm. But these guys who had to go out on deck in the peak of the storm to corral and secure the booms, I was worried about them. They did one hell of a job. If you can imagine the drama of the ship pitching and rolling in big seas, with hurricane force winds, and seawater sweeping over us, and these two cargo booms ready to go any which way. It was tense until we could get the booms secured and the men off the deck. What made this storm so dangerous was that it wasn't anticipated and when it arrived it blew continuously from one direction, mostly northerly, and this caused the seas to build higher and higher." Seawater found its way into the bridge and pilothouse, and everything was still dripping wet when the *AKL-43* docked in New Bedford. Captain Salmon summed it up by saying; "That was one hell of a storm."

The experience and difficulties that the licensed professional mariners encountered, in their United States Navy Cargo ships, adds further weight to the severity of Neptune's Nor'easter.

There are some who are critical of the training and certification of fishermen and especially fishing captains. They imply that fishing captains are some type of second-class mariner. They base this on the fact that they were not required to pass a formal test and obtain a certified captains license. This is another example of disrespect directed at the fishermen. In fact, they were held to a strict and demanding test method, known as peer approval and peer respect. This is a test method that usually takes years to complete. The path to the wheelhouse on a fishing vessel was obtained by a system which is known as completing an apprenticeship. You had to demonstrate a mastery of all tasks that a crew member on a fishing vessel was required to perform. You would then be eligible to move to the position of mate and allowed to run a watch. If successful as a mate, and only by invitation and approval of the captain who trained you, would you be eligible to be considered for the position of captain.

In the aftermath and review of Neptune's Nor'easter some shoreside "experts," intimated that the storm was not as severe as the fishing captains claimed. The implication being that fishing captains we not educated gentlemen, they were just uneducated commercial fishermen. The experience of the licensed professional mariners that manned the USNS *AKL-43* would suggest otherwise.

A United States Navy helicopter lifted seven Navy sailors from a steel radar tower in the Atlantic, twenty-eight miles southwest of Bermuda. The evacuation was done as a precaution, as waves were reaching 60-feet high with winds blowing consistently at 60-mph. Damage was detected on the lower part of the steel structure. The area of the tower above, where the men lived and worked, was deemed to be safe.

Neither, Texas Tower#2, or Texas Tower #3, were evacuated during Neptune's Nor'easter. Wind gusts of more than 60-mph were logged at Tower #2, but the towers are built to withstand 125-mph winds. Typically, when winds exceed 55-mph, the towers are evacuated for safety reasons. However, the Air Force did not request the evacuation of their personnel because the U.S. Weather Bureau did not forecast the actual intensity of this storm.

The U.S. Air Force was in a dilemma concerning the evacuation of the Texas Towers. The preference was not to evacuate the towers, the reason being that in 1962, the United States maintained a twelve-mile territorial limit, and this meant that the Texas Towers were sitting in international waters. These towers were crammed full of our most advanced radar and aircraft detection systems. Since they were in international waters, leaving the towers unmanned left them vulnerable to occupation by any foreign entity. Since the Soviet Union had a large contingent of "fishing vessels," working on Georges Bank, the risk of the unauthorized invasion of the towers was high. However, Texas Tower #4, off the coast of New Jersey, had collapsed in a severe storm in January of 1961, with the loss of twenty-eight men. So, it was a double-edged sword that the Air Force officers faced. Evacuate the tower and run the risk of the Soviet Union boarding the tower or leave the men on the tower at serious risk during a severe storm. The Air Force took this decision seriously, and if they had known the actual strength of this storm, they stated that they would have ordered the evacuation of the towers.

Chapter 14

The F/V *Moonlight*
&
The F/V *Santa Cruz*

FV *Moonlight*

Leaving New Bedford Harbor

In November of 1962, the F/V *Moonlight* was an 80-foot long, New Bedford based fishing vessel that is rigged and engaged in fishing for scallops, or as she is known in New Bedford fishing jargon, she is called a "Scalloper." Fishing vessels rigged to trawl for groundfish (cod, haddock, yellowtail flounder, grey sole) are called "Draggers." After battling the storm all night, Captain William Fielder placed a call to the Coast Guard just after dawn, on November 15th. He reported that he was located 120-miles east of Chatham, Massachusetts, and he indicated that winds were blowing 75-mph, with 50-foot seas. Captain Fielder further reported that he was; "Experiencing severe heavy weather during the night that is imperiling the vessel, part of the deck is stove in, and the boat is leaking badly. The crew is hand bailing in a bucket brigade, and we are having difficulty keeping up". The captain then declared an emergency and requested immediate assistance from the Coast Guard.

The Coast Guard responded by immediately sending two aircraft to locate the position of the *Moonlight*. The Coast Guard then dispatched two ships to proceed to her reported location, at the fastest possible speed. The 311-foot Coast Guard Cutter *Barataria* reported an ETA of 10:30 p.m., that evening. The 180-foot Coast Guard Buoy Tender *Cactus* was dispatched with an ETA of 2:00 a.m., on Friday, November 16th. The Coast Guard was sending some of their largest ships to Georges Bank because they were aware that they had a significant storm raging offshore. The Coast Guard was involved with rescue attempts, and "Mayday" calls from ships to the south of the *Moonlight*, all during the night. The Coast Guard was carefully tracking the progress of this storm, as it moved north.

The first Coast Guard aircraft arrived on the scene mid-morning and made a flyover. They spotted the F/V *Santa Cruz* running in tandem with the *Moonlight*, about 200-yards off her port beam. The *Santa Cruz* had picked up Captain Fielders call to the Coast Guard, and she was attempting to stay close to the *Moonlight*, in case she began to sink. The *Santa Cruz* in the best tradition of the sea was there, and they would attempt to rescue their brother fishermen if needed. This would have been an almost impossible task under these conditions, but the *Santa Cruz* was there anyway, and she was not leaving.

The Coast Guard airplanes reported that large waves were breaking over the entire length of both fishing vessels. Since the *Moonlight* was reporting that they were taking on water faster than they could bail it out, it was imperative that they shift this dynamic in the opposite direction, and soon. If they couldn't find a way to start removing more water than was coming in, the *Moonlight* would sink, and the rescue of the crew would be challenging. They were in a race to save six men's lives. The Coast Guard aircraft attempted to drop pumps to the *Moonlight*, but this was unsuccessful, as the parachutes that were attached to the pumps failed to deploy. When released from the aircraft, the parachutes twisted in the strong winds and immediately collapsed, sending the two pumps to the bottom of the ocean. Due to the severe weather conditions, it was futile to drop any further pumps, and this option for the rescue of the *Moonlight* was abandoned. The Coast Guard flight crew could now only stand by and watch the spectacle unfold below them. They were eyewitnesses to the best of the New Bedford Fishermen's courage and tenacity. The *Moonlight* fighting the good fight, and their friends on the *Santa Cruz* sticking with them, while enduring a beating of their own from the storm. The Coast Guard pilot reported to the Coast Guard Headquarters in Boston; "Standing by, circling the *Moonlight* with life rafts, if needed. Large breaking waves completely covering both fishing vessels. Extremely Heavy Weather." The closest large Coast Guard ship was still more than twelve hours away from arriving on the scene.

The situation was dire, and the closest real help for the *Moonlight* were their friends on the *Santa Cruz*. The Coast Guard planes circling above were only valuable to direct the large Coast Guard ships toward their exact location. The rescue ships would be arriving in the darkest hours of the night. If the crew on the *Moonlight* had to go into the water, under these conditions at night, their chances of being saved would be very slim.

The situation on the *Moonlight* was that her stanchions, which support the rails on the deck of the boat, were collapsing. These stanchions were damaged during the night when the fishing vessel was hit by a large breaking wave, which crashed into the port side rail, and ripped out thirteen-stanchions and the rail with them. When the vessel rolled, which it frequently did, water would swamp the deck, and then it would rush down through these holes in the deck, and the seawater would run down into the engine room. The engine room was flooding. The crew formed a bucket brigade to help stem the tide of incoming water because the bilge pumps could not keep up with the inflow of the water. The first concern was that as the flooding increased it would eventually cause the loss of the engine. If the engine failed, the boat would have no propulsion, and it would be impossible to keep the boat headed up into the towering seas. The *Moonlight* would be helpless to defend herself against these raging seas. This would cause the vessel to turn beam to the seas, and the deck would be swamped more frequently, and this would result in more water flowing down into the engine room. The flooding of the engine room would then lead to the eventual sinking of the vessel. The bucket brigade was performing to their utmost, but they were slowly losing ground to the relentless pounding of the sea. Something had to be done, or the most likely scenario was that six men would perish when the *Moonlight* sank from under their feet.

It was at this stage, that crewman Louis Raulet, stepped up and risked his life, to save his ship and shipmates. Raulet gathered some rags, a steel rod, and a rope. He tied the rope to his waist, and with the assistance of Captain Fielder, he secured the other end to the captain, and then to the pilothouse, as his safety line. Raulet and

Captain Fielder then struggled out onto the deck of the *Moonlight* in the height of the storm. Raulet now faced the full brunt of the wind as he further proceeded out on the deck, while the boat was climbing 50-foot seas that were crashing into the bow of the *Moonlight*. With the wind howling and screeching in the rigging, this man negotiated a rolling and pitching deck in hurricane force winds. Walking in hurricane force winds on land is extremely difficult but walking on the deck of a moving and rolling ship in a hurricane would be impossible for most people. Then Raulet had to work on that moving deck to implement his temporary fix. Only a very experienced and capable seaman would be able to attempt this feat. The courage this took is hard to imagine. Raulet had decided that the only option to save the boat was to try to plug the holes in the deck. He hoped that this temporary plugging of the holes with rags, would stop, or at the very least, slow the incoming water. Raulet, when interviewed by a New Bedford Standard-Times reporter said; "No one said anything, I just decided to go give it a try. Something had to be done. Right then there were three feet of water in the engine room, and unless we could plug the holes in the deck to slow the inflow of water, we were going to sink. I've weathered two hurricanes at sea, and they were easier than this storm, this was the worst weather I've ever experienced on the banks." To the crew of the *Moonlight*, Louis Raulet made the difference, and his courage and contribution saved their lives. The *Moonlight* rolled and creaked, tossed and moaned, but she remained afloat.

Crewman Louis Raulet, the hero of the *Moonlight*, displayed courage and determination in the finest tradition of the New Bedford Fisherman!

Raulet was quoted as saying;

"Captain Fielder is the Finest Kind. I'd do anything for him."

And he did! He risked his life for his captain and his shipmates!

Louis Raulet,
New Bedford Fisherman,
The hero of the F/V *Moonlight*,
"The Finest Kind"

The *Moonlight* was escorted to the Pollock Rip lightship by the USCGC *Barataria*. At this time, the situation on the *Moonlight* was deemed to be under control, and she then proceeded on to New Bedford unaccompanied. As she came home into the harbor of New Bedford, the water was calm.

The *Moonlight* reached the dock in New Bedford, on Saturday, November 17th, more than 70-hours since she first encountered the storm. She tied-up to the F/V *Kingfisher*, at Pier 3.

Captain William Fielder had been fishing for twenty-six years when he encountered Neptune's Nor'easter. He was quoted as saying; "For the first time in my career, I felt very afraid. I came to New Bedford from New York City at age twenty to start my fishing career, and this is as close as I've ever come to being lost at sea. But it's all I know, so what am I going to do, but repair the boat and go back out fishing." The captain's stepson was not so sure, and this was his first trip fishing after getting out of the Air Force. Captain Fielder said; "He may have changed his mind about fishing. I don't want him to come in; there's no future in this business. We came in with 12,000 pounds of scallops which will net us about 6,000 dollars. We spent 26-hours on the verge of death, with 40-foot seas and 80-mph winds. I don't think if I was a young man and knew what I know now, that I'd go into this business again. Perhaps I shouldn't say that we need young men out here. But after this, I don't think I can see it. This storm shook me up. Ten years ago, I was caught offshore in a bad storm, but it was nothing like this one. That time I had confidence that we would make it. But this one, I was worried. When water is pouring into the engine room, and it's gaining on you no matter how hard you try to bail, you get worried". The captain looked at the damaged deck and wandered about surveying the boat. He then stepped over to the F/V *Kingfisher*, climbed up onto the dock, and drove home with his family.

Stanley St. Pierre, a crewman on the *Moonlight,* said; "I've been hit with other breezes during my time fishing, but this one had me scared. I'm not afraid to say this one has me shook up. You learn a lot about your shipmates in a crisis like this; everyone worked to save the boat. Even the cook took turns bailing. Manny brought whatever he could put together for nourishment, he kept the coffee coming, and he took turns bailing. The cook was Manuel Sylvia, from Mattapoisett, Massachusetts. No one quit, if one man had quit, we wouldn't have made it. When you're down there, in a bucket brigade, and the waters coming in faster than you can throw it out, it'll make you start thinking, and none of them are good thoughts. But no one threw in the towel; we just kept going." St. Pierre lived in Acushnet, Massachusetts, with his wife and six children.

The crew of the F/V *Moonlight*

Captain William Fiedler, New Bedford, MA
Arnold Gustafson, Fairhaven, MA – Mate & Engineer
Louis Raulet, New Bedford, MA
Stanley St. Pierre, Acushnet, MA
Manuel Sylvia, Mattapoisett, MA – Cook
John Nelson, New Bedford, MA – Stepson of Captain

F/V *Santa Cruz*

The F/V *Santa Cruz* was also a Gamage built boat, and she was launched in 1960. She was similar in design, to both the *Venus* and the *Midnight Sun*. The *Santa Cruz* was 70-feet long and displaced 90-tons. Captain Manual Mello, of South Dartmouth, Massachusetts, was in command of the *Santa Cruz* on this day. When he heard the "Mayday" call from the *Moonlight*, he immediately went to her aid. The *Santa Cruz* was fishing close by the *Moonlight*, and Captain Mello brought his boat into a position off the port side of the *Moonlight*. Captain Mello made radio contact with Captain Fiedler and received an update on the conditions aboard the *Moonlight*. The two captains made contingency plans based on several different options, and Captain Mello assured Captain Fiedler that the *Santa Cruz* was there with them, and they were not leaving.

Captain Mello reported to the Coast Guard, "We can barely see the *Moonlight* in the heavy seas. She's a couple of hundred feet away, but the seas are so high that they are blocking our view." Due to the vast seas, he would only catch sight of the *Moonlight* on about every third wave, when they were both at the peak of the same wave, that they were climbing. He further reported that he estimated the wind speed to be at least 70-mph and that the seas were consistently running at least 40-feet in height.

The consensus around the docks, after both boats made it home, was that Captain Mello and the crew of the *Santa Cruz* did a very heroic and noble thing in coming to the aid of their brother fishermen.

Captain Manual Mello,
The Crew of the F/V *Santa Cruz,*
Good Friends and Courageous New Bedford Fishermen.
"The Finest Kind"

Chapter 15

<u>The F/V *Florence B.*</u>

Another example of the struggle is told in the experience of the New Bedford scalloper, the F/V *Florence B.*

The *Florence B.* was fishing on the Southeast Part of Georges Bank, about 90-miles east of the *Nantucket* Lightship. She was working off a fishing buoy that had been placed by the F/V *Aloha*.

In describing the experience, Captain Hans Davidsen of Fairhaven said; "We took one big wave, about 50-feet high, a really bad one. It curled and took us into the rounding of the crest. That wave rolled right over the pilothouse. We went over quickly, 50-degrees, 60-degrees, 70-degrees, and then about 80 to 90-degrees. The force of the water pushed us right down. Only the top of the pilothouse was above the water. Then she started to come up. It took a long time, maybe one or two minutes. But we didn't get any water in the hull, and she shimmied up slowly, like a plate thrown on the surface of the water shimmies down, only we were coming up. Then the rails showed above the water, and what water was trapped on deck ran out the scuppers. But she freed herself. Very few boats could withstand the seas we took."

The survival of the *Florence B.* was only possible because Captain Hans Davidsen, and his crew, had prepared the boat when they saw the storm intensifying. The captain and his men had cleared the deck, and battened down all hatches, in preparation for the gale that was brewing, and this kept the boat airtight. This buoyancy was critical in the *Florence B.* regaining the surface by trapping air in the hull and not allowing water to flood the interior of the boat. A great job by Captain Davidsen, and his crew, and their discipline was rewarded by saving their boat and their lives.

This giant breaking wave blew out all the pilothouse windows, swept the lifeboats off the roof of the pilothouse, snapped some of the rigging, and tore the scallop boxes away and over the side.

What Captain Davidsen has just described is the massive force of a breaking wave, and this one caused the *Florence B.* to be hove down and submerged, a clear indicator of the power of this storm. The *Florence B.* and her captain and crew were very lucky to live through this experience. The *Florence B.* was underwater for several minutes, and it is a miracle that they survived and made it home.

As my father told me, in his entire fishing career, he only knew of two boats that had been, "Hove Down at Sea," and returned home to tell about it. Many others had undoubtedly suffered this same fate, but they never returned to tell their tale. On this day, in this storm, two boats would be "Hove Down at Sea" and return to tell their story, the *Florence B.*, and the *Venus*. So, in my father's fifty-year career, he now could say that he only knew of four boats that had been, "Hoved Down at Sea," and returned to tell about it. He could further say, that he had personally been aboard one of those four fishing vessels, that survived being, "Hove Down at Sea."

The *Florence B.* had been fishing, near the *Midnight Sun*, the *Fleetwing*, and the *Aloha*. The weather was so intense that it caused the *Florence B.* to be hove down. For a boat the size of the *Florence B.*, to be hove down, it would require a breaking wave of at least 45 to 50-feet. This conclusion is based on scientific experiments that were conducted in England, after the disastrous 1979 Fastnet Sailboat Race. This work, which was conducted in wave test-tanks, established that it requires a wave that is at least 65-percent of the length of the boat, to cause a knockdown in a deep-keel boat.

The *Florence B.* did not reach New Bedford until Saturday, November 17th, a full three days after the onslaught of the storm, a journey that usually takes twenty hours. Captain Davidsen was quoted as saying when asked about the *Midnight Sun*; "I hope those men on the *Midnight Sun* are all right. I know the skipper and most of her crew".

Captain Davidsen estimated winds of more than 100-miles per hour, with seas of at least 50-feet.

Captain Davidsen said of the storm; "I've never seen anything like this before in my 36-years of fishing".

I recently had the opportunity to discuss this storm with Captain Kenneth Risdal, and he recalled going down to the dock and seeing the *Florence B.* when she got home. He said; "She looked like a ghost ship at the dock. The pilothouse windows were blown out, and the shucking boxes were gone. This boat had taken a terrible beating, but she made it home." Captain Kenneth Risdal is the nephew of Captain Magne Risdal.

Chapter 16

F/V *MONTE CARLO*

The F/V *Monte Carlo* was another Gamage built boat, and she was a lobster dragger, fishing out of New Bedford. When the storm struck, she was located about 150-miles southeast of Nantucket.

On Thursday morning, November 15th, Captain Albert Dahl, called the Coast Guard and reported; "I am taking on water, we have six to seven feet of the starboard rail caved in. Large breaking waves, of at least 30 to 40-feet, at my location. Damage to the rail was caused by a breaking wave that crashed into our starboard side. I am running due south with the wind. Wind is out of the north. Are there any large vessels in the area that I could use for shelter?"
This first message was received by the Coast Guard Headquarters in Boston, at 6:57 a.m., on Thursday morning.

Captain Dahl placed another call to the Coast Guard 67-minutes later, at 8:04 a.m., and he reported; "Still running in heavy weather. Request rendezvous with Coast Guard Cutter. If things get any worse, I will be forced to issue a "Mayday." If no cutter is available, I request any other large vessel for shelter purposes."

Captain Dahl placed his third call to the Coast Guard, 41-minutes later. This time he said the phrase that every mariner fear having to say; "MAYDAY, MAYDAY, MAYDAY." The captain then reported his position and that he was heading south, running before the wind, at a speed of 6 to 8-knots, and that he required immediate assistance to get to calmer water."

At approximately, 9:00 a.m., Captain Dahl followed up his declaring of a "Mayday" situation, with the following message; "Experiencing severe heavy weather, which is imperiling the vessel."

The situation on the *Monte Carlo* was reaching a peak of intensity; a very experienced captain had just uttered all the keywords for an emergency at sea, "Mayday" and "situation is imperiling my vessel." These are the words that alert everyone who hears them, to proceed at the fastest possible speed to render all possible assistance to the captain who speaks them. This is the Mariners' way of screaming, HELP! These words are never used unless the situation is dire. Saying these words honor binds everyone at sea, and the assets of the Coast Guard and Navy, to respond immediately. It puts the lives of many others at risk to come to your aid. A captain understands this, and he only uses these words if his situation is critical, using them otherwise, would be the equivalent of the boy who cried wolf, and it would ruin the reputation of the man who would do so. Captain Dahl had assessed his situation and knew he was in imminent danger of sinking.

The Coast Guard declared the "Mayday" and broadcast it out, asking for any large vessels to proceed to the position of the F/V *Monte Carlo*. The Coast Guard further declared that winds were gusting to 75-knots, in the area around the *Monte Carlo*.

At approximately, 10:30 a.m., a Coast Guard plane spotted the *Monte Carlo* and made a low pass over the fishing vessel. The Coast Guard now had eyes on the fishing vessel and had confirmed her position, which was broadcast out by the Coast Guard rescue headquarters in Boston. This aircraft had no pumps aboard, so they could only fly above the fishing vessel and report the conditions, which they declared as being; "Extreme Heavy Weather." The Coast Guard then dispatched the 180-foot, USCG Buoy Tender *Spar*, to proceed to the position of the *Monte*

Carlo. The *Spar* got underway immediately from Bristol, Rhode Island and she had an ETA of 5:00 a.m., on Friday, November 16th. This meant that the *Monte Carlo* would have to hang on for about seventeen-hours before help would arrive, a very long time to wait for Captain Dahl and his crew.

At 8:00 a.m., on Friday, the *Spar* finally reached the *Monte Carlo*, 180-miles southeast of Nantucket. The *Spar* reported that the six-man crew was all okay, but that it appeared that the *Monte Carlo* had suffered hull damage. Wind strength was now diminishing, but seas were still running 20-feet. The fishing vessel was only making three knots of speed, and she was proceeding slowly toward New Bedford, with the Coast Guard following her back to port. The *Monte Carlo* finally limped into the New Bedford harbor, on Sunday afternoon, November 18th, a full four days after first encountering the storm.

Now, here is an excellent glimpse into the life of a commercial fisherman. What do you think the crew of the *Monte Carlo* did after stepping up on the dock and greeting their anxious, but happy, loved ones? You guessed it, they went back aboard the boat, like it was business as usual, and proceeded to off-load their catch. They went back to the work of being a fisherman.

When his vessel was secured to the dock, Captain Albert Dahl jumped onto the pier from the boat and greeted his family. He talked briefly to his loved ones, and other well-wishers, before returning to the boat to supervise the unloading of their catch. Before he went back to the boat, he praised the crew and called them; "Good fishermen, every one of them, they're the Finest Kind."

Shortly after the *Monte Carlo* tied-up to the dock, three trucks pulled up, and the crew began off-loading the lobsters. Some of the lobsters were damaged from the jolting ride that they had been subjected to, along with the crew. The men and their catch were equally bruised and beat up from their shared battle with the sea. Some of the crew said that during the time from, 3:00 pm. to 7:00 p.m., on Thursday, it was a very touch and go situation, and one man said that he didn't think he would ever see New Bedford, or his family again. During this time, the storm seemed to be at the peak of its' intensity, with hurricane-force winds and seas consistently at 40-feet in height. Many times, the boat rolled so far that the rails were completely under water. A dory was torn from its' mounts on top of the pilothouse, three doors were stove in, and all the pilothouse windows were shattered by the force of the breaking waves.

Romeo Lemire, the Engineer, was quoted in the Standard-Times as saying; "There was a point when I was prepared to go if I had to. But I was so busy operating a pump, and patching doors, that it kept me from dwelling on my thoughts that we were not going to make it. I give the Coast Guard a lot of credit. They flew a plane right into the storm, and she came in low, and she hung right close to us. It gave us courage during the worst part of the storm that the Coast Guard was right there with us, and that help was on the way. Those pilots did a great job, and you can believe that we appreciated it."

After the lobsters were unloaded, a man on the dock, asked Lemire if he would keep on fishing after this experience. Romeo paused and answered; "Why not? We're realistic. I've been fishing for 15-years. We all know things like this can happen, and it might happen again. This storm was the worst weather I've seen in my 15-years fishing, but why should I quit? I'm a New Bedford fisherman, and this is what we do."

That ladies and gentlemen is perseverance and courage, and that is what it takes to be a successful offshore commercial fisherman!

<u>The Crew of the F/V *Monte Carlo*</u>

Captain Albert Dahl, Fairhaven, MA
Romeo J. Lemire, Engineer, Freetown, MA
Grandison Taber, New Bedford, MA
John Freitas, Cook, New Bedford, MA
Alden Ryan, New Bedford, MA
Tore Pubin, West Warwick, RI

To further highlight the danger of offshore commercial fishing we can look at the prior experience of five of the six crew members of the *Monte Carlo*. Grandison Tabor and Tore Rubin were both previously aboard the lobster/dragger, the F/V *Robert W. Griffin*. In 1958, the F/V *Griffin* was run down and sank. The British freighter, the M/V *City of Karachi*, ran down the *Griffin*, 70-miles south of Martha's Vineyard. The area was blanketed in thick fog, and the collision took three lives, Captain Warren B. Vincent, Engineer Milton Taber, and Cook John Paulsen. Four other crew members were rescued by the Coast Guard including, Mr. Taber and Mr. Rubin. Captain Albert Dahl was the skipper of the F/V *Shannon* during the time of this accident, and he witnessed the collision on his radar. Captain Dahl and his fishing vessel *Shannon* were one of the first boats to reach the scene of the collision and render assistance.

In 1960, the *Monte Carlo* had another close call, when she was in danger of sinking. A faulty valve in the boat's cooling system had caused the engine room to flood. The crew operated the pumps, and they were able to save the *Monte Carlo*. Aboard the *Monte Carlo* were Captain Dahl, Romeo Lemire, Grandison Taber, and John Freitas, who were all still with the *Monte Carlo* in November of 1962, during the battle with Neptune's Nor'easter. These three incidents, over a six-year period, highlight the danger that the fishermen faced on a routine basis, and demonstrate why offshore commercial fishing is consistently ranked as one of the most dangerous jobs in the world.

Another factor that influences and heightens the impact of a boat lost at sea are the family ties and friendships that develop out of becoming a member of a crew on a fishing boat. In the New Bedford fishing community, fishermen come together and bond when they respect each other's ability and trustworthiness. This bond develops a team mentality, where each member of the crew depends on his shipmates to do their job, every crewman's life and livelihood depend on it. Consequently, on boats that are successful, the crew tends to stay together, and these men often work together for years. This makes any loss that much worse because the families of these men also become friends. This long-term work history builds friendships between the crew and their families, and this magnifies the impact of any loss.

F/V *SUNAPEE*

A report was filed with the Coast Guard that the F/V *Sunapee* was not heard from on an expected call in time. A Coast Guard plane was sent to her last known position, and the fishing vessel was found sixty-miles south of Nantucket. Radio contact was made between the F/V *Sunapee* and the Coast Guard aircraft, and the fishing captain reported that the boat and her crew were all in good condition. He reported that they had been pushed back forty-miles while riding out the storm.

Many other New Bedford fishing boats also received damage in this storm.

Chapter 17

THE SAGA OF THE *MIDNIGHT SUN*

Saga is an old Norse word that originally meant simply a story. However, from its association with the kind of story that the ancient Norsemen liked to tell, it has come to mean a story of heroism and endeavor, and of adventure at sea. This is the story of the F/V *Midnight Sun* and her captain and crew of modern-day Norsemen.

The F/V *Midnight Sun* was launched on April 9th, 1960, at the Harvey F. Gamage Shipyard in South Bristol, Maine. The *Midnight Sun* was heralded as representing the latest in design and equipment of the new series of fishing boats joining the New Bedford scallop fleet. She was a state-of-the-art fishing machine, for the year 1960. An article in the June 1960 edition of the trade publication, the <u>Fishing Gazette</u>, touted her design and planning as exhibiting the best of safety and efficiency in North Atlantic fishing trawlers. A photograph from the day of her launching, as she is being backed out of the building shed, with the builders on her deck, highlights her beautiful sheer line as she slides down the ways into the water. Another photograph from the launch day, captures a proud Captain and Mrs. Magne Risdal, alongside their daughter Linda, who was acting as the sponsor for the launch.

The *Midnight Sun* was 72-feet in length, had a beam of 17-feet, and a draft of 9-feet. Her keel, frames, and planking were all oak with decking of pine. All fastenings were galvanized. Her main engine was a General Motors marine diesel, Model-12V-71, rated at 335-horsepower. The auxiliary engine was a Lister diesel SL2, a two-cylinder air cooled engine. The Lister drove a 32 D.C. generator, a 2-inch bilge pump, and a 2-inch deck pump. She was also equipped with a 2-inch Edson hand operated pump. Storage batteries were 32-volt Surrette Type 8, for lighting service and electronic equipment and a 30-volt Surrette type-6 battery set was installed for engine starting service. She had a 4-inch diameter bronze propeller shaft with bearings and stuffing box manufactured by Hathaway Machinery Company, all connected to a 5-blade 52-inch by 38-inch propeller. The main deck winch with 20-inch drums was also produced by Hathaway Machinery Company, located in Fairhaven, Massachusetts.

The lifesaving equipment included, two wooden dories, and one life raft stored in a container on the roof of the pilothouse. Coast Guard required life jackets, life rings and buoys were all aboard the boat. All Coast Guard safety equipment was in place.

The foc'sle had eight built-in berths, a folding mess table, a Shipmate oil burning stove; two galvanized freshwater tanks with a capacity of 400-gallons. A stainless-steel sink with a hand pump for fresh water supply and a built-in refrigerator. The berth fronts, dish rack fronts and all trim work in the foc'sle were finished in mahogany.

The aft cabin contained two built-in berths, and the aft cabin was trimmed in mahogany. A Shipmate hot water boiler was connected to radiators in the pilothouse, the captain's stateroom, the after cabin, and the toilet room, known on a boat as, "the head."

The pilothouse was equipped with the following electronic gear; one radiotelephone, one Bendix depth sounding machine, and two Lorans for a navigational fix.

In October of 1960, this was as state-of-the-art, as a New Bedford fishing vessel could be built. All who saw her, and all who examined her agreed, this was a great fishing vessel. Captain Magne Risdal, had put together an excellent fishing machine, built by one of the best boat builders in the business.

In November of 1962, the *Midnight Sun* was two years old and was one of the top boats in the New Bedford fishing fleet. She was regarded as an able boat, with an able captain and crew, all of whom were of Norwegian descent. The Norwegian boats have always been considered as being among the best run boats in the fleet.

The *Midnight Sun* and her crew of eleven-men left Kelly's Shipyard in Fairhaven, Massachusetts, on Wednesday morning, November 7, 1962. They were accompanied out from Kelly's by a 74-foot dragger, the *Venus*, her sister ship, also built at the Harvey Gamage shipyard in Maine. The *Venus* was a new boat only two months old. She also had an able crew and was considered a top-notch new boat.

The *Midnight Sun* was last heard from on Wednesday, November 14th, in the afternoon and Captain Risdal reported to the F/V *Aloha*, that he was finishing up the trip and was heading home to New Bedford.

Late Wednesday and into Thursday an unexpected storm rolled in, with winds of 90 to 105-mph and seas as high as 60-feet. The vessels on Georges Bank took a beating, and they filtered back into New Bedford throughout the weekend. The men and boats that returned from this ordeal were damaged, bruised, and exhausted. They all reported that they had survived an extreme storm and that they had all come very close to death in the process.

The *Midnight Sun* never returned to New Bedford. When she did not return and had not been heard from by Saturday, the F/V *Midnight Sun* was officially listed as missing. The Coast Guard dispatched an airplane to her last known position to start a search, but the weather conditions were still so severe in this area, that the plane had to return to base. Two Coast Guard aircraft were then sent out on Monday, November 19th, and ships were also being sent out to join the search. The search party for the *Midnight Sun* now included the following assets of the Coast Guard; Three Coast Guard Cutters, the *Acushnet*, the *Mendota*, and the *Mackinac*, and four Coast Guard airplanes. The search began at the last known location of the *Midnight Sun* and these units began a search pattern about 120-miles southeast of Nantucket.

The last reported radio contact occurred on Wednesday, November 14th, between 1:00 p.m. and 2:00 p.m., in the afternoon. Captain Risdal spoke with John Isaksen, who was the mate on the scalloper, *Aloha*. Isaksen reported; "Captain Risdal said he was on the way home. He didn't say where he was, but from talking with him, I figured he had started for New Bedford about an hour before our conversation. He did not indicate that anything was wrong. She was fishing in the same general area as the *Aloha*, *Fleetwing*, and the *Florence B.*, about 90-miles ESE (east-southeast) of Nantucket. The *Edgartown* was a little to the south of us. The trip home would generally take eighteen to twenty hours in good weather, but because of the storm, it took us sixty hours to get home. We headed in about 1:30 p.m., on Wednesday, November 14th, and we docked in New Bedford at 4:00 a.m., on Saturday, November 17th."

THE *ALOHA*
Captain Nils Isaksen
Mate John Isaksen

THE *FLEETWING*
Captain Karsten Gundersen

Meanwhile, as the search began, everyone on the waterfront in New Bedford was concerned, and speculation ran rampant. All hoped that the *Midnight Sun* had survived and that she might have just lost the use of her engine, due to a lack of fuel after battling the storm, and she might be drifting in deep water south of Georges Bank. This theory was backed up by the experience of the F/V *Palmers Island* that was adrift for three days after a winter storm in 1940. The F/V *Palmers Island* was eventually found by the Coast Guard, and she was subsequently towed back to New Bedford. Everyone hoped that this was the case with the *Midnight Sun* and her crew of eleven men.

Captain Karsten Gundersen of the scalloper *Fleetwing* offered the following; "I was not in radio contact with the *Midnight Sun*, but the last time I observed her was when I saw her on the radar, on Wednesday, November 14th in the afternoon. I believe we were both headed home around the same time." Most of the fishermen who were out in this storm, were very critical of the weather service, for lack of warning about the hurricane force winds that they experienced.

THE CREW OF THE *MIDNIGHT SUN*

Captain Magne Risdal, 55, Fairhaven, MA
Olav Ferkingstad, 34, Mate & Engineer, New Bedford, MA
August Larsen, 33, Cook, Brooklyn, NY
Jans Ferkingstad, brother of Olav, New Bedford, MA
Osjborn Pedersen, New Bedford, MA
Sam Lund, 55, New Bedford, MA
Gordon Kallestein, nephew of Captain Risdal, Fairhaven, MA
Jon Nilsen, 18, New Bedford, MA
John Wagner, Gloucester, MA
Arne Lindanger, 53, New Bedford, MA
Torgils Holmen

The storm takes another vessel,
the total is now 36-men and 6-vessels,

Rest in Peace,
F/V *Midnight Sun*

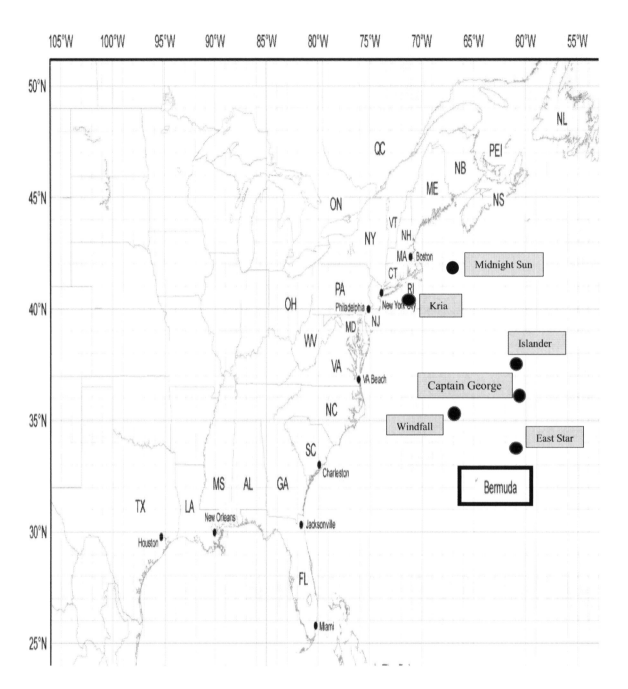

NEPTUNE'S NOR'EASTER
SHIPS LOST DURING STORM
November 14 – 16, 1962

6-Ships and 36-Men would never come home again!

Chapter 18

THOSE LEFT BEHIND BY THE F/V *MIDNIGHT SUN*

THE PAIN THAT NEVER ENDS

Mrs. Karry Risdal was the wife of Captain Magne Risdal. She had lost her first husband in the famous 1938 Great New England Hurricane, on September 21, 1938, when the F/V *Ariel* never returned home. She was now experiencing this nightmare for the second time in her life. The agony and grief that this woman had to endure are painful to even contemplate. There are no words that can adequately convey the terrible burden that she must have felt. Every time that I think about her loss, I am sad, and I struggle with the idea of how did she cope? I can only use her life story as an example that illustrates the sacrifice and burden that a fisherman's wife endures. It's the loss and hurt that is felt for the remainder of the lives of the loved ones who are left behind.

Mr. Hallvard Stoll was the regular cook on the *Midnight Sun*, but he decided to take this trip off. Hallvard had been battling a persistent cold, and he chose to sit out this trip, to give himself time to recover from his lingering cold, before the winter weather set in on the fishing grounds. This would turn out to be a decision that would save his life.

Mr. Stoll was quoted in the New Bedford Standard-Times newspaper as saying; "I think she'll be found. The boat is a good one, she's one of the best in the fleet, and one of the best I've ever been on in my twenty years of fishing. There's little chance that she would take on water."

When interviewed by the Standard-Times on November 18th, while the search for the *Midnight Sun* was underway, Mr. Stoll offered two possible scenarios for what might be happening; "First, she might have lost power, and she is drifting. There's a good possibility that she'll be found way down in the canyons." The canyons are on the southern side of Georges Bank. "The second possibility is that she is still fishing. The boat left New Bedford on November 7th, and there were high winds (the Kria Low) not long after they left. There's a good chance that they didn't get an opportunity to fish until November 11th. In that case, the eight-day limit for the boat would not expire until November 19th. If they lost the use of the radiotelephone, there's a good chance that they would remain at sea and fish out the limit before heading in. The boat has never been missing before. The previous trip was a rough one. We had 80-mph winds, and the boat took it with no problem. All but two of the crew are very experienced men, and this is a very well-run boat. They know how to handle rough weather."

When asked if he had any feelings about missing this trip, Mr. Stoll replied; "If you get saved from one trip, you get a chance to go out again, and the breaks are the same. I doubt that any of the men on the *Midnight Sun* will give up fishing when they make it in." Unfortunately, Mr. Stoll's shipmates on the *Midnight Sun* never had the chance to make that decision. Mr. Stoll's wife was not so sure if she agreed with her husband's assessment, and she was grateful that he had decided to take this trip off and was safe at home.

A Standard-Times reporter also interviewed another crew members wife. She had difficulty speaking to the reporter, but she offered the following; "I'm sorry, but I can't seem to compose myself. My husband has been missing before, but never for this long. When it was first reported that they were missing, I just hoped that they weren't using the radio because they were saving the batteries to keep the pumps running. I'm still praying for that."

In the past, she did not worry if the boat was overdue. Her husband told her not to worry because the *Midnight Sun* was a good boat and the captain and crew were the best in the fleet. She continued; "I didn't think about it. But this time it has been too long." She then excused herself from the room and returned a moment later with a small slip-over sweater. She continued by saying, "My mother-in-law in Norway just sent this over for our one-year-old son. You should have seen my husband when we got it, he was delighted." Her son had been sick when her husband left last Wednesday. "He kept me awake all night; it's funny how both things happened at the same time. The boy misses his father; he kept going to the door all day crying for him."

She had expected a call from her husband at the end of the week. "It was my birthday. He always remembers. You can't know what this is like unless you've been through it. All I can do is wait." This is the same agonizing waiting, which I watched my aunts endure when I was a young boy. It is a horrible sense of feeling helpless, and the waiting, waiting, and seemingly endless waiting, while deep down knowing the actual reality. It can only be described as a long agonizing terrible ordeal for the families back at home when a boat is lost at sea.

Knut Nilsen waited for news about another member of the crew, his 18-year-old cousin, Jon Nilsen. The two young men lived in a rooming house, along with Jon's three brothers. Jon came to the United States, in August, and this was his sixth fishing trip. Knut said that Jon's mother back in Norway had not been told that he is missing. "He is the first one in the family to ever be missing at sea. I guess all we can do is wait and hope." More pain and grief, and a mother far away who has no idea that she has lost her eighteen-year-old son.

Fishing is a dangerous business, and the specter of the sudden unexpected death of a loved one haunts everyone involved, both offshore and onshore.

Chapter 19

THE F/V *VENUS*

IN A FIGHT FOR HER LIFE

"Then captains courageous, whom death could not daunt."
The Ballard of Mary Ambree

THE ROMAN GODDESS OF LOVE AND BEAUTY

The heroine of Neptune's Nor'easter

"The Finest Kind"

The captain stares out the pilothouse window openings, and all he can see are shades of grey, and big breaking waves everywhere he looks. He glances down at his watch, but he cannot read the time, his eyes are blurred by the rain and salt water that is on his face, and that covers his watch. He pulls a bandana out of the red and black checked flannel jacket that he is wearing beneath his oilers and wipes his eyes and face, and then he cleans the face of his watch. It is 7:20 a.m., and it is now technically daylight. It has been almost four hours since he came back on watch after the boat was hove down. He has been battling the big breaking waves during the darkness of the night, where you can feel and hear the waves, but you cannot see them until they crash into the boat. It is now light enough that he can assess the sea conditions. He looks at the leaden sky, and it almost blends into the ocean. It is difficult to see where the sky stops, and the ocean begins. Everything is varying shades of gray and black, with specks of white where the tops of these monster waves are being blown off by the hurricane force wind forming spindrift. The sky and the ocean look angry and cold. The seas are as tall as a five or six story building, and they are as wide as a New York City block. They are marching toward the boat in a never-ending formation that looks like they are an oversized freight train, running on an invisible track, and they are on a collision course with the *Venus*. The onslaught of the waves seems endless. He thinks it looks like the end of the world, and he says to himself; "What are we doing out here?"

As the waves build, the 100-mph wind shears the tops off the waves and along with the heavy rain it makes visibility very limited. To make matters worse, this mixture of rain and salt water is invading the interior of the pilothouse, because the window openings are without glass. All the glass was blown out when the *Venus* was hove down four hours ago. The men in the pilothouse have their foul weather gear on, to keep from being soaked. The fishermen call their foul weather gear, "Oilers," which harkens back to the old days when they wore cotton fabric that had been oiled, or waxed, to give it some water repellency. He has a random thought that this was the way it was, in his father and grandfather's days on the schooners. The schooners had no pilothouse to protect the man on wheel watch. The thought of his father floods his mind, and he can hear his father's voice in his head, offering encouragement and advice. He hears his father repeating some of his lessons on navigation and boat handling in severe weather. It seems like his father is standing right next to him, in the pilothouse, but he knows that right now he is probably eating breakfast at his home in Falmouth, on the Cape.

The captain engages in a silent conversation with his father, in his mind, and he hears his father offer; "Just ease her up and jog into these big seas and ride it." He silently answers his father, "No Pa; I cannot, the Cultivator Shoal is close to the south of us, I'm not sure exactly how far. I can't let her be pushed backward, or we will founder and sink on the shoals. I can't swing off to the east, or the west, because we are boxed in by Neptune's Trident. My only option is to drive her north, to get above the Trident, and then I can swing her off and gain deep water, in the channel, to ride this out." His father answers him, "Alright Louie, but be careful with your boat speed when you start down the backside of these seas, be careful not to get her going too fast and pitchpole. These big seas are curling and breaking with incredible force, so be careful how you attack them, do not get beam or quarter to these seas, if you can help it. You can do this Louie, it won't be easy, but keep your wits about you boy, and remember these men are counting on you, you're the captain. Show them confidence and calmness. We're all here with you." The captain answers silently, "Thanks Pa, I will."

He has a plan. The captain looks out the window openings. He reaches back and grabs his Black Sou'wester hat and puts it on his head. It makes him feel closer to his father. Old school, only Black Sou'westers for real offshore fishermen, never yellow. He needs any edge he can get, and like all fishermen he is superstitious, so wearing this Black Sou'wester seems right. It's a sign to Neptune that he's up against real fishermen today.

He issues a command to the man on the wheel on how he wants to attack the seas, and he gives him a course to steer. The captain is not a big man, but he has unusually large hands and fingers for a man his size. These hands have been swollen and toughened from years of work in salt water. He braces himself with his left hand and grips the throttle firmly with his right hand. He is now controlling how fast they will climb these waves, and how he will minimize the boat speed as they surf down the backs of these monsters.

He is realistic in their chances and allows his mind to reason that their chances are not good. He thinks that this might be his last day alive. He can feel the boat hesitate when she rolls to port before she comes back level. He senses that the *Venus* has been wounded in the fight when she was hove down. He puts this thought out of his mind, as it does no good to dwell on it, and he returns to the task at hand. A captain must be calm and confident. He takes a deep breath, and he is suddenly acutely aware of the sea and wind noise. The wind is screaming through the rigging, and it sounds like Neptune has unleashed a thousand screaming banshees heralding their demise. They seem to be hollering at him; "Why are you here?" "This is Neptune's Trident, how dare you enter this area, you will not escape!" The voices of his father and his ancestors seem to come back into his mind, and they rally in his defense by offering encouragement. He somehow remembers the Breton Fisherman's Prayer. His ancestors originated from Breton, and the Loire Atlantique of Northwest France, and later Acadia, now known as Nova Scotia, in Canada. They have been men of the sea for centuries. He quietly recites the "Breton Fisherman's Prayer," while he looks out into the storm;

"O' God,
Thy sea is so great, and our boat is so small,
grant us your help and your mercy!"

The howling seems to increase, and it is evident that Neptune is angry, and that this storm is out to kill. The wind velocity continues to rise, the seas build higher, and together they scream at the captain; "You cannot withstand our fury." The noise is both deafening and eerie, and the storm is all powerful with the fury of Mother Nature on a bad day. The captain then gathers his strength and determination, and he looks back out the pilothouse window openings into the teeth of the storm and says;

Neptune!
Our boat is strong and beautiful,
Her name is *Venus*,
We're New Bedford Fishermen,
We've been tested before,
We will not go down without a fight!

And with that, the battle is joined!
Venus versus Neptune,
It would last twenty-five hours,
Eleven men's lives hung on the outcome!

The fishing vessel *Venus* was 74-feet long and displaced 80-tons, she was built at the Harvey F. Gamage Shipyard in South Bristol, Maine. The layout and dimensions of the *Venus* were very close to those of the *Midnight Sun*. Harvey Gamage had a basic design plan that he constructed all his fishing boats around. The owners could make modifications and adjustments to this basic plan to suit their individual preferences, but all Gamage built fishing boats began with this one basic design. The F/V *Venus* joined the New Bedford fishing fleet in September of 1962, and Captain Thomas B. Larsen, of New Bedford, was the owner.

Captain Larsen was a long-time experienced fisherman, and he built the *Venus* by utilizing a new government funding program. This program was designed to assist fishermen in purchasing new boats to modernize the domestic fishing fleet. The *Venus* was the first dragger in the New Bedford fleet to take advantage of the federally subsidized boat loan program, and she was built for a cost of $117,700 in 1962, or the equivalent of about one million dollars in 2018, a sizable investment for any individual. Captain Larsen next went about securing a competent crew to help him man his new boat and make her profitable.

My father had just finished the swordfishing season, as the striker on the F/V *Comber*, with Captain Willie Isaksen, and he was looking for a site on another boat.

The *Venus*, like her namesake, the Roman Goddess of Beauty, was in fact, a very handsome vessel. When my father first laid eyes on her, he was immediately in love with this boat. She was a new boat, shiny and bright, with all new perfectly functioning gear. Freshly painted, she still had that fresh paint smell. For men that use machines to make their living, the *Venus* was a state-of-the-art fishing machine. She looked the part with a perfect sheer line and a wide beam. A strong, and rugged boat, built to get the job done, and able to take what the ocean would give her.

Captain Larsen and my father had known each other for many years, and they both saw an opportunity unfolding that could be beneficial to all concerned. Captain Larsen proposed a plan to bring my father on as the Captain of the *Venus*, and he would fill the position of the Mate. The further understanding is that they would later alternate the position of captain, from trip to trip. This would help ensure that the *Venus* got off to a fast start, as they could both bring their experience to the enterprise. This arrangement would involve using my father's long experience as a captain to help develop the fishing strategy for the *Venus*, along with Captain Larsen. A win-win for all involved, and a solid move in building a winning team.

Although they didn't know it then, having more than one experienced man in the pilothouse was an arrangement that would soon save their lives.

By November 7th, 1962, this new boat had made four trips since coming into the fleet, and she was off to a fast start. As the *Venus* was preparing to make her fifth trip to the fishing grounds, it was decided to take her to the Northern Edge of Georges Bank to fish for grey sole. This decision was influenced by the fact that grey sole was bringing about five-times the price of yellowtail flounder at the daily fish auction. Going after the higher value fish was a way to maximize the earnings of the boat. But, to find grey sole they had to go to the Northern Edge of Georges Bank because this is where grey sole would be found in November. This is also where a high degree of danger would be found, due to the shallow water at the Cultivator Shoal and Georges Shoal. These shallow waters on the bank are why fish accumulate and grow here, but this shallow water is also what makes the north side of the bank such a dangerous place in the winter. The prevailing winds in the winter, especially the prevailing storm winds in this part of the world, are from the north. If you are fishing the north side of the bank and a storm brews up, it will come at you from the north, northwest, or from the dreaded northeast, known to all in these parts as a nor'easter.

If you are fishing the Northern Edge of Georges, and if the wind comes from a northerly direction, it will drive you onto the shallow part of the bank. If this happens, you will die. A good sea boat can take a lot of beating if she has enough water under her keel, but if she doesn't, she will rip her bottom out and sink like a rock. In the winter, in this frigid water, a man might last fifteen minutes without a survival suit. In 1962, there were no survival suits; it was an invention of the future. The *Venus* was built to be a good sea boat. This was still the time of wooden boats and iron men. The accommodations were spartan compared to the new steel boats which the fleet sails in today, but make no mistake, these were proven sea boats.

The next thing that you need to understand is why anyone would go to the Northern Edge of Georges Bank in the winter if it's so dangerous? Many boats did not. A large part of the New Bedford fleet would work the southern edges of Georges in the winter. There is a part of the south side of Georges Bank, that is known as the "Winter Fishing Grounds." This was the prime destination for scallops and yellowtail flounder, the two mainstays of the New Bedford fish market. There was another reason that many of the boats preferred to fish the southern parts of the bank in the winter, and it involved safety. On the south side of the bank, if a northerly storm brewed up, you would be driven to the safety of deep water, as the water south of the bank gets very deep and this is good for the survival of the boat and her crew. These deep hulled sea boats were built to ride out rough weather because they saw it often. Winds of 70 to 80-miles per hour, with big seas, are not uncommon, especially during the winter months. The boats and crews knew how to handle these conditions if they had deep water to ride in. The men who ventured to the Northern Edge in the winter did it for the oldest reason in the world, the root of all evil… money! The boats on the south side were fishing for yellowtail flounder and scallops. The boys on the north side were after grey sole and other ground species which would fetch a higher price at the fish auction, due to supply and demand. The classic risk/reward dilemma. If your skill as a captain was good enough, and if you thought your boat was strong enough, you went to the Northern Edge to get the bigger value trip. More money for the boat owner, and more money for the crew. Captain Larsen and Captain Doucette, of the F/V *Venus*, had a brand-new boat, and they were well regarded as skilled, experienced fishermen. So, on this late fall day, they were off to the Northern Edge of Georges Bank, to get a big trip. The same plan that the Gloucester "Georges Men" had in the 1800's. The *Venus* and her crew had decided to go "dancing" with the tip of Neptune's Trident.

On Wednesday morning, November 7, 1962, the *Venus* was ready to go fishing. The supplies were aboard the boat, the fresh water and fuel tanks had been filled, and the fish hold was filled with fresh ice. The crew said their goodbyes to their loved ones, who were on the dock to see them off, and then they jumped down onto the deck of the *Venus*. The big GM diesel engine was sufficiently warmed up, and Captain Larsen gave the order to let the lines go. Captain Doucette was at the wheel, and he swung the *Venus* off the dock, with the aid of a spring line, and the fifth trip of this new boat was underway. Once clear of the pier, the bow was swung off to starboard, and the throttle was increased to line the *Venus* up to steam off to the mouth of the New Bedford harbor. The F/V *Midnight Sun* was just ahead of the *Venus*, also on her way out to George's Bank. There was no Hurricane Barrier in place at the harbor entrance as there is now. The approval to start construction on the barrier to protect the harbor would take place while the *Venus* was at sea on this trip. The *Venus* proceeded up the New Bedford Channel, with the green cans to starboard, and the red cans to port, past the Butler's Flat Lighthouse, on a compass course southeast through Buzzard's Bay on her way to the Woods Hole Passage. Once through Woods Hole, she continued eastward to proceed through Nantucket Sound, heading to the Great Round Shoal Channel, and then she was off to the Northern Edge of Georges Bank to commence fishing.

The watches were set, and as the *Venus* proceeded out to Georges Bank most of the crew was below resting, as the pace would soon pick up when they arrived on the fishing grounds. This boat would spend the next eight-days fishing twenty-four hours per day, with the crew working in shifts for eight hours, and then they could go below for four hours, to eat and sleep. This would be the schedule for eight straight days, weather permitting. This watch schedule was typical on a New Bedford dragger and was known as "eight and fours," and this required the fishermen to work sixteen hours out of every twenty-four hour day. About twenty hours after leaving New Bedford, the *Venus* arrived at the designated part of the grounds to commence fishing. It was now 9:30 a.m., on Thursday, November 8th, the trip clock was set, and by this time on November 16th, the *Venus* would be required by union rules to end the fishing trip and head back to New Bedford. The *Venus* was now located just north of the Cultivator Shoal, in a depth of about 118-fathoms of water. Captain Doucette had picked this spot because he knew that this was an excellent place to catch grey sole in November. He also knew that this was a dangerous place to fish in November, so he was extra alert to the weather. The net was made ready and placed over the side, and the *Venus* was turned hard to starboard to set the net, and then the first tow of this trip was underway.

On the afternoon of Saturday, November 10th, a weather front (The Kria Low) moved through the area, and the *Venus* stopped fishing for a few hours, but then the winds died down, and the fishing resumed. The grey sole was coming on board at a good rate, everything was proceeding as planned, and another good trip was in the works.

On Wednesday evening, November 14th, 1962, at 11:10 p.m., Captain Doucette was on watch in the pilothouse, the net was in the water, and a tow was underway. The gang had cleared the deck, and they had gone below to get a cup of coffee, known in the fleet as a "mug up" before it was time to haul back the net. Captain Doucette dialed in the marine weather forecast that the Weather Bureau in Boston broadcast over WOU radio, for the offshore waters of Georges Bank. This marine weather report was transmitted twice per day, at 11:10 a.m., and then at 11:10 p.m., and lasted three minutes each time. A grand total of six minutes of weather information for the fishing fleet per day. In 1962, this was the only weather forecast and weather report that the fishermen would get. There were no weather satellites, no instant on-demand internet weather updates, no automated weather buoys, and no weather fax information. In 1962, all they had was six minutes from the Weather Bureau per day, and their ability to read the sky and the sea and to study the ship's barometer to anticipate changes in weather conditions. The forecast predicted winds of 35 to 45-mph, with seas running 15 to 20-feet during the overnight hours for Georges Bank, and then moderating with winds of 20 to 25-mph, with seas of 10 to 15-feet, shortly after daybreak. At 11:10 p.m., Captain Doucette observed that the wind was building rapidly, and the barometer was dropping fast, and he estimated that the wind was already blowing 25 to 30-mph. It was already getting rough. Captain Larsen was coming on watch at midnight, and since the fishing was so good, Captain Doucette kept the *Venus* fishing. He decided that he, and Captain Larsen, would discuss the weather in 45-minutes when the boat owner came back on watch.

The next chapter will pick up this story from this point, in my father's own words as he told it to me, and as he recorded it on his tape recorder.

Chapter 20

Captain Doucette's Story

The Encounter with Neptune's Nor'easter

(In His Own Words)

This is my story of being "Hove Down at Sea" on Georges Banks. I took three hurricanes while at sea, including the famous New England Hurricane of 1938. I was out to sea on the fishing grounds in the '38 Hurricane, in a 55-foot boat, the F/V *Sankaty Head*, which was owned by the legendary Captain Dan Mullins. The Blue Hills Weather Observatory outside of Boston recorded sustained winds of 121-mph, with peak gusts of 186-mph. The Hurricane of 1938 has been rated as one of the four worst hurricanes to ever to strike the United States mainland, and the worst to ever hit this far north. Hurricane forecasting, as we now know it, was a thing of the future. There was no warning; it came up so fast, that people did not have time to prepare.

On the morning of September 21, 1938, I realized that a hurricane was approaching by reading the sky, the sea conditions, and the barometer, as my father had taught me. Pa had told me, that if it was late summer or early fall, and if I started to see big swells building and a rapidly dropping barometer, I should think hurricane. I ordered the crew to prepare the boat for the storm that I knew must be coming. This was critical, as it gave us time to put all loose items away and to batten down the hatches. At the height of the storm, I estimated the seas to be 70-feet in height. By preparing the boat before the hurricane hit, it allowed us to ride out the storm and survive. Two New Bedford fishing vessels, the F/V *Arial* and the F/V *Charles Carlson* never returned, with a total loss of nineteen men. The destruction onshore was massive. It was estimated that about two-thirds of the boats in the New Bedford harbor sank. The Palmers Island lighthouse keeper's home was destroyed, and his wife drowned during the storm. The storm surge in New Bedford exceeded eight feet. The 1938 Hurricane was a massive, terrible storm that I was able to survive, even though I was offshore on the fishing grounds in a small boat. I thought at the time, in 1938, that this was the worst heavy weather event that I would probably ever encounter in my fishing career. But twenty-four years later, I would encounter weather, that for me, was worse.

I saw a lot of bad weather during my fifty-year career, but this unexpected storm in November of 1962, was the most dangerous experience of my fishing career. For 48-hours during this raging nor'easter, I was quite sure that we were all going to die, on the Northern Edge of Georges Bank. I had never been hove down before, but after November 15th, in 1962, I could no longer make that claim.

Our problem on the *Venus*, was that we didn't have time to prepare for the storm, as I did in 1938. We had no warning that it was coming. The weather report did not forecast any weather of this severity, and when it did hit our location, it was in the darkest hours of the night. We were caught totally unprepared to handle weather of this intensity. The fact that we were in a brand-new quality-built boat was a significant reason why we survived. The *Venus* took a terrible beating, but she brought me home.

I was born on Martha's Vineyard, and I first went to sea with my dad as a little boy of eight-years-old, on his fishing catboat. I always went fishing with my father during school vacations. As I was growing up, I would go fishing with my father on his new boat, the fishing schooner *Gleaner*, when he was dory fishing out of Edgartown, Massachusetts. He taught me how to navigate a ship at sea before I was 12-years old. He used to call me out when we'd be making Cape Cod, coming in from Georges. The back side of the Cape is hazardous, the water shoals very fast as you approach Cape Cod. In thick weather, snow storms or fog, you must be very careful. As we would be making the back side of Cape Cod, my father would call me up to the pilothouse and say to me; "What light is that flashing, Louie?" I was a young kid, and I would count the flashes, look at the colors, or look at my watch and count the time between flashes, consult the charts, and then I would say to my father, that's Nauset Light, or that's Chatham Light. He was teaching me navigation and boat handling skills so that when I was old enough to take a vessel to sea, I would know what to do. In November of 1962, I was going to need every bit of the knowledge my father taught me to get out of this trouble with my life.

We were fishing the Northern Edge of Georges Bank chasing grey sole, which is a large flatfish that all the fish buyers wanted, they are a wonderful fish to eat. The consumer was hungry for grey sole, and we were hungry for the money. The holidays were coming, and we needed the money. Even after surviving this trouble, I still went back to this area to fish for grey sole. Most of the New Bedford and Fairhaven boats were fishing on the southern side of the bank, during the winter. Most of them worked the south side because if you get the northerly and easterly wind, you are better off on the south side of the bank, as it offers you plenty of sea room. You can "heave the boat to" and let her lay, and ride out a storm, you can go for miles. But on the northern side of the bank, you had to be on the lookout for severe weather all the time. Now, I had been fishing on the north part of the bank for years. I had a boat out of Gloucester, and in my other boats, I had always fished the Northern Edge of the bank. I knew it was risky business, but grey sole was bringing a price about four or five times that of yellowtail flounder. You also got a little other groundfish with the grey sole in this area. So, this made a big difference and gave you a higher average price when you returned to port to sell your trip. We were fishing in an area just north of the Cultivator Shoal and Georges Shoal, in 118-fathoms of water. You can go from 120-fathoms to 20-fathoms in a matter of 15 or 20-minutes, that's how close the edges are.

On this trip, the owner was acting as the captain, and I was serving as the mate. As the owner came on watch he said; "Looks like it's getting too rough to fish." I said; "Yes, it is getting too rough to fish." I then filled in Captain Larsen on the details of the 11:10 p.m. weather report. He said; "I'll finish up the tow and then steam her into the edge, into 20 or 30-fathoms and let her lay." I said; "Tommy, I don't agree, the tide has just turned to the south. The tide will take us in there fast enough without our steaming in that direction. If anything, steam to the west'ard for 2 or 3-hours, and then you'll be safe to heave-to in the channel." Captain Larsen replied; "I'll finish the tow, get everything secure on deck, let the boy's go below, and see what the weather looks like then before we make a move."

Four hours later, I would discover that he did not do as I suggested, he did not heed my warning. The captain finished the tow, and then he let the boat lay. Because the tide had turned to the south, within 20 or 30-minutes, we were in the 20-fathom area. Beyond this 20-fathom mark, the bank goes even more shoal, down to as low as, one and one-half fathoms. Very shallow water. The owner had let the boat lay for four hours. We were now in a dangerous place on Georges, in a storm with hurricane force winds.

At 3:00 a.m., the *Venus* was taking a beating, the wind was at hurricane force, with seas exceeding 40-feet in height. While I was down below sleeping, a giant wave slammed into the boat and broke right over the deck, blowing out two pilothouse windows in the process. Water and wind were now blowing straight into the wheelhouse and glass was all over the floor. The engineer was up in the pilothouse when this happened, and he grabbed several pin-boards and nailed them into the broken window areas, to reduce the inflow of water and wind. Engineer Jack Landsvik then headed to the engine room to check on the operating condition of the diesel engine and the bilge pumps. He also planned to wake me up and fill me in on the current situation topside.

At 3:26 a.m., the engineer called me to come back on watch. He said; "My God Captain, we're in shoal water and we're in a terrible fix." He knew himself that this was a place we should never be. When I went off watch at midnight, the weather service had predicted 35 to 45-mph of wind from the northwest. When I got up to the pilothouse, it was blowing at least 100-mph, from the north. The weather service later confirmed that the wind peaked out at 104-mph. We couldn't be in any worse place, on the banks with this wind.

I was still in the aft cabin when the *Venus* was hove down. My bunk was on the starboard side of the aft cabin, and the engineer's bunk was on the port side. Jack was sitting on his locker, in front of his bunk. While I was putting on my clothes to go up to the wheelhouse, Jack was filling me in on the conditions topside. Jack said; "Please hurry 'Cap and see what you can do. It's a mess up there, we have water in the wheelhouse, broken glass everywhere, and the wind is blowing a gale. Visibility is nil, and the skipper is under extreme pressure. Captain Larsen needs your help." I was getting my gear on as quick as I could, and while I was doing this, she went down on her port side. When she went horizontal, she threw me over on top of Jack, and we were both pushed into his bunk. I knew we were lying over on our side; I knew we were "Hove Down." I couldn't right myself immediately, and we stayed like that for a few minutes, which seemed like an hour. Then the boat righted herself, and she came back up on her feet. When a boat is hove down, you never know if she is going to come back up on her feet, or if she is going to continue over and "go turtle." She was a strong boat, and she came back up. It was a good thing that we didn't take another big breaking wave right then, or this story would have never been told.

When I finally made it up to the pilothouse, I quickly surveyed the scene, and it wasn't very good. The pilothouse windows were blown out, glass was everywhere, all the electronics were down because they had been soaked with seawater during the knockdown. The boat and the crew were fighting this storm, and the storm was winning the fight. The captain was sitting slouched down in the corner of the pilothouse, with his head down, hanging onto the compass supports. He was muttering that we were going to lose a brand-new boat and a whole gang of men. Captain Larsen was not himself, and I quickly realized that he had been badly hurt during the knockdown. I asked what happened to Captain Larsen, and Ronnie Lahey who was at the wheel, told me that the captain had been standing on the starboard side of the wheelhouse when she was hove down, and the sudden quick jolt of the boat had thrown him through the air, and over to the port side of the pilothouse. The storm had dealt Captain Larsen a knockout punch, and it was clear that he was injured. I spoke to Tommy, and he was like a boxer who has had his bell rung. I was sure that he had hit his head during the knockdown and that he had probably suffered a concussion. His breathing was labored, and I figured that he might have broken some ribs in the incident, as well. The crew in the wheelhouse all looked at me, and someone said; "You have to take over." I replied that I wasn't the captain on this trip and that I couldn't take over unless the captain relinquished command. Captain Larsen looked at me and said; "Go ahead Louie, if you think you can do anything, go ahead and try." I knew that I had to take command and thankfully the skipper had agreed. He was obviously in no condition to continue; he was badly injured. I give the man a lot of credit for realizing his condition and being able to decide to relinquish command of his vessel. It was now up to me.

When you go skipper of a vessel, and you're in danger, you cannot show any emotion, most certainly not fear. If you do, the crew will get out of hand. Even if you know that your situation is almost hopeless, you cannot say it. You keep the men calm with your confidence, this is one of the many things that my father taught me.

When you encounter a storm of this type, your visibility is zero, and on top of that, it was the middle of the night so we couldn't see the seas that were coming our way. The wind was howling and blowing the tops off the waves; this was another thing that was working against us. The only break that we got was that it was not freezing weather. If we had been making ice, we would have never recovered from the knockdown. Due to the damage in the pilothouse, we had no long-range navigation capability; the Loran was not working, and the Sounding Machine (depth finder) was down. The only thing that we had to navigate with was the compass. Since we couldn't pinpoint our location with the Loran, and since I had been down below sleeping for the last four hours, I could only guess at our position. It was vital that I know the depth of the water under the boat. If I knew the depth, I could estimate where we were located on the bank and have some idea of how to navigate the boat. I had been fishing this area for so long that the charts were burned into my brain. I knew those charts like I knew my name. I surveyed the situation in the pilothouse and then I began to issue orders to rally the men. I was now in command, and our lives were in my hands.

I called over to Jack Landsvik, our engineer, and I gave him two orders. First, and foremost, it was imperative that he must keep the engine and the bilge pumps running. If we lost the engine and had no propulsion we would turn beam to the sea, and we would be pushed down very quickly onto the Cultivator Shoal, and then it would be all over. We didn't know it at that moment, but we had no life raft or dories on the top of the pilothouse, they had been swept away in the knockdown.

Second, did he have any ideas on getting the sounding machine back up and running? Jack confirmed that he understood, and then he said; "Louie, I'm going to take the guts out of that sounding machine and try to dry it out." Jack said that he had a type of spray that was used to dry out electronics that have been exposed to water. Jack took the main part of the sounding machine down to the engine room. I then turned to the man who was at the wheel; he was a big strong fella and a young man, his name was Ronnie Lahey, from Newfoundland. I asked Ronnie if he could handle the wheel and take my direction without any questions or hesitation. He replied that he would. He did everything I asked him to do through this whole ordeal. So, I had a good man on the wheel and a good man in the engine room. I now had the pilothouse, and engine room organized and focused on the task at hand.

Since we were somewhere in-between the most dangerous shoal water on Georges Bank, I had no choice but to drive the boat north, directly into the teeth of this fierce storm with mountainous seas. There was no alternative. We ran six hours against the wind and the sea when Jack came back up to the pilothouse with the sounding machine. Jack said; "I'm not guaranteeing anything, and don't get your hopes up, but I'm going to try to start the sounding machine." After a few minutes, he pressed the button, and I had my eyes glued to that machine. I needed that sounding machine to help me navigate out of this trouble. The sounding machine, and the information that it could provide was crucial to our survival. She spun around three or four times and then boom she flashed. Jack was going to shut the machine off, but I said; "No Jack, let it go, let's see what happens." She went around three or four more times and then she flashed for the second time. This time the machine indicated that we had 17-fathoms of water under the keel of the boat, and this was like a 100-fathoms to me because I knew that we had moved in the right direction. After another twenty minutes, the sounding machine indicated 20-fathoms, then over time it was 22, then 24, then 27-fathoms, this was an answer to my prayers. I looked at Ronnie, and he said; "I guess by the big grin on your face, that's good news, eh 'Cap?" I said; "Yes, it is, I know about where we are, and we're headed in the right direction, just keep her going north and we're going to get out of this mess." We beat against the weather for another 12-hours with zero visibility. Seas were running very high; I estimated that winds were blowing 100-mph. We only had one way to go, to get out of the shallow water, and that was to the north, which was directly against the wind and the sea. You couldn't run to the east, or the west, because you would run out of water. Shoal water trapped us in a configuration like the shape of the letter, "U," or the shape of a horseshoe. I had to keep her going to the north because I wasn't sure how close I was to the Cultivator Shoal. There was deep water just on the west side of the Cultivator Shoal, but I couldn't risk turning for it because the Cultivator blocked us, this is the reason why the sounding machine was so critical. We had to push to the north to get above the horseshoe to escape the trap. I needed the sounding machine to check the charts, and give me an idea of where I was, and how much water was under the boat. It was critical to know where we were on the banks. I wanted to take the boat out to 120 or 130-fathoms. I knew that if I could get to this depth, I would be far enough above the horseshoe to be able to swing the boat off to the southwest and be able to clear the Cultivator Shoal.

A lot of boats have been lost in my time in the area between the Cultivator Shoal and Georges Shoal by staying too long, and then not being able to get out of there. At about 11:00 p.m., on Thursday, or 19-hours since I came up from the aft cabin, we were getting readings of 122 to 124-fathoms. Ronnie asked me; "Do you still want to keep pushing to the north, Captain?" I said; "Yes I do." Ronnie and I hadn't talked for hours. He was handling the wheel, and I was controlling the speed of the boat with the throttle. There was no need for idle chatter, as we were all focused on getting out of this trouble, with our lives. I was very concerned that when we were coming down the back side of a large wave, our boat speed might get too fast, and we could "pitchpole." This is a condition where you bury the bow of the boat into the next wave in the series, and the speed and momentum of the boat somersault the boat over, and you are done.

When we got to 128-fathoms, I was ready to swing her before the wind. The course I was going to have to use to swing by the Cultivator Shoal, off the port side of the boat, was nothing under southwest. I also needed to stay, as best I could, before the wind, or that is, with the wind coming from directly behind us. The minute you ran her more to the starboard, or west, you got more beam or quarter to the sea, and that is a configuration that I wanted to avoid. In these big seas, it could cause us to be hove down again. This meant that I had to be sure that I was in deep enough water to steer a course that would allow me to, "run before the wind," and still be able to clear the shallow water of the Cultivator Shoal (the left spoke of Neptune's Trident) off to our port side. So, the course had to be just right, too far one way, or the other, and we ran the risk of running out of water on the port side or risked being hove down again, on the starboard side.

With the wind now blowing from the northeast, I needed to run a compass course of nothing under southwest. When we swung her before the wind, she buried herself, and I mean like a submarine. She put the bow entirely underwater, and this was when we took a lot of water into the foc'sle; water just poured down through the ventilator shaft. When this happened, the sea water extinguished the fire in the stove and put water up to the lockers. The lockers are about a foot and a half higher than the deck in the foc'sle. The men trapped in the foc'sle had no vision of what was happening topside. We had no way to communicate with these men. They had been riding out this storm with no way of knowing our progress, and they were taking a beating down below for more than twenty hours. When this water came down on them, they were sure it was all over, and the boat was sure to sink at any moment.

After we made the turn and had the boat running before the wind, I was looking for 46 or 47-fathoms. After over an hour of run time, we came down from 128-fathoms to 47-fathoms, and I knew that if we could hold that depth for thirty minutes, we would be on our way out of danger. I would then be able to pinpoint where we were on the bank from these depth readings, and this is known as "Dead Reckoning Navigation," as taught to me as a young boy, by my father. Knowing where we were, would allow me to plot a course that would take us to safety. Every time that I got a sounding that was the depth that I was looking for, I was as a happy as a kid at Christmas. Ronnie would look at me and say; "Cap is that good?" and I'd say; "So far so good, but we need to run another half hour to be sure. If we keep getting these soundings, you won't have to ask me, you'll know by looking at my face." We ran her down the bank until we got near the bottom of the Great Round Channel. Finally, I said; "Ron, we're going to swing her around and heave her to." This was around 5:00 a.m., the next morning, Friday, November 16th, or about 25-hours since I had come up from my bunk.

We now had time to assess the damage that we had incurred. The *Venus* was brand-new, she was only two months old. We had an eight-man life raft attached to the roof of the pilothouse. Big stainless-steel straps ran across it to hold it in place, and the straps were bolted down to the pilothouse roof. These straps were five inches wide. The life raft was gone, it was ripped out of its securing straps when she was hove down, and that raft has never been seen since. We had a wooden dory on top of the pilothouse, and it was gone as well. We had two lobster boxes on the port side, well aft. They were both ripped from the deck of the boat when she went down, and they were both gone. One of the lobster boxes took part of the lazzerette with it when the lobster box went over the side, and this was also where the toilet was located, so it was gone as well. One good feature of this boat, being a new boat built by Gamage is that she had a camel-back. Because of this camel-back, it was possible to move from the engine room to the pilothouse without going out on deck, and this was important because it allowed the engineer, and myself, to make it to the pilothouse. During the height of the storm, going out on deck would have been nearly impossible. The camel-back contributed to our survival because it allowed the engineer to go back and forth, from the engine room to the pilothouse. When we got the boat stopped, our priority was to check on the condition of the men in the foc'sle. We hadn't seen these men in over twenty-five hours. I was very concerned about them, and I prayed that they had survived this ordeal while being isolated below. I immediately sent two men down to the foc'sle, to contact our four shipmates and to report back on their condition. I was sure that we had taken water down into the foc'sle. One of them came back immediately and said; "The men below are a little beat up, but they are okay, and you can't imagine what a mess we've got down forward." The four men were happy to see us, but they were well bruised and banged up. I was very relieved to find out that the men in the foc'sle were alive and had not been seriously injured. I can't imagine what it felt like to be down below for twenty-five hours, with no idea or vision of what our situation was topside. Pots and pans were all over the floor. Anything that was stored in the cabinets flew out of those shelves when she went over and smashed all over the foc'sle. Broken dishes, and coffee cups all smashed to pieces. Glass jars of mayonnaise and jam had flown out of the cabinets and shelves, and hit the side of the hull, and were smashed to pieces. Anything that was movable was thrown about; the stove was out; the Shipmate stove was bolted down with turnbuckles to keep it from moving. It was still in place as it should be, but the seas we took had sent enough water into the foc'sle to douse the fire out in the stove. I could see that everything that had been on deck that was movable had been washed overboard, it was all gone. We hadn't had anything to eat for over twenty-four hours; I knew that we were in bad need of nourishment, and it had to be something we could make quickly. I told one of the men in the pilothouse to go down forward and if possible to make toast, with butter, and a big pot of coffee. Get it all together and bring it back up here. After the ordeal we had been through, with nothing to eat for over a day, I knew we would eat like hungry wolves. The men now worked on the stove, and they eventually got it re-lit. They made the toast and coffee, and it tasted like the finest meal I had ever eaten.

Before this day, I had only known of two boats in my career that had been, hove down at sea, and returned to tell about it. One boat was fishing down in Norfolk, Virginia. We were fishing down that way also, and Pa took me over to see it, this was when I was a young man before I went, skipper. Her name was the F/V *Clinton*, and she was from New Bedford. When she went down her mast went into the water, and the mast fetched up on her nets that they had been carrying on deck. She lay at the dock in Portsmouth, Virginia, with the net hanging from her mast cross-tree. Down in the engine room, the ceiling was all covered with crude oil. The *Clinton* was a total wreck. My father brought me over to see her so that I would realize what it is like when you get hove down.

The other boat was the F/V *Huntington & Sanford*, a scalloper, out of New Bedford, and owned by Mr. Josh Murphy, Senior. When she was hove down the skipper was a Norwegian fella they called "Black Jack," a very able and experienced captain. The *Huntington & Sanford* righted herself and made it back to New Bedford. The stove was lit when she was hove down, and the covers from the stove came loose and fell into the bunk of a young man, who I knew very well, his name was Lawrence Vincent. They had to get him ashore, as fast as they could, for medical treatment. Lawrence had third-degree burns, but he survived this incident, and he later went back fishing. When a boat goes down like that on her side, usually all your storage batteries go out, and then the lights go out. The lights on the *Clinton* went out in the foc'sle. I talked to some of the men who were down in the foc'sle when she went down, and they said water was coming down through the ventilator shaft and they thought that they were gone for sure. It's bad enough if you can see what you're doing, but when it's pitch-black dark, it's impossible. The men on the *Clinton* were in their bunks, it was dark, and anything loose was flying around in the foc'sle like missiles. I'm sure it was a horrible scene for the men who were trapped there. The lights stayed on when the *Venus* was hove down, but otherwise, the scene in the foc'sle was very similar. A scene that is hard to imagine and a very unnerving event even for experienced fishermen. A near death experience for everyone aboard.

We arrived home in New Bedford, and we took out our trip of fish. Then we took the boat over to Kelly's Shipyard, in Fairhaven, to arrange for repairs. All the electronic gear had to go to the repair shop, as they were all full of salt water. I talked with the men, and I told them that Captain Larsen was in the hospital recovering from his injuries and that he had asked me to take the boat out myself on the next trip. The boys were well shook-up by the experience that they had just survived. They needed a little time to get over the ordeal. The crew was made up of seasoned Norwegian fishermen, all veterans of the banks, men who had been on the water all their lives, damned good men, their ancestors were Vikings. The crew of the *Midnight Sun* were also seasoned Norwegian fishermen and friends of my crew. Many of the Norwegians in the New Bedford fishing fleet are from the same area in Norway, so these friendships and family ties have deep roots. Fishermen, in general, are somewhat superstitious, and the men saw these two events, in sister ships as somehow being linked. They felt that they had been spared, while their friends on the *Midnight Sun* had not been so fortunate. We talked things over at one of the waterfront bars. There was a feeling that perhaps they shouldn't push their luck, maybe they should move on to another boat. The real issue that the crew had was that they felt that the owner had made a bad decision. They couldn't understand why he stayed near the shoals, instead of running off to the safety of deeper water. When they heard from another member of the crew, who was in the pilothouse at watch change that night, that I had advised Captain Larsen not to stay, but to jog off to the west'ard in case the storm intensified, they lost their trust in the owner's decision making. I told them that Tommy made his decision based on a bad weather forecast and that this could happen to anyone. In fact, many other New Bedford captains had been fooled by this faulty weather forecast. It was a judgment call, the type of decision a captain makes hundreds of times. It was just that the weather forecast was so far wrong, that it became a disaster for everyone who was on the bank that night. The crew felt that the owner had put money above their lives. The sea bags were going ashore; the entire crew said they were going to quit the boat. I thought they might change their minds after a couple of days ashore. I didn't blame them, but there was nothing I could do. I was almost ready to do the same thing, but Christmas was coming, and I needed the money. So, I stayed for another trip which would be the sixth fishing trip of the *Venus*. We had done very well in this boat; we had some nice trips. But, I was almost ready to stop going to the Northern Edge of the bank myself.

The owner was supposed to spend some time in the hospital, but he was only there for a couple of days. He didn't realize that the crew held him responsible for their ordeal. When the crew saw him back around the boat, this was the straw that broke the camel's back. They wanted no part of returning to sea with him in command. They were not going to come back. So, we had to hire a new crew to man the boat, and this was a little difficult because everyone on the waterfront heard what had happened. However, this boat was a money maker, and we were soon able to find fishermen who were hungry for a site on a money-making boat. Fishermen are money motivated.

I lost a good friend that night. We left Kelly's Shipyard together, and both boats were built at the same shipyard in Maine. Captain Magne Risdal, was the skipper and owner of the *Midnight Sun*, and he was a friend of mine. Magne was to the south of me in the storm, he was scalloping, and we were dragging. The *Midnight Sun* was about 50-miles to the south of our position. I don't know what happened there, but I know what the conditions were like at my position, and since he was less than 50-miles from me, I have a good idea of what Magne was fighting. The *Midnight Sun* was lost with all hands, eleven-men total, and it was a terrible loss for our fishing community.

I know what it is to lose men at sea. I had a brother who was a U.S. Navy Seabee in World War II; he was at Saipan and Guam. He had been working in the Charlestown Navy Yard as a rigger, building and repairing Navy ships. His job was declared to be critical to the war effort, so he was deferred from joining the military. This was the same for fishermen, our jobs were declared as being crucial to the war effort. People were kidding Herbie about not joining up, so he got mad and went down and joined the Navy. Herbie didn't have to go, he had a critical civilian job. He was assigned to the 13th Seabees Special, and after training, he shipped out to the Pacific. My brother survived the war and came home, only to be lost at sea with my brother-in-law. They had a total of eleven-men on that boat, her name was the F/V *Doris Gertrude*. She was lost in January of 1955, with all hands. It's bad enough for a wife to lose her husband, but she knows that this is the business, and this is the risk, but it's the kids. How do you explain it to the kids? How do you explain it to the young children, that their father got in his truck, like he always did, to go down to the fishing pier to make a trip of 8 or 10-days, but this time he'll never come home? In the case of my brother, he had a son and a daughter, and his wife was pregnant with another son. My brother-in-law had two young boys at home. This is the way of the sea and fishing, you leave home, and you never know if you're coming back. I never left my home without giving my wife and my children a kiss. We said nothing, no premonitions, that was it. We all knew the score. Some things are better left unsaid.

The next trip that we took out the *Venus*, we got in trouble with her icing up. The owner was back on board. The conditions were cold, and the boat was making a substantial amount of ice. The boat was acting very cranky. She would roll to port and hesitate before she would slowly come back up, and with us making ice, and after our experience on the last trip, this was very unnerving. I guessed at what the problem was, and I was sure that it all went back to when she was hove down. I figured that the ballast must have moved. I asked the owner if the ballast was all cemented down, and he said that it was. I knew from the way the boat was acting that it couldn't be. I knew that the ballast must have moved during the knockdown. I told the owner that we needed to stop fishing, as I was afraid the boat was going to capsize. I ran the *Venus* up under the lee of Cape Cod, so we could hack the ice off her, and wait for conditions to improve before we went back to fishing. We made for the back side of the Cape, and when we set out the anchor she rolled heavily to port, I didn't think she was going to come back up, but the anchor caught, and she finally did come back level. We later finished the trip without further incident.

When we got back home, we knew that we had to inspect the ballast. Captain Larsen went under the water tank and had a look. He found that 5,000-pounds of ballast had moved, and it was now jammed up against the port side toward the bow of the boat. It had moved out of position when we were hove down, and that was why she was hesitating when she rolled to port; the boat was out of design balance. We hired four lumpers from the fish pier to assist us in correcting this ballast problem. We moved the 5,000 pounds of ballast that were on the port side forward, and we moved it aft and centered, where it was designed to be located. This repair made this boat behave as she should. This imbalance complicated things during the storm, I knew she wasn't handling correctly, but I never said anything to the men while we were going through the storm. I hoped I was wrong and there was no need to unnerve the crew further while we were fighting the storm. Adding one more worry would have served no purpose, but after what happened on the next trip, I knew she wasn't acting right. It amazed me that this boat, even with her ballast out of position, had fought her way through the worst storm I ever encountered, and brought us home. The *Venus* was a great boat, and I felt that if my arms we long enough, I would wrap them around her, and give her a hug. I loved this boat, and she saved my life, she was the "Finest Kind."

In November of 1962, I used every bit of skill and judgment that I was taught by my father to save the *Venus*. He was a wonderful man, and he was very skilled in boats. He had sailed on big sailing ships as a young man. I had a lot of help in bringing the *Venus* out of the place we were in; I don't think that anybody, including myself, could ever do that again. We had a one in a million chance of making it out of that area of Georges Bank, and we hit the jackpot, we were rewarded with our lives. But, I know that somebody was helping me along. I could feel my father's presence, and I could hear his voice in my head encouraging me, as I thought of some of the skills that he had taught me. There's no question in my mind; I know the good Lord and my father were there with me. We didn't beat the storm, but it didn't beat us either, it was a draw. We all came away with even more respect for our boat, the men who built her, and for the power of the sea.

- Captain Louis A. Doucette, Jr.

In 2004, after I had written the short story of my father's experience aboard the *Venus*, I sat down with him to discuss the story in further detail. Forty-two years had passed since he survived this storm, and I wondered if he had any additional thoughts and insight on this story.

I first asked my dad to elaborate on the exchange that he had with Captain Larson at watch change, at midnight, on November 15th, 1962. The following is his answer:

"A few minutes before midnight, Captain Larsen came into the pilothouse from his stateroom. He observed that the weather was getting nasty. We discussed the weather forecast, and Captain Larsen declared; "Looks like it's getting too rough to fish, what do you think Louie?" I agreed that it was time to secure the deck and get the men below for the night, and since the weather forecast called for better weather in a few hours, we both decided that this was the correct decision to make." Captain Larsen said; "I think I'll run her into the edge, just let her lay, and ride this weather out until it breaks." I replied; "I don't think that's a good idea, Tommy. The tide has just turned to the south, and this wind is building from the north. If we do that, and it gets blowing harder, the wind and the tide could have us down on top of the Cultivator and Georges Shoal in 30-minutes, and that would be a bad place to be if this weather forecast is wrong. I'd suggest that after this tow, you steam her off to the west for two or three hours, and then you can let her lay. This way you'll be well clear of the shoals and have plenty of deep water in the channel to ride it out." My father told me that he just had a feeling that the weather forecast was wrong. The wind was piping up fast during his watch, and because they were fishing in the most dangerous part of Georges with a northerly wind, something gave him a bad feeling. This is called experience and instinct, honed over more than 25-years of going skipper on boats, at the time of this storm. My father turned over the watch to Captain Larsen and made his way to the aft cabin, and his berth. After storing his gear, he climbed into his bunk and was soon asleep. It had been seven days since they had left New Bedford, and he was exhausted.

While my father was sleeping, Captain Larsen was in command, and he was taking stock of the situation. After reviewing the information from the last weather report, and since the wind was now blowing at the speed that was predicted by the Weather Bureau to be the peak strength, he surmised that this was as bad as it was going to get. He concluded that it had come on earlier than predicted, and it was now going to drop in intensity a little sooner than the weather report had predicted. If true, this would mean that they could resume fishing sometime soon. The *Venus* was coming to the end of the union mandated eight days of fishing before returning to port. The eight-day rule was made by an agreement between the Fisherman's Union and the boat owners. Since this agreement would mean that the *Venus* would be required to turn for home soon, and since the fishing was so good in this area, Captain Larsen concluded that the worst of the weather was past them. He based this on the weather report, and if they could let the boat lay in place, they could then resume fishing in a few hours and get a few more tows in, before having to turn for New Bedford. These were reasonable conclusions, and good fishing strategy if the weather forecast was correct. It was not. The current weather conditions were terrible, but it was going to get much worse. In the next few hours the wind quickly exceeded 100-mph from the north, and when the tide turned to the north, you had the classic opposing forces that create large waves. That being tide running up against and opposing the wind. This condition builds big powerful seas. These sea conditions were similar, to those that the schooner *Curlew* faced earlier in the Gulf Stream, near Bermuda. But, to make things even worse, the shoals were just south of the *Venus*, and this made the conditions extremely dangerous. Neptune's Trident was just south of their position waiting to snag any boat that dared to enter his territory.

I asked my father, why did the crew quit the boat, and why did everyone seem to blame Captain Larsen for this near-death experience? Dad was clear in his answer. He said, "We all blamed Captain Larsen because he was the captain, and the captain is responsible for everything that happens on a vessel at sea, both good and bad. I was upset with him because I had strongly suggested that he move away from the shoals at midnight, and he did not take my advice. We were all shaken and emotional, we had come close to being lost at sea, and we were looking for someone to blame. However, looking back on this event after many years, I can now say that the real cause was simply the intensity of this weather, it was unlike anything that I had ever experienced in my fifty-years of going to sea. The second cause was the fact that we received no warning that a storm of this magnitude was headed our way. If we had been warned by the weather service, even by a few hours, we could have prepared the boat and found deep water to ride it out. Every boat out on Georges that night was caught unaware, and we were lulled to sleep by an inaccurate weather forecast. Captain Larsen wasn't the only one who was fooled by the weather report. In fact, this weather report influenced Tommy's decision to stay in place. The weather report that was broadcast at 11:10 p.m. would make you believe that the moderate storm that was forecast, was on its way by us. Looking back at these things, I can admit that we were a little hard on Captain Larsen, he was a good fisherman and a friend. He was deeply affected by this incident, and to me, he was never quite the same after this storm."

A captain carries a heavy burden to make prudent decisions while at sea, he must balance safety with the need to catch fish so the trip can be profitable. A captain who doesn't operate a profitable boat will be replaced. Now on this trip Captain Larsen was both the captain, and the boat owner, and this made the pressure on him even more intense. Tommy had just taken on the debt of over one million dollars to build the *Venus*, so he carried an immense burden on this night.

My father continued; "Even though Captain Larsen was injured during the knockdown, he had the presence of mind to turn over his new boat to me, because he realized he was unable to continue to skipper the boat at that moment. This was a courageous thing to do, and it was critical to our survival."

This is an interesting point, and it speaks volumes about how Captain Doucette was trained by his father. This is an absolute tenant of the sea; "The Captain is the Captain," his commands are law, there is no debate. A vessel at sea is not a democracy, it is a dictatorship, and it must be this way, especially in a tight spot, because the captain must make the critical decisions, and there is no time for debate. The captain is in charge. I gave my father, Sebastian Junger's book, The Perfect Storm when it first came out, and he thought it was excellent and that the author had done a good job. My niece took him to see the movie of the same name, and he was not too happy with how Hollywood portrayed the interaction between the captain and the crew of the F/V *Andrea Gail*. The scene where the crew is arguing and debating with the captain he found to be ludicrous. "I never saw any such thing on any boat I was ever on, nor would I tolerate any such shenanigans from any crew."

I had the first-hand experience with my father, concerning this rule of the sea being, "The Captain is the Captain." We were crossing Buzzards Bay after exiting Woods Hole on our way back to New Bedford, in my 30-foot sloop rigged sailboat. We had spent the weekend in Edgartown, on Martha's Vineyard, with my friend, John Bowman, as the third member of the crew. I had the GPS up running a course back to New Bedford, but I was steering the boat manually. It was an overcast, foggy dark day, and John was down below at the chart table watching the radar, looking for any possible traffic as we crossed Buzzards Bay. I noticed that the GPS indicated that I should be steering a course more to the northwest, but my instincts told me I was right, and the machine was wrong, a big mistake on my part. I thought I was heading toward a buoy that I wanted to pass to starboard. When I didn't see my mark, I looked over to port and saw a buoy some distance away that looked like the one I was aiming for but on the wrong side. Out of curiosity, I asked my father, who was observing this entire episode with hawk-like intensity, if that was indeed my mark. He said; "Captain, are you asking for my assistance?" I said; "What?" He said again; "Captain, do you require my assistance?" I thought to myself, oh I get it. So, I replied, "Yes Captain, I am requesting your assistance, am I headed for New Bedford?" He said: "No, New Bedford is up there, exactly where that fancy machine of yours is pointing." He was pointing to the northwest, which was exactly the direction where the GPS said I should be going. I said; "Why didn't you tell me that I was heading wrong?" He said: "This is your boat, and you're the captain, it is not my place to interfere with the running of your boat. I am not the captain of this vessel, you are!" Even at our advanced ages, he was teaching me. I always wondered if he would have let me pile up on some rocks if I hadn't asked for his help. I wasn't sure how far he would be willing to go, to teach me about navigation and being the captain. But, this was a rule of the sea, as he had been taught by his father, a man who had sailed all over the world. "The Captain is the Captain; there is no debate."

So, turning over of the command of the *Venus* was a pivotal moment, and it was critical to the survival of the boat and her crew. I asked dad what he would have done if the injured Captain Larsen had not relinquished command. He said, "Tommy was a good man, and he made a courageous decision to turn the boat over to me. But, we were in grave danger, if he hadn't, we probably would have had to take over, because he was just not able to skipper the boat at that moment, he was injured. Thankfully, that wasn't necessary."

I next discussed the subject of being hove down at sea, I was curious to find out what he was thinking in those moments when he realized that he was hove down. He told me the following; "I was talking to Jack and I could feel the boat rolling heavily, and in the next instant she went over hard on her port side, and I knew instantly that we were hove down. I knew right then that the odds were high that we were going to die. Even though I was in the aft cabin below deck, I could visualize what things probably looked like, if you were looking down at the *Venus* from above. I knew that the waves had to be huge, and the winds had to be blowing at hurricane force to cause this to happen. I knew the *Venus* was now in the most vulnerable position that a ship can be in. I knew that at least some of her keel was out of the water and most probably her mast was in the water. I was calculating the odds that she would right herself, because there was nothing we could do in those minutes that she was capsized, except wait and pray and have faith our boat would shrug this off and get back on her feet. I loved this boat, and I was confident that she would fight her way back up. However, I also knew that four things could happen next and three of those four possibilities were dire and fatal.

One, she can continue to turn over and go upside down, known as "turning turtle," to the 180-degree, or 6 o'clock position, then fill with water and sink. Second, she can lie in the knockdown position and fill up with water, and sink. Third, she gets hit with another breaking wave, while lying on her side, which will make her "turn turtle" and sink. Or fourth, the weight of her keel and the righting momentum of her design can flip her back on her feet, to the zero-degree position, or 12 o'clock position and you live, at least for a while. As you can see, when a boat gets hove down, most of the next possible things that will happen are fatal. Your chances of recovery are only one out of four possibilities, and the odds are not good that you will survive."

I then asked my father to explain to me why some, "so-called experts," and later a federal judge, had said in the newspaper that the correct tactic to take in a storm of this type, was to "lay to" or to "heave the boat to" in these storm conditions. My father's response was quick; "If we had let the boat "lay to" in the location and conditions that I found us in at 4:00 a.m. on November 15th, I would not be sitting here right now talking with you, I would be dead."

The term, "letting her lay," refers to a condition of "heaving the boat to," and this is a deliberate act of seamanship to let a boat ride out rough weather. This can be accomplished on a sailboat by placing the mainsail in one position and backwinding the jib, to allow the boat jog along at a slow speed with its bow pointing into, but slightly off the wind to ride out bad weather. In a fishing boat, this can be done by positioning the bow in the same type of configuration and using the engine and/or a riding sail to accomplish the same jogging motion. The other way to accomplish this in a sailboat, or a fishing vessel, because they are deep keel boats is to, "let her lay beam to the sea," and ride the waves like a duck. My father explained that is was not an option on the *Venus*, because, on this night, they were dangerously close to very shallow water, just to the south of their position. The wind and the waves were pushing the boat towards these shoals. He knew that if the weather conditions became more severe than predicted, they would need to get away from the shoals and find deep water if they were going to survive. He also felt that in this storm, the sea and wind conditions were so severe that laying beam to the sea was not a practical option in any depth of water.

The last item that we discussed was what was he thinking might have happened to the men who were trapped in the foc'sle. He said; "Well we had no contact with these men for over 24-hours, and I was concerned about what may have happened to them. I knew that we must have taken a large amount of water down through the ventilator shaft when we turned the boat to run down the channel. I kept thinking about the men that I spoke to on the F/V *Huntington & Sanford* in Virginia after she had been hove down and made it back to port. I was busy battling the storm, but I was worried about what we might find when we got the boat stopped. It was bad topside, but at least we could see what was happening and gauge our chances, they were blind to our progress. They were down below, and they were along for the ride, and there was nothing that they could do, except hang on. I knew they were enduring a horrible ordeal that lasted 25-hours. I was afraid that we were going to find these men badly injured at the least, and perhaps even dead. When I got the boat stopped, I sent two men forward to check on these men, and I was holding my breath until they came back to the wheelhouse and reported that they had survived. It was a huge relief."

Arne Edvardsen was one of these men in the foc'sle, and he told his daughter, Kirsten Bendiksen, and his son-in-law, Captain Reidar Bendiksen, that when the boat made the turn and water was pouring down the ventilator shaft, they were sure that the boat was going down. It was at this moment that the men in the foc'sle all shook hands and said their goodbyes to each other. An experience that is hard to imagine, but again an example of the courage of the New Bedford fishermen. I can imagine a similar scene taking place on a Viking ship, somewhere crossing unknown oceans centuries before, playing out in much the same way. The Norwegian fishermen are a stoic and courageous lot; it's in their genetic make-up. They are fine shipmates, excellent seamen, and as calm a bunch as you will ever see in a crisis. My father always spoke highly of the temperament and coolness of the Norwegian fishermen in an emergency. They seemed to take it all in stride like they had seen it all before. They also are not a boastful group, and they have never been accused of being overly verbose. I am sure that they have lots of stories to tell, but they tend not to talk about their close calls.

To the men, who were aboard the *Venus*, on November 15th, in 1962, there was no question that the man who brought them home alive was Captain Doucette.

My brother told me a story that occurred a few years after this storm. Al was walking down the dock with our father, at the D.N. Kelly Shipyard in Fairhaven, when he saw a large man approaching them with a big smile on his face. This man walked up to my father and said; "Captain Louie, how are you?" He then grabbed my dad in a bear-hug and lifted him right off the ground. When dad was finally released, he introduced my brother to Ronnie Lahey, the Newfoundlander who was at the wheel on the *Venus*, on that fateful night in 1962. Ronnie then turned and shook hands with my brother and said; "If it weren't for your father, I and everyone else who was aboard the *Venus* would be dead, he saved our lives."

Arne Edvardsen told this same thing to his daughter, Kirsten Bendiksen.

Captain Louis Doucette, Jr.

New Bedford Fishing Captain

The man who brought the F/V *Venus* home from her near-fatal encounter with an Extra-Tropical Cyclone at Neptune's Trident!

My Dad

"The Finest Kind"

The following four photos are of a chart that belonged to my father. The notes which are in red ink were made by him when he was explaining this story to me. You will notice the following notes in red ink.

- Bottom right corner –
  - Visibility – 0 (zero)
  - North later NE – Wind started out from the North then later from the Northeast (Classic Nor'easter)
  - Nov 1962 – November 1962 (we reviewed this chart in 1995)
  - 104 Mile per Hour Winds

- Middle Right – Nov 1962 – *Midnight Sun* – Lost (11)

- Middle left –
  - 5 a.m. – position of the *Venus* at 5:00 a.m. on November 15, 1962 – right between the Cultivator Shoal on the left and Georges Shoal on the right.
  - Dual red lines indicate the course that they took to escape Neptune's Trident. The reason there are two-course lines is that he did not know for sure his actual course line, but it was somewhere between these two lines.

- Middle Left lower –
  - The dotted red line indicates the course they ran after getting clear of Neptune's Trident when they were "running before the wind" to the safety of the Great South Channel.
  - 5 a.m. – This is the spot where they felt safe enough in the deep water, to "heave the boat to," to check on the damage and the men who were trapped in the foc'sle. It was now 25-hours since this ordeal began.

- You will notice that I have placed a set of parallel navigation rules on the first photo to hold the chart in place. These parallel rules belonged to my father, and they were aboard the *Venus* on the night of this storm. My father brought his navigation tools down to my sailboat, on a summer day when he was 86-years old. I will never forget that he handed me his navigation kit and said, "I'd like you to have these, they served me well for many years. I won't be needing them anymore." I was grateful that he entrusted these items to me, but I was also sad because he was admitting the fact that he would never be taking a boat out to sea again. I have kept these parallel rules next to me, during the four-year odyssey of researching and writing this book. They have given me strength and helped me persevere, as every time I hold them, I can feel his presence encouraging me to tell his story.

Chart #1

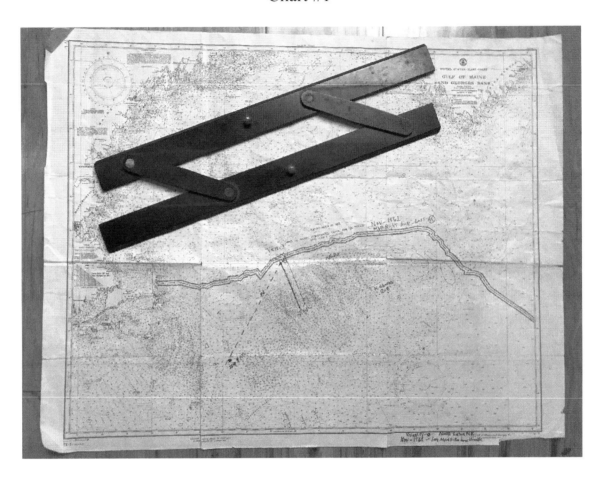

175

Chart #2 – Close-up

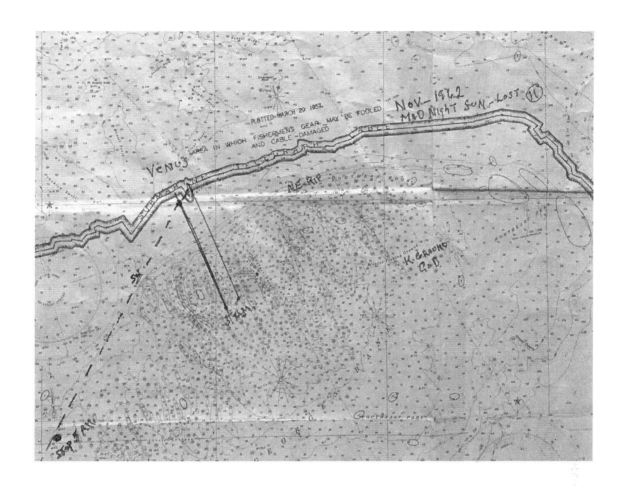

Chart #3 – Neptune's Trident

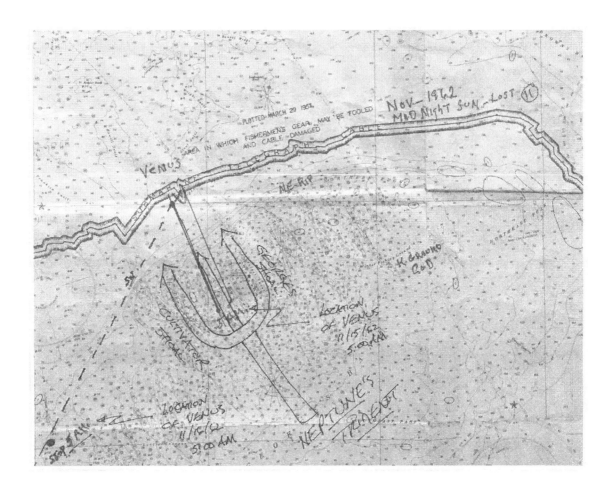

176

Chart #4 – Start & Stop Positions

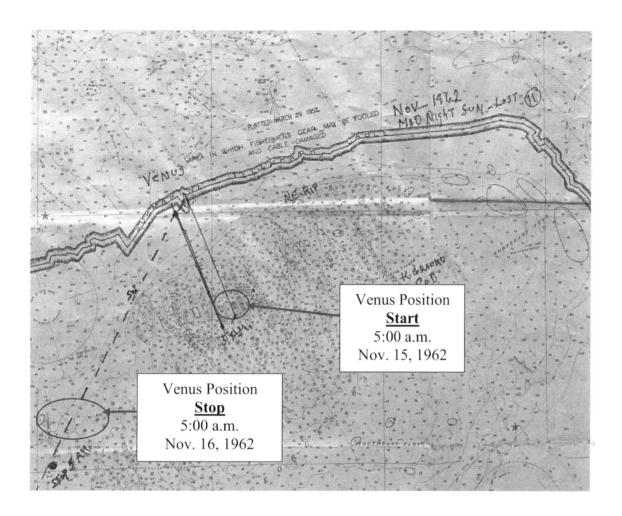

Venus Position
Start
5:00 a.m.
Nov. 15, 1962

Venus Position
Stop
5:00 a.m.
Nov. 16, 1962

Bound for Edgartown on Martha's Vineyard,
in a rain storm aboard the S/V Fleur de Lis.
My father is at the helm and I am observing.

This was when I was taught,
"The Captain is the Captain; There is No Debate."

THE F/V *GAY HEAD*
1940

IN WITH A TRIP OF FISH AND ALL ICED UP
AT KELLY'S SHIPYARD – FAIRHAVEN, MASSACHUSETTS
A YOUNG CAPTAIN LOUIS A. DOUCETTE, JR. (4th from left)
Age 29

United States Weather Bureau Chart
November 15, 1962
1:00 P.M.

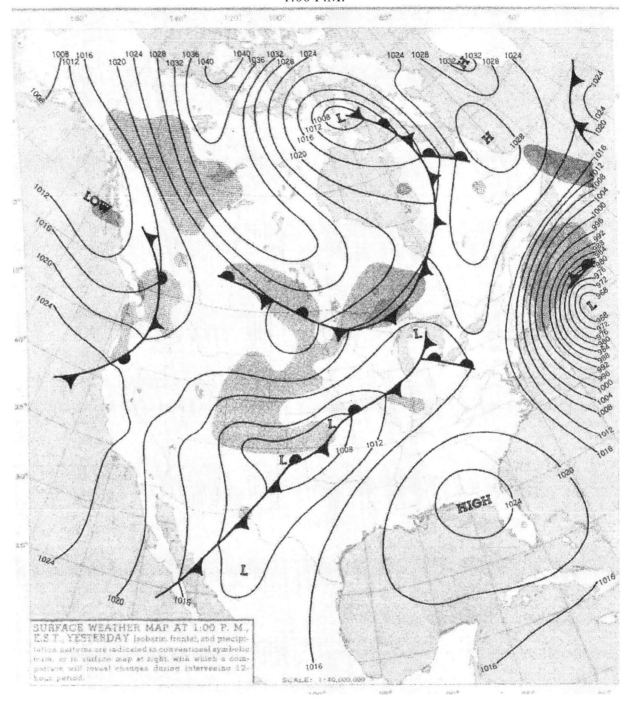

THE MONSTER ARRIVES
FULL BLOWN BOMBOGENISIS
ON GEORGES BANK

Chapter 20

<u>The Storm – Neptune's Nor'easter</u>

The United States Weather Bureau Chart for November 15, 1962, at 1:00 p.m., clearly shows the center of the low-pressure system sitting directly over Georges Bank. This low-pressure system recorded a reading of 968-millibars at its' center. Also, notice the very tight bands of pressure rotating around the center. The closer the bands, the higher the wind speed. You will also notice two high-pressure systems sitting just above and below the Georges Bank storm, and further three low-pressure systems behind the high-pressure systems, squeezing them towards our storm. Wind runs from high pressure towards low pressure and moves with the rotation of the earth in accordance with the Coriolis forces, and the jet stream, and this is nature's way of trying to restore equilibrium in the atmosphere. Nature has built a bomb, and that bomb is exploding directly over Georges Bank.

A low-pressure reading of 968-millibars is consistent with a Category-2 Hurricane, with expected wind speeds in the range of, 96 to 110-mph and waves heights of greater than 45-feet. These are significant numbers to remember because in the aftermath of this storm, the fishermen who were on Georges Bank in this storm, will be questioned about the accuracy of their wind speed estimates. Their estimates of 100-mph winds and 50 to 60-foot seas, will be challenged and refuted by the very same Weather Bureau who provided these readings and produced the above chart. A United States District Court Judge will also deny their claims about the intensity of this storm. But the science will prove that the fishermen were in fact very accurate in their estimates, as indicated by the above official United States Weather Bureau chart and data.

Another factor that made this storm more intense was the fact that the "Kria Low," came through this area two days before, with a low-pressure reading of 996-millibars, which would have generated wind speeds in the range of 65 to 75-mph from the north. The "Kria Low" then stalled over the Canadian Maritimes, and continued to funnel northerly winds over Georges Bank, until our "Bomb Storm" hit, which only increased the size of the waves, and these are the reasons why the fishermen were reporting wave heights of 50 to 60-feet.

This storm was not technically a hurricane because it did not form in the tropics. Therefore it was not followed and tracked. This monster storm did not develop until it was just southwest of the island of Bermuda, technically in the mid-latitudes. The storm was in fact what meteorologists today would now call, an Extratropical Cyclone with Explosive Cyclogenesis, a Bombogenesis Storm, or simply a Weather Bomb.

When the New Bedford fishing fleet limped back into port, and after the fishermen had time to decompress from their ordeal, and check in with their fishing friends and associates, anger began to grow among them. The main question being, why didn't we receive some advanced warning from the Weather Bureau? Surely, someone knew this thing was coming. They were all experienced seamen who had weathered many storms, gales, and in some cases multiple hurricanes. But, to a man, they all agreed that this storm was the worst storm that they had ever experienced. The low-pressure readings, the tightness of the low-pressure rings, the constant wind direction from the north and northeast, the extremely high seas, and a drop in low pressure of 24-millibars in twenty-four hours, these things explained why they felt that this was the worst storm of their fishing careers. My father always said that this storm was the only time in his 50-year career that he thought he would not make it home. Why were they caught so unaware? Their anger focused on the inability of the Weather Bureau to issue any advanced warning. They felt that the Weather Bureau had let them down, and it had nearly cost them their lives. As the days passed, and it became apparent that their friends on the Midnight Sun had indeed paid for this mistake with their lives, their anger intensified.

"I just may go to the Weather Bureau in Boston and retire a few of those so-called weather forecasters." Captain Albert Dahl of the F/V *Monte Carlo* was quoted as saying.

And this sums up the feelings of all the fishermen who were out on Georges Bank on November 15th and 16th, in 1962. The fishermen who lived through this extreme storm, held the U.S. Weather Bureau in Boston, responsible for not anticipating and issuing an adequate warning to the fleet.

At 11:00 a.m., on Thursday, November 15, 1962, Captain Albert Dahl and his crew of five men were struggling against 80 to 100-mph winds, with seas reaching 50-feet. Ten minutes later, at 11:10 a.m., the Weather Bureau broadcast, over the WOU ship to shore wave-length radio, a forecast of 40 to 55-mph winds, with seas of 20 to 30-feet. The weather forecast could not have been more out of whack with the reality on Georges Bank.

"This is no picnic that these guys are forecasting for, this is a matter of life and death for us. We depend on their forecast to make life and death decisions." Captain Albert Dahl.

The captains, who were out in this storm, shared the opinion that the Weather Bureau was derelict in their duties, and that they should have provided more warning about this storm, and they were right! The Weather Bureau should have been aware of the carnage that was happening earlier to the south of Georges Bank. The Coast Guard and Navy were involved in rescues all around the island of Bermuda hours earlier. They should have been in better coordination with the Coast Guard. They missed an opportunity on the November 14th, 11:10 a.m. forecast, to warn the fishermen of what was heading their way. The M/V *Captain George* and the schooners *Curlew* and *Windfall* were already in trouble, 800-miles to the south of Georges Bank. The Coast Guard and Navy were already engaged in rescue missions for these vessels. This information was known, but not to the Weather Bureau forecasters in Boston. If the fleet had been issued adequate warning in the Wednesday, November 14th, at 11:10 a.m. forecast, they would have had time to prepare, and if not enough time to return to New Bedford, they could have made for Nantucket, or found deep water with plenty of sea room to ride out this storm.

But even on Thursday, November 15th, in the 11:10 a.m. report, they still had it wrong. The conditions were much worse than the forecast, even then. It was too late to do any good, but it was never the less still wrong. Not by a little, but by a lot.

One fisherman who was out in the storm stated that the Coast Guard had planes flying over the boats and that they could certainly see us bobbing up and down in the storm. Why can't they get that information to the weather authorities in Boston?

As the search for the missing New Bedford scalloper, the F/V *Midnight Sun* continued, Congressman Hastings Keith (R-MA) called for an investigation of the; "Obviously inadequate weather warning system for the fishing fleet."

As criticism of the U.S. Weather Bureau's forecasting of the storm continued, Congressman Keith scheduled a meeting in New Bedford, on Saturday, November 24, 1962, for all interested parties.

Scheduled to attend the meeting were Weather Bureau officials, boat owners, fishing captains, Coast Guard officers and officials of the New England Telephone company.

Congressman Keith emphasized before the meeting that the purpose of the meeting was; "Not to criticize the weather bureau, but for bureau officials to obtain information which will result in revisions of present rules and regulations, or the drafting of legislation, if necessary, to correct conditions." There was some concern that a room full of angry fishermen could get out of hand.

Several captains appealed to Congressman Keith for correction of what they have termed late and often inadequate weather forecasts. Keith discussed the problem with the Assistant Secretary of Commerce, J. Holloman, and was promised the department's full cooperation. Mr. Holloman prepared a letter for Congressman Keith, expressing his concern about this problem. The message said; "We offer this information, together with our pledge of cooperation for you to present at your meeting with fishing interests in New Bedford, on Saturday. Signed; Assistant Secretary of Commerce, J. Holloman."

Mr. Holloman held a position that was created by Congress to coordinate and encourage the proper use of existing facilities in weather forecasting and broadcasting.

Congressman Keith also spoke with Paul Kutchenreuter, Assistant Chief of the Weather Bureau for technical services. Kutchenreuter was formerly in charge of forecasting in Boston, and he was therefore intimately aware of the problems of forecasting for the fishing grounds and the limitations of the Boston Weather Bureau. He expressed the opinion that a lot of good could come out of this meeting.

Captain Dahl and others had called Congressman Keith to complain that the Weather Bureau had failed to predict the intensity of the storm. Fishermen claim that the winds reached 80 to 100-mph, while the Weather Bureau anticipated winds of 35 to 45-mph.

When contacted for comment, the Chief of the Boston Weather Bureau was quoted in the newspaper as saying that he did not believe that winds in the storm exceeded 55-mph. He said claims of stronger winds were probably only estimates.

THEREIN LIES THE PROBLEM!

The fishermen who are stuck out in the weather obviously don't know what they are talking about, just estimates from a bunch of uneducated rough necks. The arrogance of this statement is criminal. Some of these men have in their DNA, the genes handed down to them from Vikings, who roamed the world's oceans when most people thought the world was flat. The genes from the Portuguese explorers, who defined the world. The genes from the Breton fisherman of Northwest France and the genes from the Basques, who ruled the salted codfish market in Europe for hundreds of years. The genes from the English and Irish fishermen, who worked the dangerous North Sea with the Scandinavians, and many others. All men who had salt water in their veins, and who over the centuries paid for that knowledge of the sea, with their ancestor's blood. These fishermen obviously don't know how to evaluate weather conditions. No, that requires a trained meteorologist sitting in an office in Boston, looking at charts and data, some of which is obviously flawed.

In spite, of the comments, by the Chief of the Boston Weather Bureau, winds of 75-mph were recorded at Texas Tower #3, which is located sixty-two miles southeast of Nantucket. However, the head of the Boston office of the U.S. Weather Bureau says; "I don't believe that the wind exceeded 55-mph."

The severity of the storm also caught the Air Force off-guard at Otis AFB, on Cape Cod. An Air Force spokesman said; "The weather forecast at 7:00 p.m., Wednesday, predicted a mild storm with winds of 45-mph. But, during the evening the storm intensified, so that by 7:00 a.m., on Thursday, we were beyond the point of the safe evacuation of the men on the Texas Towers. We left the men on the Towers throughout the storm. If the true nature of the storm had been predicted, we would have evacuated the men."

Chapter 21

NEPTUNE'S ANGER

It was a terrible week for mariners across the globe, as 155-seamen lost their lives due to an unprecedented rash of extreme weather. Also, more than 100-seamen were rescued from vessels that sank or were severely disabled. Beyond the loss of 36-mariners in the Western North Atlantic, the carnage continued throughout the rest of the world during this week. The God's were angered by how careless, and stupid mankind had behaved in coming so close to destroying the planet, with all-out nuclear war. Neptune was their messenger, and he was tasked with displaying the God's displeasure, by creating violent storms at sea, during this week. It was an attempt to enforce the need for humanity to change its' behavior before it was too late.

Forty-eight hours after the storm left the Western Atlantic, the weather system that supported Neptune's Nor'easter made its way across the Atlantic, and extreme weather barreled into Europe, with similarly disastrous results.

The following are stories of accidents that occurred due to this weather system reaching the Eastern North Atlantic of Europe.

ENGLAND

In England, nine people drowned when the fishing coble, *Economy*, found herself in distress off the east coast of England at Seaham Harbour. A coble is a traditional open cockpit fishing boat that has been used for many years in this part of England. The fishing coble had a crew of four men and a nine-year-old boy, who was the son of one of the fishermen. The young boy was out with his dad and his shipmates for a typical day of fishing. They had no reason to expect extreme weather when they set out for the day, and they were fishing close to shore. The storm struck without warning, and soon the fishing coble was in distress. Since they were within sight of land, some townspeople saw the trouble and called for help.

The RNLI Rescue Lifeboat, named the *George Elmy*, with a crew of five men, was alerted and put to sea to rescue the fishermen. The lifeboat crew managed to get all five people safely into the lifeboat, as the fishing coble was sinking, and then they headed back towards Seaham Harbour. When the lifeboat was 200-yards from the town wharf, it was struck by a massive wave and capsized, spilling all ten occupants of the lifeboat into the sea. They all vanished in the blink of an eye, right in front of the townspeople on the beach, who were observing the rescue operation. The only survivor was one fisherman, he was the father of the nine-year-old boy. Nine lives were lost in this mishap, five members of the RNLI lifeboat crew, three fishermen, and a nine-year-old boy. The grief and responsibility that this father must have felt for the death of his young son are hard to imagine.

The Royal National Lifeboat Institution (RNLI), is a charity which maintains lifeboats and trained rescue personnel in 350-locations throughout the United Kingdom. The Seaham Harbour lifeboat, RNLI *George Elmy*, later washed up on the beach and was taken out of service after this disaster. It has now been restored, and it is on display in Seaham, England, as a memorial to the men who lost their lives in this tragic incident.

At the same time, the F/V *Faithful* was in distress off the Farne Islands, seventy miles south of Seaham, in Northumberland, England. Two RNLI lifeboats were launched and went to the aid of the fishermen. The weather was so severe that they were unable to take the men off the fishing vessel. The F/V *Faithful* and the two RNLI Lifeboats decided to anchor the three boats under the shelter of one of the islands, to ride out the storm. A Royal Air Force helicopter was directed to attempt a rescue of the nineteen men if possible. At first, the helicopter was unable to lift off the ground, because the winds were so severe. When it was found that one of the fishermen had a heart condition, the helicopter made another attempt and this time was able to get off the ground and go on to rescue the man with the heart condition. The helicopter took the one man to the hospital in Seahorses, England, and then proceeded back to the rescue site. The storm intensity had increased during this time, and the decision was made to lift the remaining eighteen men and shuttle them to one of the Inner Farne Islands, where they would have to take shelter and wait out the storm. This was completed without incident and no loss of life, but a very close call for all involved.

Meanwhile, off the North Devon Coast, on the west coast of England, the Royal Fleet Auxiliary (RFA) Oil Tanker, the *Green Ranger*, went aground a few miles south of Hartland Point. The Tug *Caswell* was towing the *Green Ranger*, from Plymouth, England to Cardiff, Wales. On Friday night, November 17, 1962, the weather began to deteriorate, and the *Caswell* and *Green Ranger* anchored off Clovelly, England to ride out the storm. On Saturday morning, they restarted the tow, but they encountered even more intense weather and had to drop the tow or run the risk of both vessels sinking. The *Caswell* proceeded to Lundy for shelter.

The *Green Ranger* drifted and eventually went aground on the rocky coast near Hartland Point. The Point is 325-feet high, and it marks the western limit on the English side, of the Bristol Channel. Two lifeboats put to sea, the RNLI *Appledore* and the RNLI *Clovelly* to come to the aid of the seven-man crew of the *Green Ranger*. The *Clovelly* soon became swamped and had to retire back to base. The *Appledore* was able to stay through the night but found it impossible to remove the crew. The following day the seven-man crew were taken off the *Green Ranger* safely by Breeches Buoy.

A fleet of Russian and Polish fishing trawlers was forced to shelter off Folkstone and Hythe, in the Southeast corner of England, due to the storm conditions.

The English Channel ferry service was suspended due to the weather and Scotland was inundated in heavy snow with road and train service disrupted.

This weather is consistent with an Extra-Tropical Cyclone, and very much like the experience that occurred in the Western North Atlantic, forty-eight hours earlier.

SPAIN

The F/V *De Jesus*, a 130-ton Spanish fishing vessel, with a crew of twelve Spanish fishermen vanished. The captain reported that he was taking on water due to the storm conditions. He stated that their location was approximately eight miles from San Sebastian, Spain. The Spanish Navy immediately sent air and sea assets to the scene, but no trace of the *De Jesus* was found.

ITALY

In Naples, the British freighter *Ashanti Palm*, sank after she was ripped from her moorings and smashed against the rocks in gale force winds. Captain Robert Anderson was the last man off the ship out of a crew of 47-men. As Captain Anderson stepped into a lifeboat, he saluted his wrecked ship and watched her sink three minutes later.

ELSEWHERE AROUND THE WORLD THIS WEEK

This week around the globe, Neptune was busy, and an additional ninety-eight mariners were lost due to the weather. The single most substantial loss being the collision of two oil tankers in Japan, with a total loss of forty mariners. The entire 36-man crew of the Japanese gasoline tanker, *Munakata Maru* were killed in a blazing inferno, when their ship caught fire, after a collision with the Norwegian tanker, *Tharald Brovig*, in the narrow Kawasaki Canal, which was shrouded in dense fog, twelve miles from Tokyo. One member of the Norwegian Tanker was killed, and forty-six others were rescued. Three Japanese crew members of a barge were also killed in this incident. The Japanese Tanker was loaded with 950,000 gallons of gasoline at the time of the collision. This accident resulted in a loss of forty seamen.

Neptune was angry, and he was trying to send us a message!

PART IV

THE AFTERMATH

Chapter 22

CONGRESSMAN KEITH'S MEETING

CONCERNING THE WEATHER BUREAU FORECAST

The meeting concerning the inadequate weather forecasting for the fishing industry was held at the New Bedford Free Public Library. This is the downtown building with the Whaleman Statue out front, adjacent to the City Hall. Maybe the lance scared the Chief of the Boston Weather Bureau, or perhaps someone talked sense to him because his story changed from the arrogant stance that he took only days earlier in the newspaper.

Attending were personnel from the United States Weather Bureau, from both Boston and Washington D.C., Coast Guard and Air Force officers, fishermen and fishing captains, boat owners, and Fishermen's Union officials.

The meeting was orderly and cordial, though many fishermen were upset about a forecast that failed to anticipate the hurricane-force storm that raked the fishing grounds.

It was stated by the Chief of the U.S. Weather Bureau, that his office has been unable to provide complete weather forecasts for the Georges Bank fishing grounds, because of limited access to the marine radio channel. The Chief of the Boston Office said; "During any twenty-four-hour period, we give only six minutes of weather predictions directed to the Georges Bank area. He admitted his office failed to correctly predict the intensity and direction of the storm." He emphasized; "That bureau employees were earnestly striving for accuracy, in the bounds of an inexact science. We are unable to put out all the forecasting information that we would like to use. When you only have a three-minute window, twice per day, you try to do the best you can." Solving a problem only starts when you accept that you have a problem. It has been said, that a problem that is defined is halfway to becoming solved. So, it was nice to hear that the Chief of the Boston Weather Bureau, accepted that his office failed to predict the intensity of this storm. But, then he turns around and says, well it's not really our fault, it's the telephone company's fault, because they only give us three minutes, twice per day, to broadcast the weather report for the offshore fishing grounds. If they failed to predict the storm, it wouldn't have mattered if he had an hour to broadcast an incorrect weather report. I've seen managers pass the buck and blame anybody else they can, and say it's not my fault, it's his fault, or my favorite, it's "their" fault. I have seen this tactic employed many times in my management career, and it's the mark of a weak manager. I'm surprised one of the fishermen in the audience didn't run outside, pry the lance off the Whaleman Statue out front, and jab the Boston Weather Bureau Chief in the posterior with it. However, I will agree that weather forecasting, in 1962, was an inexact science. It's easy to look at weather forecasting, as we know it today, and ask, how could they miss this large of a storm? Many of the scientific weather instruments that we take for granted today were not in existence in 1962. The job of weather forecasting for the offshore fishing grounds was undoubtedly more difficult than it is now. However, when you have a storm raging 800-miles south of Georges Bank, in the area around the Island of Bermuda, and the Coast Guard is engaged in rescue missions down there, the Weather Bureau should have had some knowledge of this fact.

Several captains who were out in the storm listed their grievances about forecasts and broadcasting procedures. Ideas were then solicited on how the Weather Bureau could receive more complete information, and how it could be interpreted and relayed to the fishermen with greater frequency. Paul Kutchenreuter, Assistant Chief of the Weather Bureau for Technical Services, in Washington, D.C., conducted the meeting. He was tasked with discussing these suggestions with officials back in Washington when he returns to his office. He will also present a formal report to Congressman Keith, within 21 days on an action plan, and in the meantime, he will initiate whatever procedures are possible in Boston to facilitate better forecasting.

Many of the complaints by the fishermen were also leveled at WOU, the marine channel of the New England Telephone Company. Weather forecasts are compiled and taped at the Boston office and are then broadcast at regular intervals by WOU. The broadcast time is donated by the telephone company as a public service. You can read into this problem that it is all about money, and you would probably be correct. While several weather broadcasts are given over WOU daily, only two are directed to the fishing grounds, and they are of a duration of three minutes each.

The fishermen also complained that the reception is often blurred, and that it often merges with the channel used by the Federal Bureau of Standards, and that the forecasts are very short and lack adequate detail. My father and brother told me that many times when you could not hear the broadcast. The reception was often garbled and unclear. You would then attempt to contact another fishing boat, and inquire if they had listened to the weather report, and ask them what it said? Often, they couldn't hear it either, so you did what fishermen always do, you observed the sea and sky, and you lived by the barometer. The fishermen have always understood that they are out there on their own. The problem being that you come to depend on the official weather forecast, and a flawed forecast can cause you to make bad decisions. One captain stated that it caused him to go against his instincts. Clearly, this is precisely what happened on the F/V *Venus*.

One waterfront official offered the observation; "When the forecast was broadcast live, instead of on tape, the announcer would repeat forecasts, and take pains to emphasize storm forecasts and the possibility of storm conditions developing. He also seemed to have more time. He would often give additional information, such as the highs and lows across the nation, so the captains could do some forecasting of their own. It's too short now."

The District Manager, for the New England Telephone Company, who was in attendance, said it was unlikely that his company would go back to the live broadcast system. He indicated it would probably require four or five additional employees to run the live system, and that the phone company had already made a substantial investment in the automated equipment. It is nice that Mr. Smith told the truth here, but it is frustrating beyond belief. The fact is, the telephone company donated the air-time for a whopping six minutes per day, for the weather forecast that is directed to the fishing fleet. And by the way, we bought some fancy automated equipment to do this job, because we had to employ five or six people to do this work in real-time, and now it only takes one employee. I've been involved in managing manufacturing plants my entire working life, and I understand cost-saving projects probably better than most people. The automation of this service, and the reduction of labor costs to provide it was some managers cost-saving project. I get it, but in 1962, the New England Telephone Company was a monopoly. If you wanted a phone they were the only game in town, you had to get it from them, and you paid what they told you to pay as they had no competition. A lack of competition breeds corporate arrogance. What is the price of the men's lives that depend on your service? These men and their families are also your customers. What value should be placed on the eleven men lives aboard the *Midnight Sun*, who perished in this storm, because the Weather Bureau and the Telephone Company failed them? It's always about money, which many times makes us do the wrong thing, instead of the right thing!

Allow me to use my imagination; I can imagine a scene that may have played out in real life. Perhaps, when the weather forecaster, who missed the storm forecast, or maybe the telephone company manager, who came up with the cost savings idea to make the broadcasting of the weather report more automated. Perhaps, when they got home from work, after complaining to their wife about how hard they had worked that day, and what genius thoughts they had shared with their colleagues, during their long and exhausting workday. They probably then asked, "Honey, what's for dinner?" The wife might have replied, "Oh, I picked up a couple of nice pieces of codfish at the market." To which our managers replied, "Great, that sounds delicious!" In the meantime, the very men who caught that fish are out on the fishing grounds, paying the price for their incompetence and arrogance, while they enjoy their codfish, with a nice glass of white wine, in the warmth and comfort of their home. Even fifty-six years later, it annoys me to no end.

After the comments by the Weather Bureau and the Telephone Company representatives, Congressman Keith should have called timeout and ordered in some buses. He should have loaded everyone present on those buses and reconvened this meeting at the State House in Boston. The meeting should have been set up in plain view of the "Sacred Cod," to remind all the officials present, that it was the codfish and the men who caught them, that built the Commonwealth of Massachusetts. There is a deep meaning in the word commonwealth, it means for the common good of all who reside in this state. In reading the summary of this meeting, it appears that some of those present did not understand or embrace this concept. You can almost feel the arrogance of some of the attendees when reviewing these meeting minutes. Most of the fishermen were not highly educated and were looked down on, as being a bunch of rough necks, a northern maritime version of the famous southern redneck. These men may not have been highly educated, but dumb they were not, especially about ships, the ocean, the weather, and how to catch fish. To dismiss their observations about the weather that they encountered is wrong. These men spend their lives in the weather, on the ocean, and their observations are not "guesstimates." They are based on a lifetime of hands-on experience. These men are also courageous, determined, and extremely loyal to their friends. Just look at Captain Manny Mello, of the F/V *Santa Cruz* as an example. To those who take the time to get to know them, they are indeed good friends to have.

My father dropped out of high school during the Great Depression to go fishing, because his father needed help on the boat. My father was a smart, but uneducated man, but he was a man who valued education. He preached the value of education to me, during my youth, almost every day that I was in his presence. My father was in awe and had respect for educated people; I am sure that this was his motivation for insisting that I receive a college education. He didn't want anyone talking down to me, due to a lack of knowledge; he wanted me to be one of them. This weather forecast meeting has a tone of the educated speaking down to the uneducated. The author, Anthony Brandt, wrote an excellent book called, "The Man Who Ate His Boots," which is the story of the British obsession to find the Northwest Passage, via the Arctic Ocean. It was the "Holy Grail" of nineteenth-century British exploration. In an interview with Amazon, Brandt was asked if these missions were a fool's errand? His response was; "Yes, but the map of the world was blank above 80-degrees north. It was unknown territory to most of the civilized world, and there was a belief that a Northwest Passage existed". However, some already knew better. Those that absolutely knew better were the Whalemen, who chased whales up into the area of Greenland and Alaska, into the Arctic Ocean. Many of the Arctic whalers hailed from New Bedford and London. When the whalers told these explorers that they were wrong, these highly educated gentlemen dismissed them. They were not scientists; they were not gentlemen, they were just commercial fishermen. What did they know? They were just a bunch of uneducated, simple roughnecks. These explorers were educated British gentlemen. So, they ignored the Whalers observations and experience about the Arctic Ocean, and because of it, some of these gentlemen went to their death, and some had to eat their boots to survive, which was a very ungentlemanly act. Perhaps, they should have listened to the uneducated commercial fishermen and respected their practical knowledge. This was the state of the nineteenth-century class system. When reading the minutes of Congressman Keith's meeting at the New Bedford Public Library, you can certainly hear these same undertones, and realize that a class system was still alive and well, in America in 1962, and it cost some good men their lives.

Kutchenreuter, who seems to be one of the few officials who grasps the severity of the problem, proposed that it would be best if a full-time transmitting facility is established that could beam weather information around the clock. He noted that an FM wavelength is used in this manner, in New York and Chicago, to provide this information to vessels in those locations. However, he also noted that this FM signal is a line of sight device, which would not reach from the mainland to Georges Bank. But, it might be possible to use this method, if it was established on one of the Texas Towers. He also urged the fishermen to report their weather observations to the Weather Bureau in Boston, so that this information can be used in preparing the forecasts. Most of the information now used by the bureau comes from the Navy, Coast Guard, and merchant vessels at sea. You can read into this, that the masters of those vessels are licensed, professional captains. Information from the commercial fishermen was not solicited, because they were not educated, gentlemen. More evidence of a class system alive and well, in 1962. It was also suggested by the weather bureau officials that an automated machine be placed on the Texas Towers to gather temperature, barometric pressure, wind velocity and direction. At present the Texas Tower personnel report weather conditions to the Boston Bureau only between 7:00 a.m. and 7:00 p.m., nice convenient gentlemen's hours for the weather bureau employees. The men out on the Texas Towers were members of the United States Air Force; they were on duty 24-hours per day, so gathering the information and relaying it to the Boston Weather Bureau would have been easily accommodated by the Air Force.

Members of the audience also inquired if the Federal Government might consider taking responsibility for a twenty-four-hour forecasting system. Perhaps, placing a weather ship in a strategic Atlantic Ocean area, to gather weather forecasting information and report current conditions.

Congressman Keith indicated that speculation on suggestions offered during the meeting would be premature until Kutchenreuter compiles the formal report. You can read into this comment from the Congressman, that he didn't want to make any promises that he might not be able to keep. The reason being that securing funds for any additional projects might be a problem. It's always about money. But, I give him full credit for understanding the need and trying to get something done to improve the weather forecast for the fishermen.

It is easy to look back at this storm and the woefully inadequate weather forecast, and dissemination of weather information to the fishermen, and other mariners in 1962, and wonder how could this happen? Based on today's technology it seems hard to understand. The Weather Bureau did not have the tools that we have today, so it is not a fair comparison. Weather information was passed along by local meteorologists, from west to east, as the weather moved across the country. This worked well for the mainland of the United States, but it left great masses of the ocean unreported. Today, with weather satellites circling the earth, we see everything in real-time, and there are no weather black-out spots, even across the seas. However, when we look closely at this storm, even with the technology that was available in 1962, you must ask yourself, if the weather was so bad in Bermuda, 800-miles to the south, how was that information not known by the weather authorities in Boston? How was that information not relayed to the fishermen on Georges Bank? If the fishermen had known that a dangerous storm was hitting Bermuda on November 14th, it would have given them time to safely return to port.

The real reason that this information was not available was that it wasn't a priority for the government and weather authorities. The fishermen represented a miniscule percentage of the population. They had no voice and no political clout. As the British Arctic explorers said about the Whalers in the nineteenth century, they were not gentlemen, they were not scientists, they were just commercial fishermen, and in the same way, fishermen are viewed by some as risk-takers who are expendable. I would like to point out, that if not for risk-takers there would be no United States of America. Taking a risk is central to what being an American is all about.

Progress is not possible without risk, the fishermen and other risk-takers like them, are a national treasure, they are not expendable!

Congressman Keith concluded the meeting by saying, "I think this meeting was most productive. Everyone involved now has a clearer understanding of the problems we face. There is a spirit here that I think can correct the shortcomings in this system."

As the meeting attendees filed out of the New Bedford Free Public Library, past the Whaleman Statue, the hunt for the missing fishing vessel, the *Midnight Sun*, and her eleven-man crew continued offshore.

The following day, the Coast Guard called off the search for the *Midnight Sun*, after an extensive seven-day search, involving multiple ships and planes, and covering an area of 63,000 square miles.

If the men who had assembled in New Bedford, at the library, twenty-four hours earlier, had collectively found a way to address the weather forecast shortcomings sooner, it might have been prevented. Eleven brave New Bedford fisherman might have made it home.

If he could have, the bronze Whaleman Statue, standing his silent sentinel in front of the New Bedford Free Public Library, would have surely shed a tear.

It didn't have to happen!

The Whaleman Statue
"Shedding a Tear"

Chapter 23

THE COURT CASE

THE FINAL STORM FOR CAPTAIN MAGNE RISDAL
AND HIS *MIDNIGHT SUN*

Three years after the loss of the F/V *Midnight Sun*, a case was heard in United States District Court in Boston, Massachusetts. This court is a Federal United States District Court with territorial jurisdiction for the Commonwealth of Massachusetts, and it was established in 1789. One of the areas that it adjudicates is Admiralty Law.

A summary of a decision issued by a United States District Court Judge, in the matter of the loss of the F/V *Midnight Sun* will follow. This is the finding of the judge, after reviewing the facts of the circumstances of the sinking of the *Midnight Sun*, and the liability in claims made by the families of the dead crew members. I struggled with the decision of whether to make this part of this book. I finally decided that it had to be included, the reason being that in my research this item popped up immediately when I searched for information on Captain Magne Risdal. This judgment has become important in legal circles because it has been used in other cases to establish liability, regarding who is considered a family member in maritime losses. This importance to the legal community is the reason why this case comes to the surface when you search the internet for information on Captain Risdal.

After reading this court finding, I was outraged at the conclusions that the court found, and I felt that the integrity and ability of Captain Risdal were unfairly attacked. I thought that the court had gotten the facts of this case very wrong. I asked myself how did this conclusion come about? What were the circumstances that created a summary, that in my opinion, was so inaccurate? It was at this point that I realized there must be reasons and that I was very ignorant of Admiralty Law.

My first area of research was, who was this District Court Judge Andrew Caffery, the man who wrote the summary and the judgment? I quickly found out that Judge Caffrey served in the U.S. Army Signal Corp, Intelligence Branch, from 1942 to 1946, during WWII. After the war, he graduated from Harvard Law School in 1948. He was appointed to the District Court in 1960, by President Eisenhower. He then served as the Chief Judge of the court from 1972 to 1986. He then moved to Senior Judge status until 1993. Apparently, this was an intelligent man and was a highly regarded Federal Judge, and without a doubt an expert on the law. This gave me pause, and I realized that I would have to look closely into the details of this case, that seemed so wrong to me on first look.

The second area that I examined was why did the families take this legal avenue and sue the boat? These men were all shipmates and the F/V *Midnight Sun* was a high earning boat, one of the best in the fleet. I am sure that during their lives, they were all were proud to be part of her crew. Further, the crew was mostly made up of men of Norwegian ancestry, mainly from Karmoy, and therefore had family ties that probably went back generations. On closer look, this became very easy to understand. The families had no choice but to proceed in this direction. Fishermen were basically independent contractors; they were paid based on the amount and value of their catch. There were almost no benefits for these men, such as health care, life insurance, vacation time, or even workmen's compensation. Fishermen are financially dependent on their ability to catch fish, there are few fringe benefits, and this is the reason why it was so essential to be on a high earning boat. When the *Midnight Sun* was lost, it must have been financially devastating to the families. I can only imagine what would have happened, if my father had been lost in this storm, my life would have probably turned out very differently. Congress understood this problem for seamen, and in 1920 passed the Jones Act, and the Death on the High Seas Act, to give seamen and their families a means to gain some compensation for their lost loved ones. But this required that they pursue their claims in court.

The third item which I needed to understand, was what does Admiralty Law say, and what are the options to be pursued? Maritime law recognizing the inherent risk of setting a ship upon the sea differentiates among three fundamental causes for all ship disasters:

- First, an "Act of God," such as a violent storm that can sink a seaworthy ship, for which no man can be held accountable.
- Second, negligence of the crew beyond the knowledge or power of the shipowners, that can cause the loss of a ship, for which the shipowner cannot be held liable.
- Third, a shipowner can be found fully responsible if a ship is lost because it is found to be "unseaworthy," or if a shipowner allows his ship to be handled in a negligent, or illegal manner.

The Death on the High Seas Act covers dependents when the seaman dies three or more miles out to sea, from the coast of the United States. Dependents filling a claim under this law must be able to prove that their loved one died because of a wrongful act, or negligence related to the vessel being unseaworthy.

Unseaworthiness has a broad definition, and the burden of proof is relatively low. What most would consider a seaworthy vessel, can easily be found "unseaworthy," for the most minor item, in the eyes of this law.

Dependents are entitled to receive money to cover the lost financial support from the deceased's wages, payment for any funeral expenses, and money to compensate for pain and suffering, including coverage for mental health care related to the death.

So, we have reached the point where everyone is following the only options that are available to them. The families of the dead men have no choice but to comply and initiate legal action, in the hope of compensation for their lost loved ones. The judge must decide if they will receive any compensation, or not, and to do this, he must determine if this was an "Act of God," or if someone was negligent which then caused these deaths. If he rules negligence, then he is placing the blame on the crew, captain, or shipowner. It is to borrow a phrase, "A Perfect Storm," with no one doing anything wrong, but someone will win, and someone will lose. The *Midnight Sun* and her captain are caught in a legal storm, three years after her loss at sea. It seems a shame that our legal system works this way, but it is our system. For the families to receive financial compensation, someone must be at fault. While I am glad that the families received financial help, it is a shame that a good man's reputation will be tarnished in the process. Since this judgment is readily available to anyone who searches the internet, I feel that I must offer a rebuttal in defense of Captain Risdal. I also think that Judge Caffrey was aggressive and mean-spirited in his attack on the ability and competence of Captain Risdal. I took exception to the tone that the judge used in this summary, and while I understand why he ruled as he did, I feel that some of his comments were personal and unnecessary.

I also heard that one witness who appeared in court in this case, who was also out in this storm, said that he was not allowed to explain his answers and that it felt like the decision had already been made before they ever arrived in court. The judge seemed to attack the integrity and technical judgment of all the fishermen who appeared in his court on this day. The summary rings of arrogance, and it sounds to me, like another case of the highly educated talking down to the less educated. This irritates me, and I find it necessary that I must offer a rebuttal to many of the conclusions made in this court decision.

The court summary and decision will follow, along with my explanations and rebuttals.

The comments that are underlined, and marked as, "The Court:" are exactly as they were made and filed by the Federal Court in this decision. They have not been altered by me in any way.

The comments that are underlined and marked as, "Author's Explanation:" or "Author's Rebuttal:" are my comments and rebuttals.

United States District Court for the District of Massachusetts
January 5, 1966

Petition of Risdal & Anderson, Inc. for exoneration from or limitation of liability as owner of the Fishing Vessel *Midnight Sun*

The Court: On January 5, 1966, a petition was heard in United States District Court in Boston, Massachusetts. This was a petition in admiralty law for exoneration or limitation of liability with respect to the loss of the fishing vessel *Midnight Sun* and her entire crew of 10 men. Claims and answers have been filed by the personal representatives of each of the ten deceased crew members challenging the petitioner's claim to exoneration or limitation and asserting that petitioner is liable to the personal representatives of the decedents for all provable damages, under the provisions of the Jones Act, 46 U.S.C.A. 688 and the Death on the High Seas Act, 46 U.S.C.A. 761.

Author's explanation: The attorneys representing Risdal & Anderson, Inc., which was the corporation that owned the *Midnight Sun*, have asked the court to exonerate the corporation from liability, due to the sinking of the *Midnight Sun* being caused by a violent storm, which was "An Act of God" and therefore beyond the control of the boat. Failing that, they are asking for limitation of liability based on the same grounds.

The legal team for the deceased crew members families are challenging this request and maintaining that the boat is liable for the deaths of their loved ones, due to negligence. There were eleven men on this boat including Captain Risdal, the Risdal family did not participate in filing a claim for his life.

The Court: The *Midnight Sun* was owned by a Massachusetts corporation, Risdal & Anderson, Inc. The late Magne Risdal was President, Treasurer, and a Director and the principal stockholder of this corporation. The *Midnight Sun* was the sole asset owned by the corporation. Magne Risdal was the captain of the *Midnight Sun* and oversaw her last voyage. In fact, he had been the active master of the vessel since she was built and launched in 1960. No claim for the loss of Captain Risdal's life was filed in this case.

Author's explanation: The judge is establishing that Captain Risdal is the responsible captain, master, and shipowner of the *Midnight Sun*.

The Court: The *Midnight Sun* was engaged in commercial scallop fishing from her home port in New Bedford. On the morning of November 7, 1962, she left Kelly's Shipyard at Fairhaven on a voyage to the southern edge of Georges Bank in the general area of latitude 41 degrees North and longitude 67 degrees 30 minutes West. Master Risdal was her master, and the crew consisted of Mate Olav Ferkingstad, Jens Ferkingstad, Sam Lund, Gordon Kallestein, August Larsen, Jan Nilsen, John Wagner, Arne Lindanger, Torgils Holmen, and Asbjorn Pedersen. She fished close by three other New Bedford scallopers, the *Aloha*, the *Florence B.*, and the *Fleetwing*, all of which were in the same area, about three or four miles off a fishing buoy which had been put over by the *Aloha*. Fishing operations continued normally until bad weather began to make up on November 14th. By this time Captain Risdal was near the end of the eight fishing days which was the maximum permitted by union rules. At about 2:00 p.m., on November 14th, Captain Risdal communicated via radio-telephone with the mate of the *Aloha* and said the weather had become too bad for fishing and that he was headed home to New Bedford. This was the last communication that anyone had with the *Midnight Sun*, which has not been seen or heard from since, nor has any wreckage from her ever been found.

The Court: At the time of the trial the mate of the *Aloha* testified that his position was 90 miles east of the Nantucket Shoals Lightship at the time of the radio-telephone conversation with Captain Risdal, and I find, on the basis, of the fact that the four vessels were fishing off the same buoy, that the *Midnight Sun* was approximately the same distance east of the Nantucket Lightship when last heard from. At the time of this radio-telephone conversation, the wind was blowing at 45 miles per hour.

<u>Author's explanation</u>: The judge is establishing that the *Midnight Sun* was more than three miles off the coast of the United States, which is a requirement of the Death on the High Seas Act.

<u>The Court</u>: The wind intensified, and the weather kept getting worse. The mate of the *Aloha* testified that by 6:00 p.m. the wind hit 100-miles per hour. This was a visual estimate by the witness since there were no scientific instruments capable of measuring wind velocity on the *Aloha*. Witnesses from the *Aloha*, the *Florence B.*, and the *Fleetwing*, none of whom had benefit of any scientific wind velocity measuring, expressed their opinion that at the height of the storm on November 14th the maximum winds which prevailed in the area where the *Midnight Sun* was last heard from were 100 mph, 100 mph, 80 mph, 70 mph. The official weather bureau reports indicate a wind force at Georges Bank of 65 mph and a recording at Nantucket Shoals Lightship of Force 8 on Beaufort Scale, i.e., 34 to 40 mph.

<u>Author's Rebuttal</u>: The fishermen are stating that the wind speed was between 70 to 100-mph. These are estimates based on years of practical experience in evaluating weather conditions on the fishing grounds. It is true that the fishing boats did not have scientific wind speed instruments. However, in my opinion, this is expert testimony. The judge references that the weather bureau records indicate a wind force of 65-mph on Georges Bank. I ask where on Georges Bank? The area of Georges Bank is larger than the entire size of the State of Massachusetts. The weather conditions and wind speed in Pittsfield can be vastly different than in Provincetown, and it's the same on Georges Bank, it occupies a large area. He further references that the wind speed at the Nantucket Shoals Lightship was 34 to 40-mph. The Lightship was 90-miles from the area where these four fishing boats were located on the bank. The wind speed data that the judge references is from Wednesday, November 14, 1962. However, the peak wind velocity of this storm, was in fact, on the following day, Thursday, November 15, between 11:00 a.m. and 3:00 p.m., as confirmed by Captain Jack Salmon, the master of the USNS AKL-43, who did, in fact, have scientific wind speed instruments aboard his United States Navy ship. I see no evidence of Captain Salmon being called in this case, why not?

As already pointed out in a prior chapter, the low-pressure readings from the very same U.S. Weather Bureau, indicate that 968-millibars of barometric pressure was a fact. This level of extreme low pressure is scientifically consistent with winds of 96 to 110-mph. These wind speeds are consistent with a Category-2 hurricane. No, this official data from the U.S. Weather Bureau supports the estimates of the fishermen as being extremely accurate.

The Court: Petitioner urges that a finding should be made that the storm of November 14th was a technical hurricane, i.e., a storm with winds more than 66 knots, which is 76 mph. While I find that it was a severe storm I also find that it was of less than hurricane strength. In so finding I have in mind, first, the official weather bureau records; and secondly, the discrepancies in the various estimates by the fisherman who were in the area who "guesstimated" the wind velocity without benefits of any instruments, and whose testimony as to wind speeds I believe to be exaggerated and which I do not fully credit. Witnesses from fishing vessels who were out in that storm of November 14-15, 1962, was as severe as they had ever experienced, although they had been out in storms just as severe previously and had brought their boats safely home, and that they expected during the remainder of their careers to ride out other storms equally severe.

Author's Rebuttal: The Judge has just ruled that the cause of the loss of the *Midnight Sun* was not due to an "Act of God." This eliminates the request of the attorney's representing the *Midnight Sun* for exoneration of liability. This is strike one for the petitioner, two to go. It is my opinion that this storm was clearly an "Act of God," and the following are my reasons to support my conclusion, and I will highlight what I believe are the inaccuracies of the court's findings.

- The court is saying that the fishermen cannot judge wind speed and are lying while under oath. In fact, the Weather Bureau's low-pressure data supports their "guesstimates," and 968-millibars of barometric pressure would be indicative of wind speeds in the range of 96 to 110-mph. The use of the word "guesstimates" is very degrading and unnecessary. I would have expected better from the judge. Here we have another example of the educated talking down to the less educated. This is very annoying to me, and it feels to me that the judge is mocking the fishermen. These men have spent their lives on the ocean, in all kinds of weather. Their lives depend on their ability to read the weather conditions and to make life and death decisions based on these observations.

- Captain Jack Clark was a licensed professional ship captain, and he was the master of a United States Naval Ship, the *AKL-43*. Captain Clark and his crew were all licensed professional seaman, and they were on Georges Bank during this storm. However, the location of the *AKL-43* was 50-miles Southeast of Nantucket, in the general vicinity of Asia Rip Shoals, the Nantucket Lightship, and Texas Tower #3. The men who were witnesses in court were fishing another 90-miles east of Captain Clark's position. The center of this cyclone passed over their position which would mean that the storm was more intense at their position, and they would have experienced higher winds than those experienced by Captain Clark. This U.S. Navy ship did have the benefit of having wind speed devices aboard. The *AKL-43* recorded wind speeds from 69 to 90-mph. The judge has already pointed out that hurricane winds are those higher than 76-mph. These readings from Captain Clark, and through his rank and position, are therefore official United States Navy records, and this confirms that winds were of hurricane force. This information was never presented to the court and must have been missed by the attorneys representing the *Midnight Sun*. This is scientific fact, and it confirms the "guesstimates" of the fishermen. Captain Clark reported that he never thought that his ship was in danger of sinking, but that it was indeed a very severe storm. In fact, he was quoted as saying; "That was one hell of a storm." I must again point out that Captain Clark was in command of a United States Navy Ship, and he was in fact, an educated gentleman, so he must be believable, no "guesstimates" here. Any discrepancies in the wind speed estimates, from boat to boat, is easily explainable by studying the weather chart. The very tight pressure bands would explain any difference in wind speed experienced in only a short distance from one boat to another boat. A ship 20 or 30-miles away from another vessel, might experience a significant difference in the wind conditions.

- I think the judge has misunderstood the severity of this storm in the eyes of the fishermen. I offer the following as evidence, the following comments and statements are from some of our most experienced captains, who experienced this storm on Georges Bank.

    o Captain Louis Doucette, Jr. – F/V *Venus* – stated that while he had survived three named hurricanes at sea, this storm was the only time that he thought he would be lost at sea, in a fifty-year career. He called this storm the worse storm that he ever encountered. In his career as a fisherman, he never experienced another storm like this one.

    o Captain Hans Davidsen – F/V *Florence B.* – was quoted, "I've never seen anything like this storm before in 36-years of fishing."

    o Captain William Fielder – F/V *Moonlight* - Captain William Fielder had been fishing for twenty-six years when he encountered Neptune's

Nor'easter. He was quoted as saying; "For the first time in my career, I felt very afraid. I came to New Bedford from New York City at age twenty to start my fishing career. This is as close as I've ever come to being lost at sea.

- o Captain Manual Mello – F/V *Santa Cruz* - "We can barely see the *Moonlight* in the heavy seas. She's a couple of hundred feet away, but the seas are so high that they are blocking our view."

- o Captain Albert Dahl – F/V *Monte Carlo* – "Mayday, Mayday, Mayday."

- o These Captains had all spent years on Georges Bank, and to a man, they concluded that this was the most severe heavy weather event that they had ever experienced. It shook them to their core, and these are all men who didn't scare easily.

- o Contrary to the comments of the Judge, the fishermen who were out in this storm hoped and prayed that they would never experience a storm of this intensity, ever again.

- o Yes, Judge, you are correct, this was not a technical hurricane, because it did not form in the tropics. It was technically an Extra-Tropical Cyclone, with hurricane-force winds. It was in fact, an Extra-Tropical Cyclone with Explosive Cyclogenesis, also known as a "Bombogenesis" storm. I am happy for the families of the dead crew members of the *Midnight Sun* that they would receive some financial compensation for the loss of their loved ones, due to the judge ruling this storm as not being an Act of God. However, the evidence makes clear that this storm was most surely an Act of God, or probably more accurately, an act of the devil.

The Court: Petitioner elicited testimony that Captain Risdal was more knowledgeable in maritime affairs than the average fishing boat captain or owner. Despite this, the captains of two, and the mate of the third, of the vessels that were fishing with the *Midnight Sun* all testified that the proper seamanship under the weather conditions then and there prevailing was for the vessel to lay to and ride out the storm rather than try to head back to New Bedford as Captain Risdal stated he was about to do. These three witnesses, who commanded scallopers 17 to 23 years older than the *Midnight Sun*, testified that they did lay-to, rode out the storm, and safely returned to port. Indeed, the undisputed testimony was that practically the entire New Bedford dragger fleet of approximately sixty draggers was out in the storm of November 14th and that everyone returned safely to New Bedford with the sole exception of the *Midnight Sun*. No fishing vessel was lost from Gloucester, Boston, or any other segment of the fishing fleet during this storm.

Author's Rebuttal: I disagree with this entire paragraph, for the following reasons:

- As already pointed out by the court in this summary, Captain Risdal communicated with the *Aloha*, at approximately 2:00 p.m., on November 14th, and declared that the weather was deteriorating and that he was near the end of his mandated eight days of fishing, so he was heading home to New Bedford. The reported wind speed at this time was estimated to be 45-mph by Mate Isaksen. The decision to return to port was in fact, was a very normal and prudent decision by Captain Risdal. He possessed no information from the United States Weather Bureau that a cyclone was headed his way. This was just another late fall/early winter day on Georges Bank, and laying to at this point would not be an option for a boat of the pedigree of the *Midnight Sun*. His vessel was full of scallops and proceeding home in 45-mph winds was just a regular prudent decision and standard practice, especially when he had no warning of the heavy weather that was headed his way. If every boat in the fleet decided to lay-to in winds of 45-mph, the entire fleet would be sitting out on Georges Bank for the whole of the winter. This statement by the court is ridiculous. Mate Isaksen stated that four hours later they were experiencing 100-mph winds at his position, but where was the *Midnight Sun* now? Based on the time she left the vicinity of the *Aloha*, she was probably 50-miles back toward the west of the *Aloha* and was headed directly into the heart of the storm. What were the conditions there? No one knows. Was the *Midnight Sun* now laying to? No one knows. So how can the court say what Captain Risdal was doing at this point? How can the court say that Captain Risdal did not make a prudent decision, that he did not show good judgment at this point? It cannot, because the only men who know for sure what they were doing when this cyclone hit them, never made it home to tell us.

- The court also declares that the only boat lost in this storm was the *Midnight Sun*. As already pointed out previously, six ships were lost, and thirty-six men also lost their lives, in this storm. If it wasn't for the skill and experience of these fishermen, who you seem to belittle, the death toll could have exceeded 200-men.

The Court: I rule that Captain Risdal's attempt to return to port was negligent and that this negligence was a proximate cause of the loss of the *Midnight Sun*. I rule that there was privity and knowledge on the part of the petitioning corporation of the facts presented by this case in view of Captain Risdal's dual capacity as Master of the vessel and principal executive and majority shareholder of the corporation and that this negligence is imputable to the petitioner.

Author explanation: The Judge is ruling that Captain Risdal was negligent in attempting to return to port. Negligence is another point necessary in the Death on the High Seas Act, that being that the crew negligently operated the vessel, and this is strike two for the petitioner, one to go. The judge will now go on to declare that the *Midnight Sun* was "unseaworthy" as defined by Admiralty Law.

The Court: The second basis of petitioner's liability, in this case, is the unseaworthiness of the *Midnight Sun*. She was built at the Gamage Boatyard, South Bristol, Maine, in 1960, from a standard plan drawn by one Albert Gordon. She was a scallop dragger of approximately 65 feet in length, and 67 gross tons, built of wood and propelled by a 335-horsepower diesel engine. During construction of the vessel, the design was altered by Mr. Gamage at the request of Captain Risdal. This alteration consisted of lengthening the stem and raising the freeboard. No naval architect was consulted about these changes. These were not the only changes Captain Risdal made in the vessel. In March 1962, he personally directed the erection of plywood shelters over the scallop-shucking boxes located aft along the deckhouse on both sides of the stern portion of the *Midnight Sun*. The forward ends of this structure contained plywood access doors on either side of the deck, but it went completely around at the stern thus making a complete U-shaped enclosure at the stern end of the vessel. Both sides of this wooden structure contained hinged wooden doors over the shucking boxes which could be fastened either in an open or shut position. This change in the *Midnight Sun* was made at the D. N. Kelley & Son Shipyard, Fairhaven, Massachusetts. The chief carpenter, Joseph N. Richard, testified that it was built under the direction and immediate control of Captain Risdal. The hull superintendent for Kelley testified that his company had neither assumed nor accepted any responsibility for the design or safety of this addition to the *Midnight Sun* but was concerned only with the physical erection thereof under the direction of Captain Risdal. I find that this work was done without consulting a naval architect or another marine expert about the effect this structure would have on the stability of the vessel. I also find that the structure was built without written specifications, plans, or blueprints, pursuant to oral instructions of Captain Risdal.

Author's rebuttal: Author Rachel Rowley Spaulding wrote an excellent book titled, In Search of *Ellen Marie*, based on her search to find the history of the New Bedford fishing vessel the *Ellen Marie*. The F/V *Ellen Marie* was another Gamage built boat launched in 1961. In her research, Rachel confirmed that Mr. Gamage had a basic fishing vessel plan of 65-feet in length, and 67-gross tons in displacement, designed by Albert Gordon. This basic plan was offered to customers as a starting point, and then it allowed them to meet their specific needs by requesting that the boat design be lengthened, or shortened, according to their requirements. By adding or deleting frames, this basic boat plan could be built from 50-feet to 100-feet long. The following chart illustrates the specifications of 66-fishing vessels built from 1941 to 1980, at the Harvey Gamage Shipyard. Most, if not all, of these boats, were constructed from the basic Gamage design plan to start the process. Only seven of the sixty-six fishing boats were made to the exact basic design specifications, and this means that eighty-nine percent of the fishing boats built at the Gamage Shipyard, were modified from the basic design plan. Gamage built boats were highly regarded from Maine to Florida, as well-built capable sea boats and they established a record of being seaworthy sturdy boats. The court is saying that by altering the basic design plan, Captain Risdal was making the *Midnight Sun* unseaworthy. If that was true, then the builder should not have offered the option of altering the basic design. Also, if this was true, then these other sixty altered fishing vessels, should have had a history of being unsafe. This was not the case, and these boats had a history of stellar performance on the fishing grounds. Captain Risdal did nothing wrong with lengthening the *Midnight Sun* to 72-feet, look at the data on the following chart.

- The issue of raising the freeboard indicates that Captain Risdal was very concerned with the safety of his crew, who would be working on deck. In the early days of draggers, and on the schooners before them, the freeboard and railings were very low, and many men were lost over the side when a freak wave washed them overboard. In the 1930's my father and grandfather lost three men in this way. It was an experience that haunted my father for his entire life, and he was always reluctant to discuss it. Captain Risdal's request to increase the height of the freeboard was made in the name of making the *Midnight Sun* safer for the crew on deck.

The following is a list of sixty-six fishing vessels that were built at the Harvey Gamage Shipyard in South Bristol, Maine. Most of these boats had long careers and were highly regarded by the men who sailed in them. If altering the basic plan made these modified boats unsafe and unseaworthy, as alleged by the court, then New Bedford would have been grieving over many more dead fishermen.

	Gamage Shipyard Boat Name	Length In Feet	Displacement In Tons	Year Built
1	Doris G. Eldridge	65	67	1941
2	Carol and Estelle	65	63	1944
3	Pearl Harbor	67	67	1944
4	Bobby and Harvey	65	63	1944
5	Pelican	72	74	1944
6	Fairhaven	78	99	1944
7	Solveig J.	73	89	1944
8	Althea Joyce	61	50	1945
9	Gannet	78	102	1946
10	Wild Duck	79	132	1946
11	The Clipper Fish	79	132	1946
12	Little Flower	61	43	1949
13	Nancy Jane	64	57	1950
14	Vivian Fay	72	76	1950
15	Brant	72	76	1951
16	Monte Carlo	66	85	1951
17	Pocahontas	79	130	1952
18	Vilanova	92	197	1952
19	Nellie-Pet	72	77	1952
20	Ruth-Moses	72	77	1952
21	Lauren Fay	72	77	1953
22	Wawenock	101	191	1953
23	Debbie and Jo-Ann	72	77	1953
24	Mother Frances	80	103	1954
25	Mary Ann	64	70	1954

	Gamage Shipyard Boat Name	Length In Feet	Displacement In Tons	Year Built
26	Rush	65	67	1955
27	Eagle	65	67	1955
28	Edgartown	79	115	1955
29	Sippican	67	92	1956
30	Stanley M. Fisher	72	101	1956
31	Carmen & Vince	83	117	1957
32	Snoopy	66	84	1957
33	North Sea	65	67	1957
34	Geraldine	83	136	1957
35	Sandra Jane	83	137	1958
36	Grace and Salvatore	76	112	1958
37	Valiant Lady	61	55	1959
38	Sea Gold	65	67	1959
39	Neptune	70	91	1959
40	Ike and Jens	76	112	1959
41	Prowler	70	94	1960
42	Midnight Sun	72	94	1960
43	Santa Cruz	70	90	1960
44	Kim	64	65	1960
45	Ellen Marie	70	92	1961
46	Four Brothers	64	65	1961
47	Antonina	70	92	1961
48	Angela W.	64	65	1961
49	Moby Dick	70	101	1962
50	Sylvia Mae	73	110	1962
51	Venus	74	80	1962
52	Explorer	73	110	1962
53	Francis J. O'Hara	88	160	1963
54	Mariner	73	103	1963
55	Jane and Ursula	86	188	1964
56	Navigator	73	104	1964
57	Zerda	86	188	1964
58	Catalina	73	105	1964
59	Harvey F. Gamage	87	158	1964

	Gamage Shipyard Boat Name	Length In Feet	Displacement In Tons	Year Built
60	Commodore	98	193	1965
61	Robert F. O'Hara	79	141	1966
62	Alexa	78	138	1966
63	Chris Ann	55	51	1974
64	Fram	70	122	1975
65	Araho	106	198	1979
66	Friendship	99	173	1980

As you can see from the above chart, most of these fishing vessels were altered in some way. If the standard design for a Gamage fishing vessel was 65-feet in length, and a displacement of 67-tons, a look at the record of the boats that were built finds numerous variations from the standard. The court's conclusion that Captain Risdal did something patently wrong by modifying the *Midnight Sun* from the basic design is just not correct.

- On the matter of the covering the scallop shucking boxes, this also was an attempt to protect the crew when they were shucking scallops aboard the *Midnight Sun*. In the past, the men would have to be exposed to the elements when they were shucking scallops. The move to provide a shelter for the men became popular, and the entire fleet moved to this idea. These shelters were made of plywood, and as mentioned by the court they had hinges so the men could fasten them open when needed. These were not extremely robust structures. The idea that this structure would capture and hold a massive amount of water in heavy seas, thereby altering the metacentric height of the vessel is improbable. If hit by a large breaking wave, this plywood structure would be destroyed and would not hold anything; it would be smashed to pieces. The *Venus* was a dragger, so she had no shelter of this type, but she had two lobster boxes, in the same general location on the boat, and they were ripped from the deck of the *Venus* and blown away when the *Venus* was hove down. The scallop shucking boxes on the *Florence B.* were also ripped off the deck during this storm. The dinghy that was covering the skylight on the schooner *Curlew* was smashed to pieces by the force of a large breaking wave. The same would most likely have happened to the shucking box shelters on the *Midnight Sun*. I understand the theory, but I disagree with the court on this conclusion.

The Court: On the basis of expert testimony of naval architects at the trial, particularly that of Dr. Abkowitz, Professor of Naval Architecture and Marine Engineering at the Massachusetts Institute of Technology, I find that it is possible prior to the construction of a vessel, once her plans and specifications have been completed, to make a computation of the metacentric height and metacentric radius of the vessel and to plot this information on a graph with other data and thus to determine her essential stability and consequently her seaworthiness. This can be done by making calculations based on weight estimates of the engine, hull, machinery, gear, cargo, and stores. After the construction of a vessel, it is possible to determine actual as distinguished from the theoretical stability of the vessel, by performing inclining tests with reference to the vessel. This was not done after construction of the *Midnight Sun*, and at no time prior to her last voyage were hydrostatic curves of the vessel computed, nor was any determination of her metacentric height ever made.

Author's rebuttal: No one did this. Most of these boats were owned by the individual fishermen who operated them. They would know in short order if a boat was unstable. These men did not have unlimited resources to spend on this type of test. These were independently owned fishing vessels, not United States Navy ships. A great idea to ponder in the halls and offices at MIT, but just not going to happen on the fish pier. Perhaps this testing should have been the responsibility of the builder. Or maybe, the shipyard should have built one standard sized vessel, had it tested, and not allowed alterations to the design. This is all speculation and second-guessing. The fact is, Gamage boats of any size were proven to be some of the most capable and seaworthy fishing boats in the Western North Atlantic.

The Court: Expert witnesses called by both sides to this controversy testified that they calculated the metacentric height of the Midnight Sun from her basic plans to be about 1.8 feet., which I find to be "moderate" absent any "degrading factors," i.e., special conditions tending to decrease metacentric height.

Author's explanation: This is stating that experts on both sides of this issue agree that the F/V *Midnight Sun* calculated out as having moderate metacentric height. This means that naval architects for both parties agree that the *Midnight Sun* was theoretically a stable vessel.

The Court: I find that the construction of the shelter under the sole direction of Captain Risdal created a condition aboard the *Midnight Sun* under which in heavy seas she tended to trap substantial quantities of seawater in this plywood shelter. I find it significant that structures accomplishing the same purpose as that sought to be accomplished by building this one on the *Midnight Sun* have been built on other fishing vessels in the New Bedford fleet, among them the *Moby Dick*, with doors fore and aft and without an enclosure going all the way around the stern. An examination of claimants' Exhibit A, which is a photograph of the *Midnight Sun*, graphically demonstrates the far greater proclivity for retaining water in a shelter of the type on the *Midnight Sun* with its completely enclosed stern as contrasted with the type of shelter on the *Moby Dick* with an open stern. I find that the shelter on the *Midnight Sun* was of such a size and shape as to trap a large amount of sea-water so that metacentric height of the vessel would be substantially reduced by a combination of the weight of the structure and the weight and free surface effect of water trapped therein.

Author's Rebuttal: As already stated above, this shelter most probably would be blown to bits in the type of large breaking waves, like those experienced in this storm. Both the *Fleetwing* and the *Monte Carlo* had sections of their rails and stanchions caved-in by the force of the large breaking waves that were being generated by this storm. The rails and stanchions are far more structurally robust and integral to the integrity of the boat than any type of shucking box structure. If the force of these waves were strong enough to damage rails and stanchions, it would surely be more than strong enough to destroy any plywood scallop shucking box.

If a shucking box was so constructed, to be robust enough to resist these types of seas, then it could also be argued that it might make the boat more watertight. Enclosed sterns are common on fishing vessels that work the North Sea in Europe, which often see extreme heavy weather events. Fishing boats from England and Norway often had enclosed areas. Some of the North Sea boats, depending on the type of fishing they were doing, even had enclosed deck shelters to protect the men and make the vessel more watertight, like you see on some lifeboats. Either way, I don't see the validity of this conclusion.

The Court: There were other "degrading factors" which reduced the metacentric height of the Midnight Sun. She had three large square scuppers amidships on each side which were fitted with ports or panels to keep them closed always except when the crew was working on deck on a catch at which time the scuppers were opened to shovel out trash from the catch, gurry, etc. In addition, there were several small scuppers around the stern which I find were inadequate to carry off any appreciable amount of sea-water which found its way to the stern portion of the deck. I find that it was normal practice on the *Midnight Sun* to keep the six large scuppers closed while underway, with the result that in heavy seas the water was trapped on the deck and this free surface condition reduced the metacentric height of the vessel by at least two feet, which alone would suffice to produce a negative metacentric height and consequently an unstable condition.

Author's Rebuttal: This makes no sense whatsoever. It is impossible to believe that a boat and crew, of the caliber of the *Midnight Sun*, would close the deck scuppers in heavy weather. No captain of any ability would do this, and no one can make me believe that Captain Risdal would do this. Keeping these scuppers open is the only way to free the deck of sea water that comes over the rail in heavy weather, and this is as basic to a fisherman, as looking both ways before crossing a street, is to a pedestrian.

Captain Hans Davidsen of the F/V *Florence B.* speaks very clear about how the seawater that was taken on deck, when his vessel was hove down, ran off through the deck scuppers.

The judge also references the inadequate stern scuppers does this mean that the boat design by the builder was in error?

The Court: I find that the absence of effective longitudinal partitioning in the fish hold tended to further reduce the metacentric height.

Author's rebuttal: This makes no sense. Where did this come from? Captain Risdal would never allow this type of bad practice to occur. The highly experienced crew on the *Midnight Sun* would not use this type of bad seamanship practice. No way this is correct.

The Court: Furthermore, the *Midnight Sun* carried two 14-foot dories on top of the pilothouse, neither of which was covered by canvas as is done by some but not all, of the fishing vessels in the New Bedford fleet, and I find that the water likely to collect in these open dories in heavy seas would further reduce the metacentric height.

Author's rebuttal:

- First, these dories would be swept from the roof of the pilothouse on the *Midnight Sun* in a storm of this magnitude. The loss of the dories located on the roof of the pilothouse happened on the *Venus*, and the *Florence B.* in this storm and those dories have never been seen again.

- Second, concerning a cover or no cover on the dories. As already stated above, this is a moot point because the dories would have been swept away. Whether they were covered is a matter of preference from boat to boat. One theory is that they would be protected by utilizing a canvas cover. Others preferred to keep them uncovered so that rain and seawater would periodically get into the dory and keep the wooden seams and caulking of the dory swollen and therefore watertight. You would find boats employing both methods in about equal numbers. It is a big stretch to think two dories filled with water would cause a vessel of the size and displacement of the *Midnight Sun*, with the fish hold full of scallops, to capsize. In the winter these boats often would become burdened with ice as they returned to port. While the crew would be required to hack the ice from the mast and rigging, these boats could carry a considerable burden of ice. It is a bit of a stretch to theorize that two fourteen-foot dories partially filled with water would cause the *Midnight Sun* to capsize. Very doubtful.

The Court: I find that these "degrading factors" eradicated the moderate 1.8 feet metacentric height of the *Midnight Sun* and produced a negative metacentric height during the storm, thereby rendering the vessel unstable and unseaworthy; and that it is more likely so than not that the *Midnight Sun* was lost during this storm because she was rendered unseaworthy by the addition of the ill-conceived shelter and as a result of her unseaworthiness capsized and foundered with the loss of all aboard. Having in mind her last known position, her unseaworthy condition, her failure to make any subsequent radio-telephone transmissions even though her engines and all her equipment were in good condition when she left the Kelley shipyard and, finally, having in mind that this was a northwesterly storm, I find that the *Midnight Sun* went down while at a distance substantially more than twenty miles east of Nantucket.

Author's rebuttal: I don't agree with this conclusion.

- I believe the *Midnight Sun* probably capsized, but it was because she was caught directly in the path of an Extratropical "Bomb" Cyclone, with winds of more than 100-mph and seas as high as 60-feet.
- She did not make a radiotelephone distress call because she most likely went down quickly.
- This was not a northwesterly storm, it was a classic nor'easter, and the proof is that it lasted for several days, which is a trait of a true nor'easter.

The Court: The petition for limitation of or exoneration from liability is denied, and the case will stand for a hearing on assessment of damages.

The opinion of the court delivered by:
Andrew Caffey, District Judge

Author's explanation: This is strike three. The legal team for the deceased crew members have won, and they are due compensation, and this is a good thing for the surviving families. The *Midnight Sun* and her master and captain have lost their last battle. However, I hope that I have demonstrated that Captain Risdal, and his vessel the *Midnight Sun*, were not at fault. Captain Risdal was an excellent and capable fisherman, and the *Midnight Sun* was one of New Bedford's best. The crew of the *Midnight Sun* were disciplined, capable fishermen with extensive experience. They were the unfortunate victims of a terrible storm. The *Midnight Sun*, her captain, her crew, and their families, were in fact;

<u>"The Finest Kind!"</u>

Chapter 24

<u>So, What Did Happen to the *Midnight Sun*?</u>

No one will never know for sure what happened to the *Midnight Sun*, but we can make some reasonable assumptions, and try to draw some possible conclusions. I can envision at least three possible scenarios regarding the loss of the *Midnight Sun*. Two of these three possibilities involve the *Midnight Sun* being hove down (capsized) due to the intensity of the weather. Since we know of the experiences of the other fishing vessels that made it home, and two of those, the *Venus* and the *Florence B.*, were hove down, it is most likely that this also happened to the *Midnight Sun*.

These are the things that we know;

- We know that the *Midnight Sun* was fishing approximately 90-miles east of the Nantucket Lightship on the Southeast Part of Georges Bank.

- We know that she was fishing, near, the F/V *Aloha*, F/V *Fleetwing*, and the F/V *Florence B*. We understand that the *Florence B.* was "Hove Down at Sea," and the *Fleetwing* and *Aloha* took 60-hours to return to New Bedford, a journey that is typically completed in 20-hours, due to the intensity of this storm.

- We know from the radio-telephone conversation between Captain Risdal and Mate John Isaksen that she left the fishing grounds on Wednesday, November 14, 1962, sometime shortly after noon, and was headed home to New Bedford.

- We know that the *Midnight Sun* was only two years old at the time of her loss and she was in perfect condition.

- We know that she was considered one of the top boats in the fleet and that she was manned with a very experienced and competent crew.

- We know that she encountered a very severe storm, technically an Extratropical Cyclone, that "Bombed Out" with 105-mph winds and 60-foot seas, and low pressure of 968-millibars.

- We know that this storm reached Georges Bank from sometime after midnight on Wednesday, November 14th, through all day Thursday, November 15th, 1962. This duration of strong wind is consistent with a classic nor'easter storm.

- It was reported that the storm seemed to reach peak intensity around midday on Thursday.

- We know that the low-pressure dropped 24-millibars, from 1:00 p.m. on Wednesday, to 1:00 p.m. on Thursday. A drop of 24-millibars in 24-hours is a "Bombogenesis" event.

- There are several options that the *Midnight Sun* could have taken to set a course from her fishing location, on the Southeast Part of Georges Bank, back to New Bedford. Whichever direction Captain Risdal decided to take, all of them would require that he proceed to the west, to reach New Bedford. The most probable course would be to head back towards the Nantucket Shoals Lightship and continue south of Nantucket and Martha's Vineyard, before heading north to New Bedford. Another hazardous area for mariners are the shoals south of Nantucket Island. The reason that the Coast Guard maintained a lightship in this area was because these shoals are so dangerous, and many ships both large and small, have met their demise in this area. The Nantucket Lightship was vital to marine traffic in this area for many years and was first placed in this location in the year 1854. The lightship was the last navigation light seen when leaving the United States when bound for Europe, and the first light that is seen when coming to the United States from Europe. Captain Risdal would have had to head towards this dangerous location to get home.

When Captain Risdal made his decision to stop fishing and end his trip, the weather was getting rough, but it was not anything serious, with winds of 40-mph from the northwest. The weather report that he would have received at 11:10 a.m., was not forecasting that any extreme heavy weather was coming his way. He was coming to the end of his mandated eight days of fishing, and he probably had a good trip of scallops in the fish-hold, so it was an easy decision to end the trip and head home. The type of decision that he had made hundreds of times in his career. As he headed west, back towards the Nantucket Lightship, and the hours ticked off, the wind began to quickly intensify out of the northwest. With the wind coming from the northwest and his course heading the boat in a westerly direction, he would have been taking the seas off the starboard side of the bow. This would put a vessel like the *Midnight Sun* right in her element, taking seas on her strong point. However, as the storm intensified, which it did quickly and without warning, the wind shifted to the north, and then the northeast, this now placed the wind on the starboard beam, and later the starboard quarter of the *Midnight Sun*. With the wind now blowing 100-mph from the northeast, and seas reported from 40 to 60-feet in height, the *Midnight Sun* was now facing the substantial probability of being "Hove Down."

Based on the time that the *Midnight Sun* left her fishing position, and with the storm intensifying as she proceeded west, and the fact that the *Aloha* departed the same fishing location not long after the *Midnight Sun*, and that it took the *Aloha* 60-hours to get to New Bedford. My best guess is that the *Midnight Sun* went down somewhere just south of Nantucket Island, probably in the vicinity of Asia Rip Shoals, or just to the west'ard, after suffering a knockdown. If in fact, this was the area where she sank it would answer the question, why didn't they head up into the wind and heave to? If in fact, they were in this area, the Nantucket Shoals, just north of Asia Rip are very dangerous and heading up into this direction would have been impossible. Some might suggest that they should have just let the boat lay-to and ride out the storm, but the intensity of this storm would have precluded that possibility in this area.

If you study the following nautical chart of the area south of Nantucket, you will see the shoals extending south of the island, reaching out like fingers, or looking something like a beard hanging off the chin of Nantucket Island. The depths are displayed in fathoms, which is six-feet, and the areas highlighted in blue are being pointed out on the chart as dangerously low water. You will also notice that there is a thin red line which outlines a box on this chart, and it is labeled as an area, "To Be Avoided." This is a warning to mariners to use extreme caution in this area. Asia Rip Shoals is located at the bottom right corner of the red box.

The reason that the Nantucket Lightship was placed in this area is to warn of the extreme danger that the Nantucket Shoals pose to mariners.

Nautical Chart of Nantucket Shoals

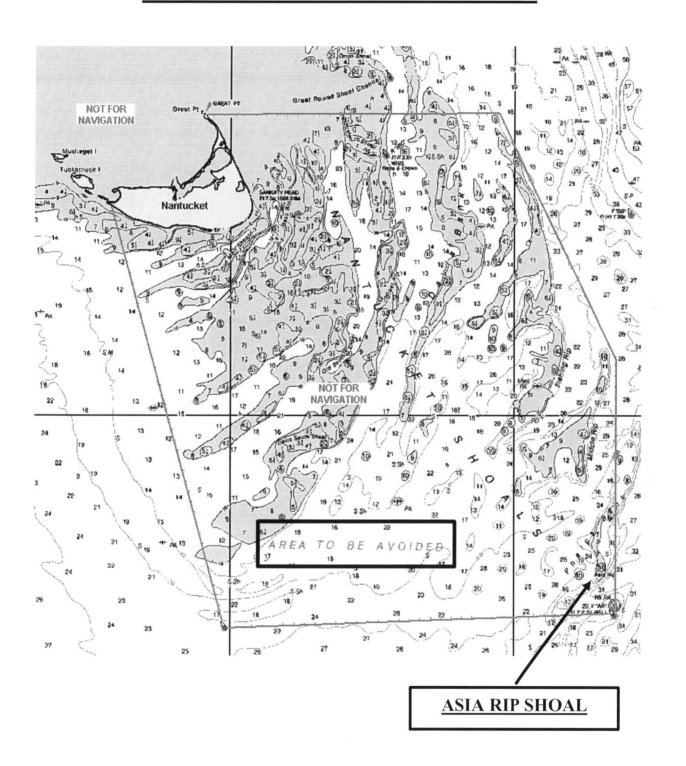

NOT FOR NAVIGATION

NOT FOR NAVIGATION

AREA TO BE AVOIDED

ASIA RIP SHOAL

In these storm conditions, the *Midnight Sun* probably encountered a giant breaking wave that caused her to be "Hove Down." Then she was probably was hit with another big breaking wave before she could recover, and she foundered and sank. This would have happened very quickly and would explain why she never made a "Mayday" call.

A second possibility is that she was hove down by a large breaking wave and then her ballast shifted, just as it did on the *Venus*, and she could not recover, and she went down.

A third possibility is that her course home would have taken her across what is known as the "Steamer Track," which is the area that the large ships use on their voyages, to and from, the United States and Europe. She could have been run down by a large ship in the turmoil of the heavy weather. Many fishing boats have suffered this fate over the years, including the F/V *Donna Lynn*, as my brother can attest.

I believe that the most probable explanation is that the *Midnight Sun* was hove down, and she was lost with all hands, due to the intensity of the storm which was a once in a lifetime storm event. I had the opportunity to discuss this with Captain Kenneth Risdal briefly, and it was my impression that this was his conclusion as well.

To further add weight to this conclusion, I also had the opportunity to discuss the possible causes of the loss of the *Midnight Sun* with Captain Reidar Bendiksen, and he recounted an experience of his own, on the F/V *Moby Dick*. The *Moby Dick* was also a Gamage built boat, launched in 1962, and is referenced by the judge in the court case, as an example of the correct way to enclose the scallop shucking boxes. The F/V *Moby Dick* was regarded as one of our finest fishing vessels. Captain Bendiksen told me a story about making the turn at the Great Round Shoal Channel, in heavy weather, while heading home to New Bedford. This put the stormwind, and large seas on the starboard rear quarter of the *Moby Dick*. Captain Bendiksen recalled; "She laid over to the point where I thought she wouldn't come back up. The pilothouse on these boats have access doors on each side. The *Moby Dick* heeled so far over that I was literally standing on the port side pilothouse door, as the door was now the floor, and my brother, who was at the wheel, was hanging onto the wheel, trying to stay upright. She finally righted herself, and we proceeded home, but it was an unnerving experience."

THE F/V *MOBY DICK*

CAPTAIN REIDAR BENDIKSEN

Added to Captain Bendiksen' experience on this occasion, is the fact that my father was very concerned about allowing the *Venus*, to get quarter to the sea, in this storm. He spoke plainly about being careful when he turned her to run before the wind. He was concerned that if he took the seas and wind on the quarter, he was running the risk of another knockdown. All boats have their own handling characteristics, and perhaps these two experiences might highlight that these boats, like most boats, were a little vulnerable when taking heavy seas on the quarter.

A boat has handling characteristics that have more in common with an airplane than an automobile. A ship can move below the surface that she is sailing on, or dive, like an airplane, of course with dire results. If the boat is weighted down unnaturally on the port side forward, as was the case with the *Venus*, she will be more susceptible to a push from a breaking sea on the starboard aft quarter. It would literally make the boat dive and roll, or be hove down, and probably go "turtle."

Added to this, is the fact that the *Venus* was hove down, and only by a miracle did she get back up and make it home. The ballast shifted on the *Venus*, to the forward port side, and this added to her difficulties and made her more prone to being hove down again, especially with seas on the starboard rear quarter. This is the reason, my father was so concerned, with not taking any seas on the starboard quarter when he turned the *Venus*.

We will never know for sure, but these are the most likely possibilities. At the end of the day, the *Midnight Sun* was taken by a once in a lifetime storm that was not forecasted. There was no warning to the fleet as to what was coming. The *Midnight Sun* was the victim of a "Bombogenesis" storm of massive intensity. It was simply an unfortunate, "Act of God."

Rest in Peace

Captain Magne Risdal
Mate Olav Ferkingstad
Jans Ferkingstad
August Larsen
Torgils Holmen
Osjborn Pedersen
Sam Lund
Gordon Kallestein
Jon Nilsen
John Wagner
Arne Lindanger

Rest in Peace,
You Sons of Norway

Hvil i fred,
du sønner av Norge

THE F/V 3&1&1
Captain Louis Doucette, Jr.

Captain Magne Risdal and his F/V *Barbara*, came to the aid of my father, and the F/V 3&1&1, off Nomans Land, saving them from certain destruction. Captain Risdal placed his vessel in extreme peril to do this.

My father had the highest respect for Captain Magne Risdal's ability and character, and my father did not dole out respect unless he thought it was deserved. In the mid -1950's, my father found himself, and his crew, including my brother, and the F/V 3&1&1 drifting off Nomans Land and about to wreck. The engine had failed, and they had put out the anchor, but it was not holding the boat against the strong tide. My father then put the net in the water, trying to slow down the boat from continuing to drift towards the island. Nomans Land is an island located close to the southwest of Martha's Vineyard. It is surrounded by dangerous rocks that will rip a boat to pieces. The tide was pushing the F/V 3&1&1 towards these rocks, and it appeared that they would soon wreck. Luckily, Captain Magne "Mike" Risdal and his F/V *Barbara* happened to come upon the scene, and he put his boat in grave peril but managed to save the F/V 3&1&1. My father even told Magne not to try, because it was too dangerous, and he might wreck the *Barbara*. Magne ignored this advice and rescued the F/V 3&1&1, and her crew, and towed them safely home to New Bedford. My father and brother never forgot him for it. He was a good friend and a brave Captain.

This is who Captain Magne Risdal was, a friend of high character, and a man who tried to do the right thing, someone who you could depend on. As my father often said, "Captain Risdal was the "Finest Kind" of a man and fisherman."

My father took the loss of Magne, and his *Midnight Sun*, very hard and he spoke of him often, throughout the rest of his life.

Captain Magne Risdal
New Bedford Fisherman
U.S. Army Veteran of WWII
"The Finest Kind"

Chapter 25

Growing up in a Fishing Family

"I would sometimes be asked, Captain, are we going to have a good trip?
I would answer, a good trip is one where we make it back to the dock."

Captain Rodney Avila
New Bedford Fishing Captain

What is it like to grow up in a fishing family? I was recently asked this question by two people. I was asked to take part in the making of a documentary film about the New Bedford Fishing Industry. Kevin Kertscher, the filmmaker, asked me this question during my interview. I was next asked this same question by Sean McCarthy, a newspaper reporter, who was writing an article for the local newspaper. I very brilliantly answered with something like, "It was just normal to me, fishing is just ingrained into our being because we're around it so much." I hadn't anticipated this question, and I was woefully unprepared to answer it intelligently. But these two men had put the wheels in motion for me to think more about this subject. They forced me to examine my being, and ask myself questions about who I am, and how did growing up in a fishing family shape me into the man that I am today. Here are my conclusions;

First, it is anything but routine when compared to the general population. It is not normal to have your father absent for seventy-percent of your young life. A fishing trip would last eight to fourteen days, and then dad would be home for three days before he left again. As a teenager, I arranged my social life around whether the "Old Man" was in (at home), or out (on the fishing grounds). The rules were a little tighter when the captain was "in" and walking the deck of the house in Fairhaven. My friends would even ask me when we would be making plans for the weekend; "Is the old man in, or out?" My curfew was a little tighter when the captain was home. On a ship the captain is often referred to as the "Old Man," and it does not refer to his age, it refers to his position as the captain.

Second, I remember the stress of how my mother had to work on a budget. The wife of a fisherman must deal with the absence of their spouse, and the pressure of keeping the home in order until he returns. A fishing family never knows precisely how much money they will have to work with, in any given month. It is all dependent on the size of the catch and the market price when they return with that catch. Many variables can adversely affect the income of the family. A string of bad luck, such as an engine breakdown, severe weather, not being able to find the fish, or the market value of your catch when you return to port. The boat owner provides the boat, but the crew must pay for the food that they eat, the ice that they need to maintain the fish that they catch, and the fuel that they use to keep the engine running during the fishing trip. These expenses are deducted from the money that the crew shares. I have seen the boat come in prematurely, due to bad weather or mechanical breakdown, with a small catch to sell, and the crew would literally owe the boat money. There is no guaranteed minimum salary, you catch fish, and you make money, or you don't eat, and you don't pay your bills. How's that for pressure? If some people feel that fishermen are a little prickly and are easily offended, or agitated, try carrying that kind of pressure on your shoulders for fifty years.

The significant stress is when the weather is terrible. I could see the anxiety build in my mother when the weather turned nasty. When the wind was howling, and rain, snow, and ice was beating against the windows of the house, and the "Old Man" was out, we would all wonder and worry about what was happening out on Georges. It takes a strong woman to fill the role of a fisherman's wife.

Thirdly, and this is the "Big Elephant" in the room. A fishing family must deal with something that we don't like to say out loud. We tiptoe around this subject by saying that fishing is a dangerous profession and other such statements. Fishermen are very superstitious, so we don't want to jinx anyone by talking too specifically about the danger. But, for the career of the fisherman, the family has a higher probability of the sudden unexpected death of a loved one, than the normal population. This higher than average probability of death, as in some other professions, such as the military, police, firefighters, loggers, and miners, leads to long-term stress. We get a brief respite from it when they return home from a fishing trip, but it starts again as soon as they head back out. It's not over until they retire from the business, which in the case of my father was fifty-years. He beat the odds, but he had several near-death experiences in the process. For the child in the family, the elephant called "Sudden Unexpected Death," grows as you grow, and you become more aware of the dangers experienced in fishing. When you go offshore fishing, you are risking your life. I learned these lessons as I grew. I slowly became aware of the danger as I learned and processed the following family events;

At an early age, I learned that my great-grandfather, Amable Doucette, was lost at sea while fishing, in the year 1880.

I knew that my Grandfather had several near-death experiences while fishing;

I learned that my grandfather was a member of the five-man crew of the 37-foot fishing sloop, *Pricilla*, based out of Edgartown on Martha's Vineyard. On January 10, 1910, the six-masted schooner, the *Mertie B. Crowley*, ran aground on Wasque Shoals, on the south side of Martha's Vineyard Island, in a blinding nor'easter snow storm. The *Crowley* was 300-feet long and had a crew of fourteen souls aboard, which included Captain William Haskell and his wife, Ida. The Coast Guard was unable to reach the *Crowley*, due to the shallow water and high seas. Captain Haskell ordered the crew, and his wife, to climb up the rigging and to lash themselves to the masts, in the hope that they could survive the disintegrating ship until they could be rescued. When the Coast Guard failed in their attempts, the townspeople of Edgartown called for Captain Levi Jackson, a skilled and daring fishing captain, who had a reputation of being a fearless seaman, and who seemed to be able to do the impossible. Captain Jackson already had several daring rescues to this credit. His reputation of defying death to save others was so established that the young boys who looked up to the five-foot, two-inch captain, had nicknamed him Captain "Ri-De-Di-Di," which translated to "Captain Ready-To-Die," in the Edgartown slang of the day. The young boys would holler it out when he walked down the streets of Edgartown, as a salute to the dynamo of a man that they admired. My grandfather was a member of the crew of Captain Jackson's 37-foot fishing vessel the *Pricilla*. The fishermen made it to the *Crowley* and anchored in the lee of the schooner, which was as close as they could get to the sinking ship. Once in position, my grandfather launched his dory and rowed to the stern of the *Crowley*. He attempted to rig a breeches buoy to remove the crew of the schooner. This proved to be impossible, and he then rowed back to the *Pricilla*. Captain Jackson realized that the only means to remove the stranded crew would be to launch three of his dories and take the crew off the sinking ship one at a time. The skill of the fishermen in control of a fourteen-foot dory in heavy seas, honed during their life fishing on Georges Bank, would now be the key toward saving the lives of the crew of the *Crowley*. This required that the *Crowley* crew members had to time their jump into the dory, as it was rising with the incoming waves, up to the rail of the schooner. The cook miss-timed his jump and fell into the sea, he desperately grabbed the rail of a dory and overturned the dory in the process. The cabin boy froze when facing the jump and had to be threatened with being left behind if he didn't jump. My grandfather was credited with making eight trips to the *Crowley* in his dory, and with safely bringing seven of the fourteen *Crowley* crew members back to the *Pricilla*. Two brothers Patrick and Henry Kelly manned the other two dories and saved the other seven members of the *Crowley's* crew. Eugene Benefito manned the *Pricilla* with Captain Jackson, while the dories were shuttling to the schooner and worked at getting the numb and half-frozen shipwreck victims out of the dories and onto the deck of the *Pricilla*.

On the trip back to Edgartown, the overloaded fishing boat nearly swamped several times. A very close call for all involved. The fishermen were all awarded the Carnegie Medal for Extraordinary Heroism, by the foundation established by Andrew Carnegie, to honor those that risk their lives to save others. The medal that my grandfather received from the Carnegie Hero Fund, is inscribed with the following; "Greater love hath no man than this, that a man lay down his life for his friends" (John 15:13). The Carnegie Medal is an award that is still bestowed by the Carnegie Hero Fund every year, to honor the best amongst us, many times posthumously. As a young boy, I would often take the medal out of its case and hold it in my hands. I understood, at a very young age, that it represented sacrifice and a heroic effort against overwhelming odds. I realized that this medal in my hands represented the danger that all men of the sea face, on a routine basis, and the fact that my grandfather has put his life at risk, to save others who were about to lose their lives.

During World War I, while swordfishing 225-miles from Highland Light, on Cape Cod, my grandfather was stopped by a German submarine. The U-Boat commander gave the fishermen five minutes to get into two dories. Then the German submarine commander gave the fishermen a compass course heading to follow to reach Cape Cod and wished them luck. The German submarine then turned the deck gun onto the fishing boat and very quickly sunk the F/V *Progress*. The two dories overloaded with the crew of the *Progress* rowed for two days before they were sighted by another fishing vessel and rescued. A close call.

I learned that in 1919, my grandfather had just unloaded a trip of fish at the Fulton Fish Market in New York City. He was at the apex of his fishing career, and he was the captain and owner of the F/V *Gleaner*, a state-of-the-art fishing boat for the year 1919. She was the first fishing boat in New Bedford equipped with electric lights. He was headed home and stopped in Bay City, New York, to fill his fuel tanks. In 1919, the engine was gasoline fueled. Due to a careless dock attendant, a spark from a cigarette ignited an explosion, and the *Gleaner* was blown out of the water. Four members of his crew were killed instantly, one of the dead crew, Fredrick Richards, was my grandfather's brother. My grandfather was blown into the water, and he hung onto a piece of chain which was attached to the pier, for several hours, before being discovered. He was hospitalized for six months due to these injuries, and it took him a further two years to fully recover.

I learned that my father had been offshore fishing in 1938, as the 27-year old captain of the F/V *Sankaty Head*, a 55-foot boat. The 1938 Hurricane was one of the most destructive to ever to hit the mainland of the United States and the worst to hit this far north. Winds were clocked at 121-mph sustained, with peak gusts of 186-mph, by the Blue Hills Weather Observatory, outside of Boston. The *Sankaty Head* did not return to New Bedford until three days after the storm had passed through, and the *Sankaty Head* was presumed to be lost with all hands. Another close call.

I learned that my brother while fishing as a young man with my father, was caught up in the scallop dredge as it was being set over the side. It was taking him down, and he went under with the dredge. If not for his ability to keep a clear head, and his strong swimming ability, along with the quick work of my Uncle Spud Murphy, and my father, I would have never known my brother.

In the 1950's, my father was the captain of the F/V *Nellie Pet*, and she fished out of Gloucester. On a visit to Gloucester, I got to view the plaques of the names of all the men who were lost fishing out of Gloucester. I counted fifteen men in the 1800's that shared my last name, out of the 3,436 Gloucester fishermen lost during that century. While these Doucette's were all Gloucester fishermen, I discovered that they all originally hailed from the southern region of Nova Scotia, which is where we came from, these men were my blood.

In January 1955, the F/V *Doris Gertrude* was lost with 11-men, while fishing on Georges Bank in a nor'easter with heavy snow. The captain and the engineer were my uncles. During the ensuing Coast Guard search, I witnessed the agony and grief of my aunts as the search moved from day to day with no sign of the boat or her crew. When it was over, we were left with no closure as we had no bodies to bury. When I entered the first grade the following September, I found that I had a classmate, Henry Zalewski, Jr., and I knew immediately that his father, and my uncles, all went down together on the F/V *Doris Gertrude*, the previous January. As we grew up, we became classmates and friends, and we both knew our shared history, but we never said a word about it to each other. It's the elephant in the room. As I progressed through school, I met and became friends with Tommy and Helger Johnson, and then Billy Gushue. Their fathers, Helger Johnson, and

Timothy Gushue were lost at sea together, with five other shipmates, aboard the F/V *Paolina*, in 1952.

In 1962, my father returned home from a trip in mid-November, and he was shaken up and told us about the storm that they had just survived, the subject of this book. While he had been through many storms at sea, including three hurricanes, he always maintained that this was as close as he ever came, to being lost at sea. Another close call. I was 13-years old in 1962, and I was starting to get it, but to me, my dad was some mixture of Sinbad the Sailor, Admiral Horatio Nelson, Admiral Bull Halsey, and maybe Superman, when he was on the water, so I thought, yes it happens, but not to him. Only a young boy of 13-years could be that naïve.

In 1966, I was a junior in high school when I learned that my sister's father-in-law, John Pendergast while fishing in heavy weather in November, had been swept from the deck of the F/V *Terra Nova*, and was lost at sea.

In 1977, while I was working in South Carolina, word reached me that my brother was aboard the F/V *Donna Lynn*, with his friend Captain Eddie Carter, when they were run down by a large container ship. Crewman Barney Lopes, a long-time experienced fisherman, was lost overboard during this incident and was a man who had fished extensively with my father. My father had such trust in Barney, and his ability, that he assigned him with the position of being the mast-headsman when they went swordfishing every summer. Barney Lopes was a good fisherman, and he was respected by all the men who went to sea with him. My brother told me that whenever there was any kind of an emergency on the boat, Barney was always the first man to run to the trouble. I have fond memories of Barney, who always had a kind word for me when I was a youngster and visited the boat. The F/V *Donna Lynn* and the remaining crew managed to make it back to New Bedford, with the assistance of the Coast Guard. Another close call for my brother.

The point is, almost any long-term fishing family can probably put together a similar list of death and near-death experiences, while fishing. This is the significant lurking threat that all fishermen and their families live under. The high probability of the sudden unexpected death of a loved one. It is like a long-term illness, and you don't know for years if you will survive it or not. It is the "Elephant in the Room," and what makes it worse, is that when someone is lost at sea, you usually have no closure, because there is no body to bury and grieve over.

This is what it is like to grow up in a fishing family.

THE F/V GLEANER
My Grandfather's Boat

The first fishing boat in New Bedford equipped with electric lights,
returning from Georges Bank and burdened with ice.
A state-of-the-art fishing vessel, in 1919.

Chapter 26

<u>NEPTUNE'S BURDEN</u>

"When you're finally up at the moon looking back on earth, all those differences and nationalistic traits are pretty well going to blend, and you're going to get a concept that maybe this really is one world and why the hell can't we learn to live together like decent people."

Frank Borman, Apollo 8 Astronaut

In October of 1962, the United States went face to face with the Soviet Union in the Cuban Missile Crisis. The world was poised on the brink of all-out nuclear war. It was a terrifying and uncertain time. I was thirteen years old, and I remember this crisis very distinctly. I recall sitting at a traffic light in the family car, at the entrance to the New Bedford–Fairhaven Bridge, listening to the latest news update on the car radio. The news was bleak, and the reporter was emphasizing how close we were to a confrontation with the Soviet Union. I recall turning to my mother, who was also in the car, and asking her if we were going to war with the Russians? Her reply was, "It certainly looks like it!" I remember the dread that I felt at her answer. Even at my young age, I realized the seriousness of the event. It was not lost on me that we lived 60-miles south of Boston, 200-miles north of New York City, and 30-miles from Otis Air Force Base, all likely enemy targets. I also realized that we lived on the coast so I could imagine that if an invasion of troops took place, we might have invaders in our streets and neighborhood. I remember that during science class every day at school, we were being lectured on how to try to survive a nuclear attack, both at school, and at home. We were sent home with building plans on how to construct a fallout shelter in our homes and encouraged to discuss it with our parents.

It was a very sobering time with constant talk and speculation about nuclear war and the Soviet Union. Thankfully, nothing happened, and the world escaped catastrophe. However, for many weeks after the two superpowers regained their sanity, the world saw savage weather events, including the subject of this book, "Neptune's Nor'easter." During the week highlighted in this book, 155-mariners were lost worldwide due to the extreme weather. As I've expressed in the book, I believe that the "Higher Powers" were disappointed with mankind for being so reckless and stupid.

Now, it is the winter of 2018, and all that we hear in the news are problems with the Russians, armed conflicts with terrorists all over the world, and the possibility of nuclear war with North Korea. We have also experienced extreme ocean generated weather events this year, with massive destruction from hurricanes in the Caribbean, Florida, Texas, Puerto Rico, and other locations, along with a constant series of nor'easters slamming the East Coast. An Iranian oil tanker, the *Sanchi*, sank in the East China Sea, after colliding with a Chinese freighter, with the loss of 32-mariners, in January 2018. This incident is reminiscent of the Norwegian and Japanese tankers that collided in the Kawasaki Canal, in November of 1962, with the loss of 40-mariners. The parallels are easy to see, it feels a lot like 1962 to me, and that's a shame.

While my personal views could best be described as middle of the road, slightly conservative. I was trained in the United States Army as an NBC (Nuclear, Biological, and Chemical) specialist. This training exposed me to the potential horrors of these types of warfare. Most of this training taught us how to identify, treat, and decontaminate, both people and equipment that have been exposed to various chemical warfare agents. It becomes evident to me, what I am watching when I see the television news showing civilians, including children in Syria, suffering and dying from chemical nerve agent. It breaks my heart to recognize first responders and civilians, trying to treat these nerve gas casualties by washing them down with water hoses, all while the victims thrash around while foaming at the mouth. None of these brave rescuers having personal protective equipment of their own, such as gas masks and protective clothing. I have yet to see anyone treating the victims with an antidote injection of atropine to the muscles of the thigh, which is necessary as an attempt to block the nerve gas agent and possibly save the victims life. How horrible it is to watch the pain and the panic of all involved, the victims, the rescuers, and often the parents of the children, all without proper equipment, or training, on how to help these innocent children. It is unimaginable, that man can be this cruel and twisted, to unleash such horror on his fellow man. There surely is a special place in hell for anyone who would do such a thing.

I then see the news on television that a chemical agent was used on the streets of Salisbury, England, a beautiful English town of 40,000 people, and the Prime Minister of Britain declaring that Russia is responsible. I hear North Korea threatening to drop nuclear weapons on the United States. I hear our President, threatening to wipe North Korea off the face of the earth. I see the Russian President giving a presentation to his nation, boasting that they have developed hypersonic nuclear missiles that are unstoppable, and showing a digital enactment of these missiles raining down on what is easily identifiable as Florida. It makes me think that the world has lost its collective mind.

I believe in the need for a strong military because I recognize that the world is a dangerous place. I doubt that anyone who knows me would describe me as a pacifist. However, I can look at these news events now, and the recent extreme weather events, and how closely they mirror the news and weather events from the last time man came close to destroying the planet, in 1962, and I ask myself, are the Gods sending us a message? Are these extreme weather events a warning? Is Neptune the messenger? It seems, not much has changed in the world, in fifty-six years. It all sounds the same, as it did when I was a young boy in 1962. In more than half a century, it doesn't look to me, that mankind has made much progress in making the world a better place.

<u>Nothing good ever comes from hate!</u>

I can imagine Neptune, somewhere on the bottom of the ocean, holding his trident, shaking his head, and wondering; what is it that we must do, to get their attention, and thinking when will these mortals ever learn?

<u>It's the burden of the messenger!</u>

<u>Will we listen?</u>

Chapter 27

EPILOGUE

Challenge, Adaptability, Resilience, and Respect

If you are reading this book, you probably selected it because you were looking to learn about a true sea story. I hope that I have provided that to you and that I have provided some insight into the life of commercial fishermen. This book is based on actual historical events and facts, and this is indeed a true story. The men, boats, and ships that I have described, and that you have read about are real, they existed, or in some cases, they still exist and live today.

I have taken the liberty of adding my interpretation of some of the events in this book, I have only done this to add emphasis to the narrative when no other source of information exists. I have introduced two mythical characters as a means, to help present my thoughts on these actual events. I believe that there are no coincidences in life, and that life is a series of journeys. I believe that those who have gone before us, are sometimes near us, and they are trying to guide us, albeit in a subtle way. We must be alert if we wish to pick up on this guidance. My beliefs in this regard are part of my personal views, and they are sometimes reflected in my writing. You may, or may not, agree with these types of thoughts, and that is your prerogative. Fishermen and men of the sea are superstitious, and they believe that sometimes there are unseen forces at work. I guess that I have inherited some of that thought process.

The introduction of Neptune as a part of this book evolved as I studied the nautical charts of the area of Georges Bank that came so close to taking my father's life. As I stared at the chart late one night, trying to collect my thoughts on how to express the inherent danger of this specific location on Georges Bank, the shape of the shoals suddenly appeared to me as the prongs of a pitchfork. There is no mistaking the shape of the area of the Cultivator Shoal and Georges Shoal on a nautical chart. The area of these shoals is highlighted in light blue, to convey the danger that they possess, it is a visual warning to any mariner who consults these charts. This area that is highlighted in blue on the chart looks like a three-prong pitchfork. My mind suddenly jumped to the thought that no, this is the ocean, so this must be the trident that is associated with Neptune. Since the fishing vessel that my father was aboard during this storm was named the *Venus*, I knew immediately that I had a connection. I decided to make the Roman Goddess Venus, and the Roman God

Neptune, central to my story, the heroine and a protagonist, for some fictional way to present and explain my thoughts, in this non-fiction work. The concept of Neptune allowed my mind to explore the ideas that I have expressed in this book, concerning why we do the things that we do, and how mankind seems to make the same mistakes over and over. I guess Neptune will be part of my journeys always, and I'm glad to have him aboard. Neptune and I have come to understand each other, and I like to think that in some small way, he is using me to convey his message.

After finishing the previous chapter, you would probably think that I am a pessimistic person. No, it is Neptune who is the pessimist, and from his perspective, I can understand why he feels this way. I would contend that I have always been optimistic, and at times I could be accused of being overly optimistic. No, I am, and always will be an optimist at heart, but I have learned to be more cautious.

While I am concerned about recent world events that seem to indicate that mankind is slow to learn, I do take solace in the fact that humanity is resilient, and we always find ways to adapt and meet the challenges that we face. Some of these challenges are global, and some are local. For most of us, the problems that we can affect are local. I would like to think that if everyone could do the best possible job with their local challenges, then we would all live in a better world.

This book had its' genesis in December of 2004, after the sinking of the F/V *Northern Edge*, with a brief short story that I wrote as a gift to my father. Ten years later, in 2014, I began serious work on researching and writing this book. This chapter marks the end of my four-year journey of following my father's sea story of his encounter with Neptune's Nor'easter. But, now I realize that this has in fact been a much longer trip. Unknowingly, I have been preparing for this project for my entire life. It has been a great experience, and it has also been one of the most challenging tasks, that I have ever undertaken. I have been asked many times; Why have you written this book? Why have you spent so much of your time on this project? I have answered this question in many ways, but here are the real reasons.

My father passed away in 2006, and as I have already explained, Mrs. Kirsten Bendiksen put the idea in my head, of writing a book about this storm, that our fathers had encountered while shipmates aboard the F/V *Venus* in 1962. Some weeks after my father's funeral my sisters gave me two boxes of papers that belonged to my dad and that he had marked to be given to me. These boxes contained newspaper articles and other documents that concerned fishing, along with two cones of fishing net twine, two fishing-net-knitting-needles, and my father's jackknife. These boxes had resided in a closet at my home, for eight years, and they had been untouched during that entire time. In 2014, I had a dream one night of my father, and I began to think about him more often than I had in a long time. I like to think that it was more a message than a dream. This message prompted me to dig out and look at those two boxes in the closet. As I worked my way through these memories that my dad had collected and kept, there was a copy of a front-page story in the Providence Journal newspaper of January 15th, 1992. The title of the article was, "Has Georges Bank Gone Bust," and it featured my father's opinions on the subject. My dad had been retired for sixteen years, on the date of the article, but he had stayed close to the fishing industry during his "retirement." He was still working making nets for the fleet at the New Bedford Ship Supply Company, with his life-long friend, Captain Eli Pothier. As he always was, my father was very clear in his thoughts about the depletion of Georges Bank. He spoke about the damage that the foreign fishing fleets had inflicted on Georges Bank, primarily the fishing vessels from the Soviet Union. He spoke about a proposal that was made in 1969, to close parts of Georges to give the bank time to replenish her stock. Dad was still actively fishing in 1969 so any closure would have hurt him badly, but he could see that something had to be done. He made a comment in the newspaper article where he said; "We have been withdrawing from this bank for too long, we need to put some deposits back in, or this bank is going to go broke." The bank he was referring to, was Georges Bank. This is a lifetime fisherman talking about conservation and the sustainability of the resource in 1969, and then again in 1992. This was not a surprise to me, as I had received a lesson and a lecture on this subject from my father in 1958 when I was nine years old. My father picked up some Russian net, that had been torn loose, and ended up in his net. The size of the mesh on the Russian net was much smaller than that of our nets. My father brought some of it home, and he hung it up in the garage. I remember my father showing me the Russian net. He was worried about this net, and he pointed out that the small openings in the mesh of the Russian net would not allow the young fish to escape, and live to grow, and become the mature fish that we would catch next year. I remember my dad telling me about the massive size of these foreign state-owned fishing vessels, some of them reaching 800-feet in length. He said to me; "Boy, they're vacuuming up the bank, and if it doesn't stop soon, we're not going to have any fish to catch." This was my first lesson that fishermen do understand and worry about sustainability.

My father loved to go swordfishing in the summer months, and I always thought that to him, harpooning swordfish was as close as he could come to having fun while fishing. Swordfish are a predatory fish, they hunt and eat smaller fish, and they are fighters. They fear no other fish in the sea. Fishermen have a high level of respect for swordfish because whether they are aware of it, or not, they both share some of the same traits. Fishermen are predators, they hunt and catch fish, and they will fight. They fear no fish in the sea or no other man on the sea. In some ways, fishermen have more in common with Mr. Swordfish, than he does with Mr. Smith, his next-door neighbor, at home.

In my father's fishing career, swordfish were harpooned. This was before the technique of long-line swordfishing was used, as you may have seen portrayed in the movie, "The Perfect Storm." Swordfishing in my father's time was closer to the technique that was used to catch whales, in the old days. A swordfish was struck with a harpoon, known as striking the fish, a line was run out from the harpoon lily that was left in the swordfish, and the other end of the line was attached to a floating keg. A dory was put over the side, and a fisherman manned the dory, he then rowed to the swordfish float. The fishermen, now in a 14-foot dory, carefully and by-hand must haul the swordfish to the surface. This fighting fish can be as long as his dory and weigh upwards of five hundred pounds. Swordfish have been known to attack the dory and punch a hole through the small dory with his sword, so this is a delicate and dangerous process for the fisherman, who is all alone in his dory. The swordfish is then secured to the dory, and the fisherman places one oar in the upright position to signal the fishing vessel that he has his fish, and he is ready to be retrieved. Sometimes the fishing vessel proceeds so far away chasing more swordfish, that the man loses sight of the fishing boat. He is all alone in a 14-foot dory, 150-miles from land, with a large dangerous bleeding and dying fish, as his only company. As you can imagine a large bleeding fish can attract all kinds of unwanted company on his own, mostly sharks. I describe the process to people, as miniature whaling. My dad lived for the chance to chase and catch swordfish every summer. He was so obsessed with this fishery that he picked up the nickname of, "Swordfish Louie." Dad was not in favor of the longline fishing of swordfish, because while he understood the efficiency of the technique, he felt that it would take too many juvenile swordfish, along with the adults. This is another example of a life-long fisherman understanding the need for conservation and sustainability.

No real fisherman wants to destroy the resource that sustains him and his family. No real fisherman intends to pull the last fish out of the ocean. When I hear comments and theories, about how fishermen have destroyed the fishing resources, and then they are blamed as the sole source of the problem, I know that those accusations and statements are not entirely correct. Real lifetime fishermen understand conservation and sustainability, and they are the ones with the most to win or lose, in this battle. If my father was alive today, I am sure that he would tell you that the overfishing of Georges Bank was primarily caused by the foreign fleets that fished our banks for years, unregulated and uncontrolled. He would then rail on about how the government was too slow to act on this issue, and how our government disrespected the New England fishermen's cries for help on this issue.

The next item that I found in my father's boxes of keepsakes were pages of yellow lined paper with words written in my father's handwriting. These were mostly his attempts to write about some of his favorite sea stories and experiences. My father dropped out of high school when he was sixteen years old, during the depression, because his father needed him on the family boat. His education had been cut short, so his attempt at writing was limited. I now better understood why he pushed me to gain as much education, as possible, and why he so valued education. He preached the value of education to me, almost every day that I was in his presence. He had been deprived of his own opportunity to further his education, due to the economic realities of his youth. It made me sad to think of my father at sixteen years old. Still just a teenager, packing his sea bag and having to turn his back on his youth, and his desire to continue his education, and going out to sea to help his family. I wonder what he might have become if he did not come of age at the beginning of the Great Depression.

As I progressed further into my father's written pages, I was shocked to find a personal letter that he had written to me. I never knew it was there, and I never knew that he had written this letter, it was buried amongst his other papers. Most of the contents of this letter are very personal but suffice it to say, that it contained praise, advice, how much he enjoyed sailing on my boat in the summer, and a message that my mother wanted conveyed to me, before her death. I treasure it as a message that was sent to me, from both my mother and my father, from beyond the grave. One of the items in this letter was his thanks for the short story that I had written about his storm experience in the November of 1962 Nor'easter, that I now call Neptune's Nor'easter. The next day, I began to seriously work on this book. The discovery of my father's personal letter was the fuel that propelled me on the journey of writing his favorite sea story.

During my research, as I was scouring newspaper articles in search of information on this storm, I was drawn to the other parts of these old newspapers. I found myself reading everything from the headline front page stories all the way through to the sports pages. This was a wonderful trip down memory lane, and it allowed me to re-focus my thoughts of this time period of my youth. I spent time at the New Bedford Public Library reading the New Bedford Standard-Times newspapers on microfiche. I obtained a digital subscription to the New York Times, the London Times, and the Boston Globe so that I could search their archives.

However, as I read the headlines and the world events of 1962, I suddenly realized how the reported news events then, mirrored many of the same news events and challenges that we face today. This was both enlightening and distressing at the same time. I must admit that I became obsessed with the year 1962, and the realization that the world is still engaged in the same type of destructive behavior now, as we did then. I have always been fascinated when I have listened to an actor describe how they sometimes get into character for the entire time that they are playing a role. These actors take on the life of that character and temporarily become that person. During the writing of this book, I have found myself, in some ways living in 1962. I have driven my family and friends crazy, with my constant talk about this storm, and the news events of that time. I could see them sometimes cringe, and the expression on their faces gave away their thought of; "Here he comes, and he's going to bombard us with information about the book." I apologize to all of them, and I hope that they can now understand that I was just in character, and for me, it was something that I had to do. It's over now, as this is the last chapter of, "the book," and you can all relax and hopefully not avoid me when I approach.

Today, in 2018, the New Bedford fishing industry is currently engulfed by the most significant and dangerous storm it has ever experienced. The outcome is unknown, and this is not a storm that the fishermen can take on alone. The very survival of our fishing industry is at stake. We stand at a tipping point and time is of the essence. The fishing industry today looks much different than it did in my grandfather's day, and this is to be expected. If there is one truism in life, it is that change is to be expected, and that change is inevitable. The question is, how do we manage change, and not allow it to destroy us? This is the challenge that the New Bedford Fishing Industry is grappling with today. The industry is far more regulated and structured than it was in my grandfather and father's days. There is now a triumvirate involved in the management and operation of the fishing industry; government regulators, marine scientists and environmentalists, and of course, the actual fishermen. As you would expect there has been a great deal of contention, accusation, and hurt feelings on all sides, as these changes in how fishing is conducted are being worked out. This is a very complicated problem, and I do not profess to understand it in detail. My family have been commercial fishermen for six generations, but today there is no member of my immediate family still in the business, so I do not have current family insight into the problems, as I did in the past.

I would like to think that everyone involved is trying to do their best to solve these issues. I would like to believe that everyone is coming from a position of concern because they all love the ocean and want to help to preserve it. Anyone who has ever seen a picture of the earth that has been taken from space, can't help but be moved by the blue color of our home, looking lonely in the blackness of space. We understand that the blue light that is emitted is caused by the oceans that dominate our planet. It is not hard to deduce that the health and protection of the world's oceans are critical to the health of the humans who live on this planet, as well as, the marine life that live in our oceans. Fishermen understand these things as they spend most of their life out on the sea. I once calculated that my father spent more than seventy percent of his working years out on the ocean. This calculated out to about 35 years on a fishing boat at sea. No mariner of any type spends more time at sea than offshore commercial fishermen. Only men who love the sea could do this for a lifetime.

Fishermen are a different breed of cat, they spend most of their lives, aboard a boat out on the ocean among similar like-minded men. Normal behavior aboard the boat sometimes is not so normal ashore and therefore they are often misunderstood. In the May 3rd, 2010 edition of The New Bedford Standard Times, Don Cuddy wrote the following: "Route 18 in New Bedford may divide the city from the waterfront, but it also defines a boundary between two very different worlds; that of the landsman and those who do business in great waters. Yet in spite of its long history and tradition, the average person ashore knows nothing about the everyday realities of commercial fishing. It is a world that exists almost as a parallel universe."

Truer words were never written!

As I promised in the introduction, I have, to the best of my ability, written this book from the point of view of the fishermen. I can only present my thoughts on this subject from what I believe my father would think about the current state of the New Bedford fishing industry. He would probably be thinking, I told you so, because he and his fishing colleagues saw this coming in the early 1960's when the foreign fishing fleets were "vacuuming up" Georges Bank. They had been fishing

Georges Bank for generations, and they had charts full of notes, denoting where the shipwrecks were located, that could tear their nets to shreds, and where specific species of fish could be found at different times of the year. My father had charts of the fishing grounds filled with information that his father had initiated, and that he had added to. The wrecks never moved, but the fish did, suddenly some areas had dried up. In William Finn's book, "The Dragger," first published in 1970, Captain Woody Bowers speaks clearly of this problem. My dad and Captain Bowers would probably say to the government regulators today; "Where were you guys when we needed you, and when this could have been easily fixed?"

The dictionary defines respect as follows; A feeling of admiration for someone or something, elicited by their abilities, or achievements, with due regard for the feelings, wishes, rights, or traditions of others.

Fishermen feel that they have often been denied respect. The first example presented in this book, is the government survey of Georges Bank in 1821, when the boundaries of the bank were defined to protect the transatlantic shipping interests, and the fishermen were told; Sorry, you're on your own out there, which then resulted in the death of 3,436 Gloucester fishermen in the 19th century.

The dismissal of the whalers' advice about the Arctic Ocean, by the British gentlemen explorers, because the whalemen were just fishermen. These educated British gentlemen then having to resort to eating the leather from their boots to survive, because they didn't respect the experience of the uneducated commercial fishermen. The U.S. Weather Bureau denying the claims of the fishermen concerning the intensity of Neptune's Nor'easter. The federal judge in the *Midnight Sun* court case denying the sworn testimony of the fishermen, labeling it as "guesstimates" and exaggeration. More recently, there has been further disrespect in how rules, regulations, and fines have been imposed on the independent fishermen. How these draconian rules have pushed the independent family owned fishing boats out of the business, and how this has brought on consolidation and more ownership by large corporations. I think you probably get the idea. Fishermen and elephants have one thing in common, they both have long memories. Showing respect is very important to fishermen, it is central to their core beliefs. You will have a hard time getting along on the fish piers, of New Bedford if you don't understand the concept of being respectful to others.

I can only say to the government officials and the scientists, that if you want to have a positive interaction with fishermen, you must come from a position of respect, and you must earn their respect. I know they can be difficult at times, and I am sure that you may have felt disrespected by them. They are strong-willed men, they must be, or they would not be able to be fishermen. They sometimes may come across as aggressive and gruff, but this is mostly the strategy of the best defense is a strong offense. They can be loud, boisterous, and very opinionated, I know because my father could be these things at times. Try to remember where they are coming from, and please realize that they have more "skin" in this game than anyone else at the table. They know that you possess information that is valuable to them. I reviewed the management structure of the NOAA (National Oceanic and Atmospheric Administration), NMFS (National Marine Fisheries Service) division, and I find it to be 4,200 men and woman strong, with a lot of highly educated smart people, and lots of lawyers. I think that some fishermen probably secretly see it as an intimidating immovable force. They probably feel like General Custer and the Seventh Cavalry, at the Little Big Horn. Surrounded and facing a numerically superior force. But, never forget, fishermen, know how to fight back when they feel they are being disrespected. The whole act of being a commercial fisherman is a constant fight, they fight the weather, they fight with the fish, they fight the machinery on the boat, sometimes they fight each other, so adding one more to the list of things to fight, won't be a problem. The true fishermen live by a code of respect and fairness. Are there some renegades who do not follow this code? Yes, of course, but the core and majority do follow the code, and all they want from the regulators is fairness and respect. While it won't be easy, everyone must work on eliminating an adversarial relationship, between all members of the fishing triumvirate.

I'll let you know a secret, deep down they have high regard for educated, smart people. I'd be willing to bet that if someone did a study of the education level obtained by the children of fishermen, it would be very high, with college level and graduate level accomplishment. This would be a true barometer of their feelings about educated people, not some comment made during a heated argument at a fishery management meeting. Commercial fishermen work hard, slacking off is not tolerated, they know how to take a calculated risk, and their core beliefs are hard work, show respect, and you will earn respect, and be fair in your dealings. They teach these beliefs to their children, and they expect the same from everyone they encounter. This is the code of the fish pier.

But, whatever you do, don't talk down to them, don't be sanctimonious and smug with them, they can smell out an insult faster than a hound dog can smell out a raccoon. Fishermen have had a lot of practice over the centuries of identifying insults. In my research, I tried to understand our fishing dilemma, and I watched a video of an NMFS meeting, and I read articles about the problems. I spent 47-years in the management of modern textiles plants, in ISO certified large corporations. I have spent more time than I care to remember attending meetings reviewing data. I am very familiar with looking at data arrays, Pareto analysis, decision trees, charts, graphs, timelines, critical paths, agenda plans, budgets, targets, you name it. In this video I observed an NMFS official droning on through a presentation with an agenda, prior meeting minutes, all printed out with numbered paragraphs, subparagraphs, revisions to previous revisions, decision trees, you name it, and in my opinion, this person was most definitely talking down to the fishermen in attendance. It made me want to pull what little hair I have remaining, right out of my head. It was one of the worst presentations that I have ever witnessed in my business career. In my opinion, this presenter needs training on how to conduct a meeting without losing your audience. There are classes that teach these skills.

As the camera panned out to the audience, you could see the fishermen sitting slouched down in their seats, with anger and disgust on their faces, and their eyes rolling back in their heads. They were being lectured to in a demeaning manner. They weren't buying the message. I can almost guarantee that I know what their thoughts were at that moment. They were probably thinking; "I've rung more salt water out of my socks than you've ever seen, you must be joking." I'd bet they were also thinking, "I'd like to see you out on Georges, with the wind blowing seventy, and thirty-foot seas, let's see how much of an expert you are then, out in our world." I must also admit that during the question and discussion period of this meeting, some of the more vocal fishermen returned some disrespect back to this official. This tit for tat exchange of insults is dangerous. It will block progress and understanding from occurring. Someone must stop this before things get worse. The way that is done is by showing and insisting on respect from all sides. This is not easy to do, but it is the only path to conflict resolution.

I also watched a video of another meeting, where Raymond and Richard Canastra, the founders and owners of the BASE New England fish auction house, are in attendance, and the frustration with the proceedings is so etched on their faces, that you really didn't need the audio portion to understand what they were thinking. I then found a newspaper article where Richie Canastra declares that some days he cannot hold a fish auction because only thirteen draggers were fishing out of New Bedford, at that time. I have known the Canastra brothers since before they were teenagers, and I would literally trust them with my life. I can see Richie in my mind when he was ten-years-old and too young to play on the basketball team that I coached, and where Raymond was our star player. Richie would come to our practices and games, and he was taking it all in, analyzing our strategies, and he knew every detail of our plays and plans. I would look across the basketball court, and I could see the wheels turning in his head. Richie was a thinker as a child, and he's a thinker as an adult. If the Canastra brothers are concerned about the future of our fishing industry, then I am very concerned.

I then watched a documentary film and viewed fishing boats with motorized conveyors on the deck, and fishermen sorting the catch, and throwing about half of the fish overboard, back into the ocean. Some of these fish are alive, and some are dead, and the reason for doing this is because they did not have the authorization to catch that species of fish. In my opinion, this is absolute madness! I understand that we need to improve the fish stocks of some endangered species. We all want sustainability, only a fool would not support the concept of sustainability. But, this system of massive amounts of paperwork, having to ask, "Please mother may I," and the tossing overboard of half of the catch, is nonsense. It is destroying the spirit of our fishermen. This current system could only be devised by bureaucrats, and committees, who have no feel for the process of going to sea and catching fish. Meetings and committees all sound terrific, but a lot of time is often wasted and people who are skilled in structured meeting warfare, often win the day and get what they want. The people with those types of meeting skills are probably not the fisherman, but the people who are skilled in meeting protocols probably are not skilled at catching fish. It's not a fair fight. Committees were how the Soviet Union was managed for decades, how did that work out?

A commercial fishing vessel is a production machine for catching fish. It is a small factory on the ocean. It must be run efficiently to produce a profit and continue to exist. These are not sport fishing boats, where you can catch and sort, and play around. Commercial fishing vessels must be run hard and run efficiently for maximum utilization. Unless your goal is to eliminate and close commercial fishing, if it is, then it looks to me that we are doing an excellent job toward that end.

These methods and policies are ripping the hearts out of our fishermen. I never thought I'd see, what I see now, some fishermen who are giving in to the inevitable, and giving up on the industry they love. They are trying to comply with impossible rules and regulations, and as hard as they try, they know it is mission impossible. It is a shame. There must be a better way to accomplish our goals.

We are all very proud of the fact, that based on dollar value landed, New Bedford is the #1 fishing port in America. This is being accomplished on the back of our scallop fishery. Scallops are carrying the load of keeping New Bedford a significant fishing port, and this is an interesting fact. My father told me that scallops were only pursued during the summer months when he first went fishing. The scallop gear was not robust and capable enough to engage in scalloping in bad weather, during that time. Everyone in the industry knew that there was an abundance of scallops available on the fishing grounds. My dad told me that there was a united effort between the fishermen, equipment companies, the fish buyers, and the New Bedford Seafood Producer's Association, to catch, promote, and market scallops. This is an excellent example of the power of cooperation and teamwork. We need to duplicate this spirit of collaboration to overcome the challenges that we face today. We need to bury the hatchet and come together, or this is not going to end well. It is a good thing that the scallop market was developed years ago, or we would be finished right now. Commercial fishing would just be a memory like whaling and textile manufacturing have become in the history of New Bedford's major industries. If you study the history of whaling and textiles in New Bedford, you will discover that they both had a prominent productive run of about one-hundred years. Then they were both taken down by the unexpected elimination, or depletion, of a valued resource, and the introduction of new technology. In the 1840's New Bedford was the wealthiest city per capita in the United States, due to its' whaling industry. At the peak of the textile run in the 1920's, New Bedford's textile mills employed more than 40,000 people. Then they were gone.

It has been 106-years since my grandfather moved his family from Martha's Vineyard to New Bedford to join the fishing explosion that was happening here. This prominent productive run of one-hundred years and our prior history in whaling and textiles tells me that we are at a critical juncture for the future of commercial fishing in New Bedford. Will fishing become the outlier and break this one-hundred-year trend? It will only happen if everyone in the fishing triumvirate work hard, work together, and most important learn to respect each other. I hope that we can. I would much rather eat fresh fish, than having to resort to eating my boots, as the educated British Gentlemen Explorers did to survive.

I can only offer some wise words to the people who are engaged in this challenge;

"Always try to do the right thing.
It will gratify some people and astonish the rest."
Mark Twain

It is easy to get discouraged and overwhelmed when thinking about the problems that we face. But, sometimes it is good to stand back and look at things from a distance, as this often illuminates the progress that we have made.

I thought about these things and our progress while attending the Working Waterfront Festival in New Bedford on September 23, 2017. On the date of the festival, Hurricane Jose was thrashing around offshore and was threatening Georges Bank. The entire New Bedford fishing fleet was in port taking shelter from the hurricane. One of the big crowd-drawing events of this festival is a scallop shucking contest which tests the speed of the fishermen who have the reputation of being the best at opening scallops. Sea scallops are pried open with a special knife to extract the edible meat while the boat is at sea. The scallop shells are then discarded overboard, and the scallop meat is put in a cotton bag and kept on ice for the remainder of the trip. The scallops are coming aboard at a fast pace, and thousands of them must be opened during a fishing trip. A fisherman who can do this quickly is a valuable man to have on any crew. The scallop shucking contest at the festival is a contest of speed and skill, and bragging rights are at stake. It is fast and furious, and the crowd really gets into the contest. It is a highlight of the festival. I received a call from Laura Orleans, Executive Director of the New Bedford Fishing Heritage Center, the night before the festival. Laura explained that she had a problem and asked if I could help her out. Due to Hurricane Jose and the fact that all the scallop boats had returned to port early to avoid the hurricane, they had no fresh scallops to open for the event. But, the show must go on, and Laura asked if I would be willing to give a brief talk about the storm that I was writing about, and she asked some others to talk about their storm experiences, as an attempt to placate the crowd. The theme being, sorry no scallops to shuck, but here are some storm stories on a stormy day. The coordinator for this storytelling section of the program was Kirsten and Reidar Bendiksen's daughter, Tove. As I made my way to the microphone, I had two thoughts that I did not share with the audience. First, while the audience was deeply disappointed that there would be no contest and that they would have to listen to me drone on about an old sea story. I was, in fact, ecstatic that all our boats and fishermen were home and safe. Sorry about the contest folks, but damn happy that everyone is home.

How far we have come in weather science in 56-years, and how different it is from 1962, and this is an example of significant progress. I thought about how in my grandfather's day, there were no weather forecasts. He had a compass and charts to navigate by, he had a lead line to determine the depth of the water under the boat and to view the composition of the sea bottom. He had a barometer to assess changes in atmospheric pressure, and he had his instincts and visual interpretation of the sky and the sea. He also had a secret weapon. He had a collision avoidance system that was foolproof and essential when anchoring up for the night in thick fog, when dory fishing, or swordfishing. He had a dog. My grandfather loved dogs, and he considered them an essential piece of safety equipment and companionship aboard the boat.

In 1962, my father had all the equipment that his father had, with the addition of a total of six minutes per day of a weather report from the U.S. Weather Bureau, which turned out to be worthless in predicting Neptune's Nor'easter. Dad had a radiotelephone, a Loran navigation system, a radar, and a sounding machine. Now that he had radar, he did not need a dog.

But, on this day in 2017, our entire fleet had good accurate weather information which allowed them to get back to port and safety. How far we have come, and I felt great that no New Bedford fishermen would be lost at sea today, due to Hurricane Jose. I also thought about how deep our fishing industry roots go and extend. Here I am being introduced to the crowd by Tove, and her grandfather and my father narrowly escaped death together, when they were shipmates on the *Venus*, as they encountered Neptune's Nor'easter in 1962. It all illustrates progress, adaptability, resilience, and the deep roots of our fishing community.

It made me think that when our problems seem overwhelming and stressful, that it is always darkest just before the dawn. It made me remember an inspiring song. In the early dark days of World War II, when Nazi Germany was marching through Europe unimpeded, and Britain was alone and the last hope of freedom and democracy in Europe. Two English songwriters came up with a patriotic song to rally the Brits. It's still an old favorite of the British today, and it's a song of pride, resilience, and defiance against staggering odds.

The title was, "There'll Always be an England."

Whenever I hear that song or that phrase, I always think of New Bedford. I think of the history of whaling and textiles, and their importance to the early development of the city. I think of how they had their time, and then they faded into history. But they left their mark in the architecture of the buildings, from the multi-story brick textile mills to the three-decker houses that housed the mill workers, to the magnificent homes and buildings that the whaling shipowners and ship captains built. But, I'm most proud of how the fishing industry came, and so far, it has found a way to stay. It's a testament to the diversity and work ethic of our people, and their ability to adapt.

While the challenges that the fishing industry faces today are complicated, with closures and quotas, permits, consolidation, politicians, government regulators, scientists, environmentalists, and of course the fishermen, I have confidence that they will all find a way to preserve our resource and not allow our fishing industry to slowly fade away. If it was easy anyone could do it, but in New Bedford, we have people who know about doing the hard tasks. To use an old cliché, if we can put a man on the moon, surely, we can do this.

I have confidence that I am correct when I declare the following;

There'll Always be a New Bedford,
And there'll always be New Bedford Fishermen,
I know, fishermen will be walking her docks,
and putting out to sea, forever!

The New Bedford Fisherman,
Second to None,
Then and Now,
The Finest Kind!

While writing this book, I found myself stuck and unable to progress forward on two of the chapters. The first was the chapter concerning the *Venus*, and the second was this last chapter that you are reading now. This final chapter block was easy for me to understand, I was trying to figure out how to tie everything together to make an ending that made sense to the reader. I had a lot to say, and it became complicated for me to determine what to say and how to say it. The chapter on the *Venus* perplexed me because the story of the *Venus* was the material that I knew the best, and that my father had passed on to me from his personal experience. I had the nuts and bolts of his experience, but somehow, I needed to incorporate and explain his own feelings of terror and uncertainty, for this important chapter. I was stuck on how to explain this part of his experience. I also felt the self-inflicted pressure of getting this chapter right. If I didn't get anything else right, I had to get this chapter right, or I would feel like I was letting my father down. Several months went by with very little progress, I tried, but I just couldn't get it done. Then one night I had a very realistic and vivid dream.

In my dream, I suddenly found myself sitting on the pilothouse floor of an eastern rigged fishing vessel. There was glass all over the floor, and the wind was howling as the boat was pitching and rolling. I got to my feet and looked around, and I was all alone. I was confused, and I was trying to figure out how, and why, was I here. More important, why was I here all alone. I looked out on the deck, and there was no one moving about, I figured whoever was aboard this boat with me, must be down below in the foc'sle. I began to frantically blow the horn, and I looked out at the doghouse expecting to see men hurrying out onto the deck and coming to my assistance. No one came! I now started to panic because the realization that I was all alone on this boat, in a storm, began to dawn on me. As my thoughts came together, I concluded that I was soon going to die. It was absolute panic, and it seemed so real, I had no idea that it was a dream, I felt that I was in this place.

Suddenly a vision appeared hovering over the deck. This was the shape of a man, and he was dressed in the robe of a priest. He was not standing on the deck, he was hovering a few feet above the deck, and he was looking back at me.

Then he spoke; You are not supposed to be here Paul, why are you here?

I replied; I have no idea, and who are you?

He answered; I am Saint Peter, sometimes known as Simon Peter.

I replied; Have you come to take me, Father?

He answered me; That was not the plan, but somehow you have managed to be here, at the wrong place and at the wrong time. There were eleven men aboard this fishing vessel, and it was their time, and they have moved on to the next life. Now we have the complication that somehow you are the twelfth man aboard this boat, and we must decide your fate. We usually have others who handle the transition for those who are moving on, but when fishermen are involved, either my brother, Saint Andrew, or I do that work ourselves. We were both fishermen during our early earthly life, and we have high respect for all who are fishermen, it is a noble and necessary calling on earth. Your friend Neptune has spoken to me on your behalf, and he informs me that you are assisting him in spreading his message. This is important work, and we would like you to continue and complete this task. We want you to help spread our concern, about the dangerous behavior of humanity towards one another, by completing the writing of your book. We also want you to highlight the power and need for respect among people. However, now that you have managed to somehow find yourself in this current predicament, our options are limited.

I replied; Can't you just send me back to where I should be? Just transport me back to my home? I promise I will finish my work.

Saint Peter answered; It's not that easy, I can only move you around if you have passed on to my realm. I am then free to do things with your soul that would amaze you, but this can only be done after your death. Have you ever felt the presence of a lost loved one? Maybe a sudden breeze in the air, or a remembrance that brings a chill to your skin? Those things are attempts to help you, from those who have passed on to the next life. I'm afraid you will have to pilot and navigate this boat through this storm if you are to survive and remain among the living.

I replied; Father, perhaps you had better take me now because it will be impossible to pilot this boat alone in a storm of this magnitude. Can't you just ask Neptune to calm the sea and then I may be able to do it?

Saint Peter said; No, I'm afraid that is not possible. While Neptune has great power, he cannot stop a storm that he has initiated. Once Neptune starts a storm, it can't be stopped. You may not know this about Neptune, but he has a terrible temper, and we have counseled him about these things. However, what I can do is this, I can send you some temporary help, to assist you in running this vessel. Once you are clear of this dangerous storm, I will have to recall them, but you will be safe. Who do I have with me, that you would like to have here to help you? If you cannot get through this storm, then I will have no choice but to come back and take you from this life.

Without a moments' hesitation I replied; Saint Peter, can you please send me my father, my grandfather, my great-grandfather, my Uncle Herbie, my Uncle Spud, Captain Eli Pothier, Captain Magne Risdal, Captain Woody Bowers, John Pendergast, Captain Eddie Carter, Barney Lopes, Captain Norman Lepire, and Captains Olav and Oddmund Tveit. That should do it, thank you.

He answered; I'll be right back, but we need to move quickly because you don't have much time.

Suddenly, St Peter was back, and he was alone. He said, we're trying to locate the men that you requested, but it's a big place and those souls move around a lot, they have a boat, and they're always out sailing around. Your time is limited, give me some other names that may be able to help you.

I replied; Okay Father, well can you send me any fisherman who has the last name Avila, and I'll take any of the fishing Sen's. If you have trouble locating any of these men, then send me anyone who spent his life as a New Bedford Fisherman, any of them will be good men. Just check that they spent more time out on the Cultivator Shoal than they did in the Cultivator Club. You know what I mean Father, I'm sure you have records on these things.

Saint Peter said; Yes, we have lots of records, and by the way, I noticed that your attendance record at church is not so good. One more thing, I don't know who the fishing Sen's are? Can you explain that term to me?

I replied; Yes, of course, Father, that would be any fisherman who has a last name that ends in the letters S-E-N. You know Father, names like Isaksen, Bendiksen, Edvardsen, Jacobsen, Ulrichsen, Enoksen, Hansen, Tonnessen, Andersen, Davidsen, Gundersen, Thompsen, Larsen, Olsen, Johannessen, Aanensen, any of those guys will do nicely. They're all top-notch good fishermen, I'll take any of them, please.

Saint Peter disappeared, and things were getting worse aboard the boat as the storm was intensifying. I then heard a loud thud coming from out on the deck, I looked, and fourteen men had landed on the boat. Twelve of them had on yellow oiler foul weather jackets, and yellow bib-type oil pants, black sea boots with wide elastic bands holding the cuff of the pants to the boot, and all of them had on black sou'wester hats. Two of them had on long black oilskin jackets, and this was the foul weather gear that the schooner men wore who went dory fishing, and I knew these two men were senior to the other twelve. They all began to move about the deck, securing loose items, making things fast, and throwing some things overboard. It was instantly apparent that these men were experienced fishermen, by their dress and by their actions.

The two men in the long black jackets headed to the starboard rail, and I noticed that part of the net, that had been on deck was loose, and it had washed overboard. If some of that net got into the propeller, we would be in serious trouble, but these two experienced men were already on it, pulling the fishing net back onto the deck. When I looked closely, I saw a large Golden Retriever dog helping them pull the net with his teeth. Even under his storm jacket, I could see that one of these men had a barrel-shaped chest and he was powerful. The old school foul weather gear, the physical shape of one of these two men, the easy way with which they moved on a pitching and rolling deck, and the dog. I knew immediately that these two men were my grandfather and my great-grandfather. My grandfather loved dogs, and he always had one aboard the boat.

A thin man, who was moving quickly around the deck, turned and looked back at me, and under the brim of his black sou'wester, I saw the face of my father. I started to rush out of the pilothouse door and run down to greet him on deck. He held his hand up in the stop position and pointed at me, and then he gestured that he wanted me to get back on the wheel, dad then turned and motioned with his hand how he wanted the bow pointed up, but slightly off the wind. I quickly got back on the wheel.

A few minutes later, another thud emanated from out on the deck, and another twelve men were suddenly on deck, the "Fishing Sen's" and the "Avila boys" had arrived. I now had my fishing family and friends aboard the boat, along with some of the best Portuguese and Norwegian fishermen to ever step aboard a fishing boat. I knew I was going to make it now, I had an all-star team of fishermen, and I was happy and relieved. I was going home, no way I was going down with these guys around.

I then saw five men from the first group heading towards the pilothouse. The pilothouse door opened, and they walked in, and the first man in was my dad, his face was as clear to me as I had ever seen it. They were all smiling at me, but none of them were talking. I was the only one talking. My dad nodded to two of the men, and they headed toward the engine room to check on the engine. As they walked past me, they lifted the brim of their sou'westers and smiled at me, and one of them winked, it was my Uncle Herbie, and the fisherman next to him had a big grin on his face, and it was my Uncle Spud. I was so excited to see them all, and especially my dad, it was just how I remembered him, clear as day. I was asking questions, and I was talking a mile a minute, but all they were doing was smiling and looking back at me, including the dog who was soaking wet, and I recognized that dog immediately, it was Jake my beloved Golden Retriever who had passed away, while in my arms, a few years earlier. He was standing next to my grandfather looking at me with that goofy smile that all Goldens seem to have.

I moved towards my dad, and as I got closer, they all began to waver side to side, and their images began to go out of focus. I took another step closer to my dad, and as I reached out to embrace him, in a flash they all disappeared, and I woke up.

I looked around, and I was in my home, in the middle of the Georgia woods. I was more than 200-miles from the nearest part of the Atlantic Ocean. My nightshirt was soaking wet, and my heart was beating fast. It was all so real that it shook me. I got up, turned on some lights and the television, changed my shirt, stepped over Lily, my sleeping Golden Retriever, walked around the house, and took a few minutes to compose myself from this very realistic dream.

I calmed down and told myself that this dream was an understandable reaction to my stress over how to write the chapter, about the *Venus*. The dream was very similar to what I was trying to write, and some of the elements in my dream matched some of the things that I knew had happened on the *Venus*, during Neptune's Nor'easter. I told myself that my consternation over how to write this chapter had induced my dream.

However, as I further thought about this dream, and how it was so clear, I knew that this was more than a typical dream. I am sure that this was a message from my father telling me that he approved of the work that I was doing with this book. My father had released my mind to continue the story and finish the chapter on the *Venus*. The terror that I felt during this dream gave me a feel for what the men who encountered Neptune's Nor'easter might have felt. This dream was the inspiration for the opening pages of the chapter on the Venus.

I have presented my view of how we got to today, and why I am concerned about the sustainability of the New Bedford fishing industry because I owe it a debt. The goal of all parents is to see their children progress and hopefully lead a life that is an improvement over the life that they led. This was my father's dream for me as he pushed me toward finding another way in life, and he was sure that obtaining a college education was central to this dream. I have led a safer more predictable life than my father did, as I did not have to risk my life to make a living. My career has afforded me the opportunity to live comfortably and to travel and see many parts of the world. I owe a debt to my fisherman father, and I owe a debt to Georges Bank for providing the cod, haddock, flounder, scallops, and swordfish, that provided our family with money. Fishing meant that as a child I could live in a comfortable house, I never remember going to bed hungry, and I always had proper clothes to wear to school. Many of my friends growing up had fathers who were fishermen, and we all owe a debt to the men who are called New Bedford fishermen.

It took me a very long time to write the last chapter of this book. I struggled with what I wanted to say in this closing chapter. I tried to bring together my thoughts and conclusions on the lessons that this project has taught me. I tried to keep this a positive book, but I also wanted to tell the truth about the way in which fishermen feel they are treated. I wanted to highlight the need for respect.

Several months went by without my being able to pull it all together. As I was trying to complete this book, I drove down to Fort Phoenix in Fairhaven. The New Bedford inner harbor is protected by a massive man-made breakwater to protect it from storm surge during hurricanes and other severe storm events. It is technically known as the New Bedford Hurricane Protection Barrier, it was constructed under the direction of the U.S. Army Corps of Engineers, and it was completed in January of 1966. Locally, we refer to it as, "The Dike." As the dike stretches across the harbor there is a gate through which ships, enter and exit, the inner harbor. This gate can be closed during stormy weather to protect the port. You can get close to the gate opening by walking along the top of the dike from Fort Phoenix. As I was looking out to sea, I saw two fishing vessels coming down the New Bedford channel headed home from offshore. I walked along the dike so that I could get a closer look at these boats, who were returning from Georges Bank. There was a small crowd of people, of various ages, gathered near the entrance gate, they were all watching the boats come and go, as dusk was fast approaching. As the first fishing boat approached and passed through the gate, some kids were waving, and a few adults were taking pictures. As I looked into the pilothouse of the first boat, I saw the captain as he waved back at the children and blew the ship's horn. I witnessed the excitement of the children and adults, some of them most probably tourists, as they observed the return home of real offshore commercial fishermen. I smiled, and I had thoughts of the many times, when I was a young boy, that I had come down to Fort Phoenix to watch for my father's return from the sea. I was facing west looking towards the New Bedford side of the harbor, and something told me to gaze up towards the sky, and there it was, the planet Venus, bright and low in the twilight sky.

At that moment, I caught a vision of my dad, at the wheel of the storm-damaged fishing vessel *Venus*, coming down the channel, returning to New Bedford from his harrowing encounter with Neptune's Nor'easter.

In the next instant, I saw a vision of my grandfather, at the wheel of his fishing schooner, the *Gleaner*, following the *Venus* down the channel, entering the New Bedford harbor with the fish-hold full of fish, from a trip to Georges Bank.

The hair on my arms and neck stood up straight, and with a lump in my throat, a tear in my eye, and pride in my heart, I now had the motivation that I needed to complete this book.

I am sure that I heard my grandpa sing out, as he flashed by in this vision;

"Finish the job boy, tighten the sails, and let her go!
Let's see what she's gonna do!
You're the son of a New Bedford Fishing Captain!
We don't back down, and we don't give up!
Finish this book, and then let her go, boy!
She's gonna fly!"

Then I heard the bark of a Golden Retriever!

I quietly replied; "Aye, Aye, Captain!"

I sincerely hope and pray that one-hundred years from now, some boy or girl will have the same privilege that I did, when they are asked;

"What does your father do for a living?"

They'll stand up straight, and look their inquisitor directly in the eye, and say proudly;

"My father is a New Bedford Fisherman!"

Pop, your story has been told!
You see, I really was listening!

Rest in Peace,
Captain Louis Doucette, Jr.

Repose en Paix, Papa

Role Reversal

Me and My Dad

In the photo on the left, I am 5-years old, and my father is 43-years old, taken at Mystic Seaport in Connecticut.

In the photo on the right, I am 50-years old, and my father is 88-years old. Out for a sail, aboard the S/V *Fleur de Lis*, on Buzzards Bay.

My brother was off serving in the United States Navy at the time of the picture on the left. Hence, I wore a sailor hat often during that time, to keep in solidarity with my big brother.

In Memoriam

On May 7th, 2017, a Sunday, I woke up early to work on writing this book. It was a little after 5:00 a.m. when I turned on my computer to begin working on this story. I first scanned the news to see what might have happened in the world while I was sleeping. A lead story declared; "Navy Seal killed in Somalia during a raid on a terrorist location." There were few details other than this fact. A chill went immediately up my spine, and I had a bad feeling that this involved the only active duty Navy Seal that I remotely knew. Over the next several hours, I kept looking for more information. A few hours later, it was revealed that this Seal, was a member of Seal Team Six, and the only Seal I knew, was a member of Seal Team Six. My anxiety and dead increased, and somehow, I just knew. I prayed that I was wrong. By mid-morning, it was revealed that the deceased Seal was Kyle Milliken, age 38, husband, and father, and was, in fact, the man that I was worried about. I knew that there was no chance that Seal Team Six had two Kyle Milliken's, but I reached out to my close lifetime friend, Gary Sykes, to see if it was true. Gary confirmed that it was the man who was a close friend of his son, Trevor. Kyle and Trevor were middle distance runners at the University of Connecticut, while in college, and the only time I was ever in the presence of Kyle Milliken was at Trevor's wedding, where Kyle was a member of Trevor's wedding party. Over the years, whenever I heard that Seal Team Six had completed a mission, I always immediately thought about Kyle and hoped that he was safe. While I didn't really know Kyle, a friend of my friends, is in fact, my friend. I admired Kyle's commitment and dedication from afar.

Kyle Milliken was a highly decorated 15-year veteran of the Navy Seals and was killed on a mission, while closing on an Al-Qaeda linked, Al-Shabaab terrorist compound, near Mogadishu, Somalia. Two of his Seal teammates were also wounded in the fierce firefight, on May 5th, 2017.

Senior Chief Special Warfare Operator (SEAL)
KYLE MILLIKEN
United States Navy
Seal Team Six

<u>A man who wore Neptune's Trident on his chest</u>

<u>KYLE MILLIKEN</u>

<u>"THE FINEST KIND"</u>

Kyle Milliken was a native of Falmouth, Maine

<u>This….is Maine</u>

In Memoriam

THE F/V DORIS GERTRUDE

Lost at Sea
January 13, 1955

Captain Joshua "Spud" Murphy

Engineer Herbert Doucette

SPECIAL THANKS

This book would not have been possible without the help of my brother,

ALBERT LOUIS DOUCETTE, SR.

My brother spent seventeen years as a commercial fisherman and escaped at least four near-death experiences, while fishing. It was after the last of these experiences that he decided to pursue his gift as an artist, and sculptor of marine life. His work reflects his intimate knowledge of the ocean life that he was able to observe up close, while fishing. He is known worldwide for his work.

Al is the first born in our family, and my father deemed that he would become a fisherman. My father took him fishing at a young age and began to train him, as my grandfather had trained my father. This was not an easy apprenticeship. I am the youngest of four children, and I always looked up to my big brother as a role model. I was always amazed at his abilities. It always seemed to me, that he could build, make, or fix anything, and his artistic talent is incredible. But it was his complete confidence when on, or in the water, which most impressed me. He sometimes seemed more like a fish, than a human. His strong swimming ability was the reason he survived being taken under by a scallop dredge, as a young man.

My brother's recollections and advice during the writing of this book, have been invaluable to me. Thanks, Al.

ALBERT LOUIS DOUCETTE, SR.

NEW BEDFORD FISHERMAN
UNITED STATES NAVY BOATSWAIN MATE
MARINE ARTIST
MY BROTHER

"THE FINEST KIND"

Photo Credit:

Fishing Vessel	Photo Credit
3&1&1	Cloutier photo
Ade Mae	Cloutier photo
Aloha	Courtesy of Steve Kennedy Collection
Edgartown	Courtesy of Steve Kennedy Collection
Fleeting	Courtesy of Steve Kennedy Collection
Florence B.	Courtesy of Steve Kennedy Collection
Gleaner	Cloutier photo
Midnight Sun	Ivan Flye photo from the Steve Kennedy Collection
Moby Dick	Ivan Flye photo from the Steve Kennedy Collection
Monte Carlo	Ivan Flye photo from the Steve Kennedy Collection
Moonlight	Courtesy of Steve Kennedy Collection
Santa Cruz	Steve Kennedy photo
Venus	Ivan Flye photo from the Steve Kennedy Collection

Newspaper References: November 14 – 22, 1962

Boston Globe
London Times
New Bedford Standard Times
New York Times
Providence Journal
Philadelphia Evening Bulletin – Temple University Library

Websites:

www.lostfishermen.com – Lost fishermen from the port of New Bedford
www.alden-schooner.com – Schooner Curlew
www.fishingheritagecenter.org – New Bedford Fishing Heritage Center

Others:

Down East Magazine – Schooner Windfall
Fishing Gazette – June 1960 – Midnight Sun
Documentary Film – Finest Kind

Reference Books:

Book Name	Author	Publisher	Date
Four Thousand Hooks	Adams, Dean	University of Washington Press	2012
The Man Who Ate His Boots	Brandt, Anthony	Anchor	2010
To the Rescue	Case, Phillips N.	Blair Manufacturing Co.	1940
Heavy Weather Sailing	Coles, k. Adlard	John de Graf, Inc.	1968
Codfish, Dogfish, Mermaids, and Frank	DeBrusk, Skip	Reginald van Fenwick Press	2006
Bravura	Ewing, Alex C.	University of Florida Press	2009
The Dragger	Finn, William	Little, Brown & Co.	1970
Perfect Storm	Junger, Sebastian		
Down to the Sea for Fish		Reynolds Printing	1936
Going Fishing	Pierce, Wesley George	International Marine Publishing Co.	1989
Astounding Tales of the Sea	Snow, Edward Rowe	Dodd, Mead & Co.	1965
In Search of Ellen Marie	Spaulding, Rachel Rowley	Archway Publishing	2014

14320269R00150

Made in the USA
Middletown, DE
19 November 2018